D0627474

LAW AND DISCIPLINE
ON CAMPUS

LAW AND DISCIPLINE ON CAMPUS

Edited by
Grace W. Holmes

The Institute of Continuing Legal Education
Hutchins Hall • Ann Arbor, Michigan

Foreword

Fifteen months after its pioneering conference on Student Protest and the Law, The Institute of Continuing Legal Education presented a seminar on Law and Discipline on Campus. The latter conference was a useful and logical sequel. Where the concern as recently as 1969 was with the use of legal procedures and devices as a response to violence and threatened violence on campus, now the concerns are management of tensions to avoid violence on the one hand and the handling of the aftermath of crisis on the other.

Areas that once were understood to be the sole domain of counselors and administrators are understood now to have legal overtones and to be subject to requirements couched in terms resembling traditional constitutional due process cases. Differences of view about the proper structure of campus discipline mechanisms themselves have become the focus of new confrontations and disruptions.

Teachers, students, administrators, and members of governing boards—and their lawyers—had keen interest in these matters and four hundred of them came to Ann Arbor from colleges and secondary schools around the country to consider the many problems involved. By this comprehensive, edited report of that conference, The Institute of Continuing Legal Education provides all who are concerned with discipline in schools and colleges with the insights offered by the distinguished faculty gathered on that occasion. In addition, the editor, Grace W. Holmes, has assembled a singular collection of legal and disciplinary materials that will be enormously useful to those who have any responsibility for drafting or applying campus rules. To her and to the faculty of the seminar the Institute is deeply grateful.

JOHN W. REED
Director

THE INSTITUTE OF CONTINUING LEGAL EDUCATION

The University of Michigan Law School

Wayne State University Law School

State Bar of Michigan

———

Executive Committee

Francis A. Allen, Dean, The University of Michigan Law School

Benjamin Carlin, Professor of Law, Wayne State University Law School

Robert E. Childs, Professor of Law, Wayne State University Law School

Charles W. Joiner, Dean, Wayne State University Law School and President, State Bar of Michigan

Douglas A. Kahn, Professor of Law, The University of Michigan Law School

James A. Park, Fraser Trebilcock Davis & Foster, Lansing

William J. Pierce, Professor of Law and Director, Legislative Research Center, The University of Michigan Law School

A. DeVere Ruegsegger, Dyer, Meek, Ruegsegger & Bullard, Detroit

Boaz Siegel, Professor of Law, Wayne State University Law School

Norman O. Stockmeyer, Jr., Commissioner, Michigan Court of Appeals

John W. Reed
Director

Table of Chapters

PART IV

THE AFTERMATH OF CRISIS

APPENDIXES

Rights, Responsibilities, and Rules

New Answers — Actual and Proposed

A Legal Remedy

Table of Contents

PART II

ADMINISTRATIVE DISCIPLINE

PART III

LAW ENFORCEMENT IN CRISIS

PART IV

THE AFTERMATH OF CRISIS

APPENDIXES

Rights, Responsibilities, and Rules

New Answers—Actual and Proposed

A Legal Remedy

Introductory Remarks

*Robben W. Fleming**

At this period in time the problems concerning student dissent appear to fall into three general categories. The first involves the adequacy of both the external law and the internal disciplinary system within universities.

Within the past year and a half there has been a great spawning of state and federal legislation dealing with student dissent. Most of this law has done little more than relieve the frustrations of the legislators. I would anticipate that insofar as the prosecutor retains judgment over which remedy to employ, the old remedies of trespass, disturbance of the peace, and assault will continue to be his chosen instruments. They are more adaptable to his needs than the many new laws.

The internal ruling system of the universities is hampered by difficulties which have long been present. One difficulty is the academic community's slow adaptation to the fact that we are no longer dealing with traditional kinds of offenses— cheating and plagiarism, for example. The violent and disruptive tactics which have been with us for some time lie outside the rubric of the traditional offenses, but only now is the academic community beginning to believe that these new tactics will not fade away. We realize that internally some adjustments in thinking must be made. Another question of equal importance is the effectiveness of the disciplinary system. Actually, the capacity of external law or the internal disciplinary system to meet a situation effectively is in large de-

---

* President, The University of Michigan, Ann Arbor, Michigan.

gree dependent upon whether the constituency to which it applies accepts it. We are not likely to have an effective rules system unless the faculty and the students view it as fair and equitable.

The second general category of problems centers upon the adequacy of the external procedures and of the internal university machinery for handling violations. A difficulty common to both is the formidable task of identifying persons involved in incidents, and the time lag frequently experienced in legal proceedings which severely limits the effectiveness of legal sanctions. Another stumbling block in devising an effective rules system, even within the academic community, is agreement on the selection of remedies. Students argue that under no set of circumstances is expulsion — which they refer to as the capital punishment of the academic world — justifiable. On the other hand, increasing numbers of people now support the view that a number of offenses, quite beyond the traditional ones, in fact, justify expulsion. The unknown quantity at this point in time is the damage suit. Around the country, damage suits are being filed both against university administrators for allegedly not performing their duties and against students engaged in certain kinds of activities. I expect that we will see an expanding use of the damage action.

The third category of problems concerns the interrelationship between the external law and the internal disciplinary system. The argument still persists that legal prosecution and internal discipline for the same offense results in double jeopardy. The concept of double jeopardy, as lawyers know it, simply has no application to these kinds of cases. Yet I find that both faculty and students have a great attachment to the double jeopardy argument, which they thoroughly misunderstand. After they study the law and find that it really does not apply, they then retreat to saying that it should apply.

In addition to the problems caused by the double jeopardy argument is the question of timeliness of disciplinary proceedings. It is argued that, in general, if two procedures are to be conducted, a university proceeding ought to be withheld pending the conclusion of a prosecution. Indeed, some time ago many people hoped that a clear choice could be made between reliance on external remedies and the use of internal remedies. Most of us have learned that in a great many cases, perhaps in most cases, there can be no choice between remedies, because both students and nonstudents are involved. Internal university disciplinary rules do not apply to nonstudents. Therefore, when students and nonstudents are involved, one is immediately faced with the fact that exactly the same incident with exactly the same surrounding circumstances involves two constituencies; the law presumably will apply to both, but the internal disciplinary rules will apply only to one—the students. Finally, additional complications arise because the student feels that it is inequitable to proceed against him on both counts while the nonstudent is proceeded against only under the law.

The three problem areas I have outlined are extraordinarily difficult. I wish you luck in examining them.

PART I

CAMPUS TENSIONS:
CHALLENGE AND RESPONSIBILITY

CHAPTER ONE

The Governing Board

*Eugene B. Power**

The question of student unrest is one which is absorbing a
tremendous amount of the energies of the academic community and of the general public as well. I am persuaded that a
substantial part of the problem which exists with the general
public arises from a lack of understanding of what is happening on the campuses. However, it is not my purpose to explore
the causes of student unrest, but to discuss governing boards
of universities.

Today many people are expressing opinions about what the
governing board of a university actually does. Some say that
university affairs are controlled by trustees who sit on corporate boards when they are not attending the monthly college
policy sessions. Others maintain that college boards are anach-
ronisms and should be abolished, if not immediately, certainly
within the next five years. Trustees have been characterized as
old, rich, totally out of touch with the world of today, and
good for nothing except fund raising. Another point of view
claims that faculty and students are so irresponsible that
trustees have an obligation to demonstrate who holds actual
power to direct university policy. All of these people are talking about the same job, and perhaps it could be said that there
is an element of truth in all of these statements. Certainly some
boards of trustees tend to equate the operation of a college
with the management of a business. I recall that one regent

---

* Chairman, Association of Governing Boards of Universities and Colleges,
  Washington, D.C.

complained because the college board meetings were not conducted in the same way as the meetings of the board of his bank. He failed to understand that a university board functions on a unique and different level, unlike the ordinary commercial or corporate board.

The university is a community of scholars and students. There is not a line of command from the board to the president to the vice president to the deans to the department chairmen. The role of a college trustee has to be entirely different. He must, for example, consider the constituency which put him on the board, especially since the money for the school comes from that source. If he serves a public institution, he may be an elected official, a gubernatorial or legislative appointee, or an alumni representative. Private schools, on the other hand, tend to have self-perpetuating boards. They may be church-appointed with alumni participation, and frequently appointment may depend on ability to contribute funds. There is a further difference. Public university boards meet at least once a month and sometimes for two days a month; the boards of private schools, particularly the smaller ones, tend to meet three or four times a year. The complex problems of the public institutions require board members to devote a substantial amount of time to their jobs. As a regent of The University of Michigan, I spent about a third of my time on university affairs. I believe other regents of the university did the same.

In Michigan the regents are elected by the voters of the state and they are sometimes not too understanding of campus disorders. This irritability is rather general. I have yet to find anything in my current reading that recognizes the fundamental problem—the lack of self-discipline. "Discipline" is an unpopular word, but until the public recognizes that discipline is essential to an organized society, we will continue to have social problems. Dr. Hayakawa has suggested that our young people need to acquire a sense of loyalty to something outside themselves, to find that the university does not revolve around them.

A new concept of human relationships is emerging and

students are in large part shaping that concept. The trustee should listen carefully and anticipate increased involvement of all of the university community in decisionmaking. If trustees do not listen, soon they will not be what they are considered to be today—the ultimate legal entity with the authority and responsibility to make the policy decisions. Ideally, matters of policy should be decided by the board and the implementation of those decisions should be left to the president and the administrative officers of the school. It is vital, however, that a board member have channels of communication which enable him to check on whether the policies are being implemented properly. Moreover, he must have sufficient background and knowledge to make accurate and intelligent decisions. Many board members do not inform themselves about campus thinking and campus needs. As a result, they may unwittingly embark upon a course of action which inflames the students and faculty, particularly the younger faculty, and precipitates disorder. In California, for example, the board has taken an intransigent position and the consequences have not been good. This simply means that boards have to be varied in their membership. One finds a distressing tendency, particularly on private boards, to have "Wasp" or "Waspo" members: white, Anglo-Saxon, Protestant, and old. Board membership should be a mixture of the young, the older, the rich, and those who are not rich.

Many institutions are placing student members on their boards. I have mixed feelings about the student membership question. Too often the decisions to be made must be based on experience and the student has not accumulated enough experience to make valid decisions. On the other hand, students have something to say and I would urge that trustees listen carefully.

The effectiveness of the board procedure is generally reflected in a more stable atmosphere in and about the institution. However, as President Fleming indicated, all contention cannot be eliminated and there is no guarantee of peace on any campus. But if the board accurately interprets the policies of the institution to the public, the alumni, and the constituency to whom they are responsible, and explains the wishes and desires of the public and alumni and others to the administration, they are effective. Further, it is incumbent upon the board to keep hands off the implementation of policy. This should be delegated to administration. If the board is not satisfied with the way the decisions are being implemented, then I would urge that the board get another president. Very few people really want to be college presidents today and the average term of office is becoming increasingly short. The board should set policy with serious thought and a thorough knowledge of the possible consequences of that policy. The administrator should be allowed to implement that policy without undue interference from the board.

There are some things a board should do which perhaps go beyond the realm of policymaking. For example, the board should make sure that the administration has touched all the bases that are essential to control of student disorder:

(1) publication of a clear and unequivocal statement of campus rules of conduct, setting out administrative and judicial procedures for dealing with violations of the rules;

(2) advance planning for the proper course of action to handle disruptive incidents, including decisions as to the remedies to be used in specific cases;

(3) advance decisions, where possible, as to the role of the police in handling campus disorders;

(4) selection of specific officials to represent the administration in negotiations with disrupters and in the settlement of such matters as the negotiability of demands and the question of amnesty.

In order to make sure that the administration has fully prepared for emergencies, the board should determine that certain specific questions have been answered:

(1) Is there a definite arrangement with legal counsel in the event of an emergency?

(2) Is personnel familiar with the proper responses and procedures?

(3) Is the administrative staff thoroughly familiar with the

law of trespass and the use of injunctive orders, temporary restraining orders, and subpoenas?

(4) Is there a definite understanding about who is authorized to summon police and for what reasons?

(5) Has a staff member been appointed to act as a liaison person in dealings with the police?

(6) Are staff members briefed as to regulations in regard to the calling of the National Guard?

(7) Have alternative administrative centers been designated for use in the event of damage to key buildings?

(8) Are specific persons authorized to call police and fire units and have code words been devised to avoid impersonations in such calls?

(9) Do the police have good maps of the buildings and grounds?

(10) Have arrangements been made for an emergency medical area?

(11) Are arrangements made for the protection of irreplaceable documents, or are they duplicated and stored elsewhere?

(12) Are there provisions for radio communication in the event telephone lines are cut?

(13) Are key buildings provided with supplies of water, flashlight batteries, first-aid supplies, blankets, and other necessities?

(14) Are staff members familiar with legal terms and the announcements which must be made to insure proper warning about violation of laws or regulations?

(15) In an emergency, who is authorized to cut off power, light, heat, and air conditioning to each building?

It seems to me that boards should question administrators about such specific preparation. As any lawyer recognizes, it is always wise, while hoping for the best, to prepare for the worst that can happen. At the very least, a concerned board of trustees will have ascertained the thinking of administration and will have an understanding of the standby measures which are ready to prevent serious, if not tragic, confrontation.

CHAPTER TWO

An Administrator's View

Robert G. Zumwinkle*

My comments will be concerned with the place of crisis in the educational process, the importance of healthy interpersonal relations in times of stress, the roles that people take or should take in relation to crisis, and the importance of communication in crisis situations.

Crisis in the Educational Process

The nature of a university defies the development of the capacity to make rapid-fire, under-pressure, police-type crisis decisions. It is my guess that universities will always be inefficient—and thus to some extent blundering, unwise, and unjust in that kind of decisionmaking—unless universities become miniature police states, or the larger political systems, including police, take over certain kinds of university decisionmaking.

Thus the greater task, in my judgment, is to prevent potential crises from reaching the extremely disruptive stage. To accomplish that task, we badly need elbow room for creativity, reason, understanding, conversation, and problem-solving attitudes at all stages of a developing crisis. By "elbow room" I mean specifically two basic elements: (1) minimal external restrictions and pressures, and (2) internal understandings concerning the nature of the educational mission and the roles of

---

* Vice President for Student Affairs, University of Kentucky, Lexington, Kentucky.

members of the university community which encourage such qualities. Given elbow room and an open, free atmosphere, crisis and potential crisis can be an opportunity for significant learning. Some scholars and educational practitioners have argued for the notion of education through crisis, but some of their thinking was formulated before the turbulent sixties. Tension, conflict of ideas, confrontation—all are acceptable; but massive disruption and coercion and violence are certainly not what people have had in mind when they have talked about education through crisis. We cannot always choose the nature, the setting, and the timing of our crisis. Nevertheless, it is clear that the way in which a crisis or potential crisis is handled is a profound and widespread educational lesson for the immediate university community and for the general public.

Interpersonal Relations under Stress

Crisis tests the reality and substance of current relationships of members of the university community, even among members of that presumably monolithic group known as "The Administration." When, for example, a vice president, because he supervises the campus police, knows in advance about student plans to occupy and lock up the administration building and thus works with campus, city, county, and state police officials to develop detailed plans for dealing with the demonstration, but fails to inform other school officials of the facts and plans until much later, there clearly exists a hiatus which is damaging in a crisis situation. The locus of real decisionmaking authority, sometimes well-screened during calmer, more peaceful times, can become badly evident in times of crisis and can strain the legitimacy and acceptability of decisions made. This is especially true where influential members of the university believe strongly that certain decisions affecting student welfare and the academic life should involve representative students and faculty in addition to the appropriate administrators, if time and other factors permit. The failure to face frankly and directly such existing strained relationships is inviting real trouble for the university when tough decisions must be made under great pressure. It may be a reason why many universities still do not have effective plans of action in the event of campus disruption. The mistrust, hostility, and strained relations may well prevent the principal parties from even getting together and getting started on the task; and the plan, if put down on paper, may fail to reflect the real (as distinct from the formal or theoretical) relationships and decisionmaking authority.

Roles in Relation to Crisis

Crisis and crisis-resolution involve dealing not only with persons but with persons in their roles in relation to the crisis. Some roles may already be present because of the nature of the crisis and of the adversaries; others may have to be devised in order to encourage a setting favorable to resolving the conflict. Effective, credible ("credible" especially to their respective "constituencies") articulation of the positions of the adversaries is essential.

Reasonably clear identification of the adversaries can be very important. The commonly heard response to an administrator's attempt to identify the leaders of a student movement, is, "We have no leaders. This is a people's movement and decisions are made by the people." Either such a response is a dodge or it reflects a fairly new development in the American social and political action scene. In any case it presents obstacles and frustrations to the establishment side of a conflict in the search for representatives with whom talks may be held. Conversely, it is not always clear to students exactly who is authorized to speak for the administration, perhaps because the president has not made a clear delegation of authority and their respective roles are not clear to the administrators themselves. In this context, I cannot resist the observation that the positions of Vice President for Student Affairs and Dean of Students may become obsolete, especially in times of crisis, given the decisionmaking assumed directly by presidents, other de facto decisionmakers, and police agencies. One effect of this confusion of roles among administrators is that the administration's side of the conflict is not told very well.

One of the almost inevitable effects of sharp conflict and confrontation is polarization of roles—to some extent necessary and desirable, but sometimes a real hindrance to resolving the conflict. On the one hand, the opposing positions should be stated sharply and effectively. On the other hand, the tendency to see all those others as the enemy and to feel that "if you are not for me you must be against me" is to fail to grasp the complex dynamics of the situation and to block from view certain potentially productive approaches to reducing the crisis. Three factors impress me as strongly contributory to the "we-they" psychology; to the taking of exaggerated, rigid positions; and to a university's inability, under pressure, to take full advantage of the multiple roles and resources available to it. I wish to comment briefly on those three factors.

(1) *Personalities of the participants.* Is it too much to expect that the principal antagonists might, even under extreme pressure, occasionally laugh at themselves and their predicament? Admit to error when error has been made? Concede that an issue may involve shadings of gray rather than black and white? Consider drastically different approaches or bring in a disinterested consultant to advise them? Perhaps it is too much to expect such qualities of any one man under great stress. I do suggest that in the process of selecting university executive officers and key student leaders and spokesmen, more careful consideration should be given to those basic personality traits and personal values which reflect openness to new ideas, fundamental respect for persons, steadiness under pressure, the value of consultation with others, and the necessity for weighing evidence before making crucial decisions. Once selected, such persons should be exposed to programs, settings, and persons that nourish and reward such qualities.

(2) *Institutionalizing certain roles and resources.* Unless other arrangements are built into the system in some way, there is great risk that the only significant input into the decisionmaking process will come from the two warring, polarized camps. I

have in mind the need to institutionalize such roles as the following:

(a) opportunities for involvement of "moderates" and other members of the university community who are concerned though not always vocal;

(b) a consultative group of nonadministrators to advise the president and other executive officers on the handling of crises and incipient crises;

(c) relevant legal counsel from an attorney acquainted with the campus on a day-to-day basis and with the established traditions of the institution and the current mood and problems of the campus;

(d) mediation by a panel of respected, trusted individuals in the university community, endorsed by administration, faculty, and student government, who can get the principal disputing parties around a table, set the stage for rational discussion of the issues, and determine points of agreement as a basis for de-escalating the conflict;

(e) more utilization of those faculty and staff members who have already established effective relations and communications with the student leaders involved—members who may be forgotten as an issue escalates to the office of the president but who, with encouragement, support, and limited negotiating authority, have the potential for being enormously useful.

(3) *Pressures from the larger society.* Although some students and faculty regard this concern as merely a bogeyman, many observers are persuaded that the current backlash against universities and against certain youth activities and movements is for real, and that we have not begun to see the full extent of repressive reaction. There is need for greater appreciation within universities of the current facts of political life in America and of the nearly impossible bind in which university presidents find themselves when campus issues escalate out of control. On the other hand, there is a compelling need for universities to do a better job of telling their stories and interpreting their missions to the public. Without hiding the fact that uni-

versities have not done some of their tasks well, and without apologizing for the disruptive, unlawful activities that have occurred on a number of campuses, a much better job must be done of telling the public the whole story of student unrest, the student's side as well as the administration's side. The public must be acquainted with the conflict of educational philosophies which lies at the base of some of the campus tensions. The public must be warned of the dangers inherent in excessive political intrusion into institutions of higher education. If we take greater initiative in educating the public, perhaps the president of an institution may gain freedom to deal with critical situations in a wise, sensitive, and creative fashion.

Communication during Crisis

In a time of actual or potential crisis it is essential that the facts, issues, university policies and rules, and possible future actions be communicated throughout the university community, and that it be done in a manner which is honest, accurate, credible, rapid, complete, responsive to the questions being asked and charges being made, and comprehensive in reaching all of the affected members of the university community. Universities must use all of the available media and must become more inventive in developing new ways of getting the word out. I refer not only to television, radio, newspapers, and mimeographed fliers, but to personal encounters offering opportunities for give and take. If, for example, a particular confrontation involves the president in a rather direct way, he must be visible as a real, live person, concerned with what the students are saying. Faculty understanding and support are crucial. This requires written and oral communication with deans, department chairmen, and faculty.

Essential Tactics

Perhaps an administrator should not speak of campus tensions and crisis without addressing himself to student codes of conduct and disciplinary procedures and contingency plans to deal with disruptions, but these matters will be discussed by other lecturers. Everyone should agree, however, that (1) every collegiate institution must have clearly formulated rules and regulations governing student conduct and disciplinary procedures which meet basic standards of justice and which are made known to each student; and (2) although contingency plans may vary from campus to campus and precise responses to given situations may or may not be specified in the plan, it is always essential that assignments of specific roles and responsibilities among designated university officials be made crystal clear.

It is obvious to most of us that universities are probably in the business of dealing with social and political conflict and potentially disruptive movements for some time to come. We must gain more institutional expertise in this field, which currently requires more time and energy than busy administrators feel able to devote to it. We have on most of our campuses a variety of faculty talents, especially in the social and behavioral sciences, for dealing with conflict. One of our tasks is to enlist those available brains and talents to prepare for crisis in advance and to make the tough decisions on the spot. I am persuaded that many members of the academic community, as yet untapped, are ready and willing to assist, but we shall probably have to seek them out and enlist them individually.

CHAPTER THREE

The Faculty

*Robert L. Knauss**

Role in General

During the past two years, faculties of universities have done a substantial amount of hand-wringing. They have been scapegoats in the news media, accused of being weak and ineffective. A look into the facts of a situation may often disclose that the faculty did, in fact, take a very strong position on an issue, but the faculty position just happened to be in opposition to the university administration. Positions in opposition are often characterized as being weak. It is true, however, that faculty roles in university-wide issues have developed only within the last year or two.

Traditionally, faculties have taken a very strong role within schools and colleges, deciding curriculum, personnel, and other matters having to do with their own departments and colleges. At the university-wide level, faculties have tended to stand apart. Most of the university battles which have made the news were described as conflicts between students and the administration. Formerly, I believed the reason that battles were not generally waged between students and faculty were because students regarded the faculty as being "good guys and somewhat on the right side." I am now aware that the students probably did not waste time battling the faculty because they believe the real power is elsewhere. Moreover, the faculty

* Vice President for Student Services, The University of Michigan, and Professor of Law, The University of Michigan Law School, Ann Arbor, Michigan.

tolerance of certain activities within the university community
has in the past been quite substantial. At The University of
Michigan the faculty showed tolerance when the Administration building was taken over; and they were calm during
the "liberation" of the ROTC building. This spring, however,
when classrooms were disrupted, many faculty decided that
things had gone too far.

What is a strong faculty organization? Many believe this
means a faculty that will support any position taken by the
president; others believe this means a faculty that stands up to
its administration at every opportunity. I believe a strong faculty is one that is sufficiently organized to be able to act
independently in times of crisis. It is able to spot critical issues
in advance and initiate positive action, as opposed to simply
reacting once the crisis has occurred. Faculties in many universities and colleges can be held accountable because they have
not been properly organized. A faculty senate composed of a
thousand faculty members, usually meeting once or twice a
year, cannot be expected to make a proper and effective response on a substantive and critical issue when suddenly called
to a crisis meeting. Such large groups may not be able to act
swiftly and effectively even when they are well-organized. But
where no committee work has been done and no preparatory
groundwork has been planned, the results will probably be
zero.

The most effective role of the faculty should center on the
ability of the individual members to recognize in advance the
issues which are likely to cause disruptive behavior and to
initiate needed changes which will reduce the tensions and
lessen the possiblity of trouble. The current faculty organization at Michigan has been developed within the past four
years. We have a representative council, a senate assembly of
sixty-five members and a full senate of more than twenty-three
hundred members. Members of the assembly are elected from
the various schools and colleges within the university. We have
a strong committee structure with committees advising each of

the vice presidents. An executive committee (SACUA) meets regularly with the president in an advisory capacity.

We have tried to emphasize that while an important part of the function of the various committees is to react to suggestions coming from the administration, it is absolutely essential that the faculty chairmen of the committees initiate agenda items to plan for the future, independent of administrative suggestions. One problem with our current organization arises from the fact that it is strictly a faculty assembly. An attempt to deal with an issue often is frustrated because the faculty has one view of the matter, the administration takes a position, and the student government expresses a different stand. The president or the regents must try to resolve the issue, hampered by all of the problems of face-saving which go with a confrontation at the top level of power. Many of the issues could and should be resolved before going to the top by having joint committees — students, faculty, and administration — at a lower level in the organization. We are trying at Michigan to develop more joint committees. The students feel that they do not have the same opportunity to speak through channels as does the faculty, despite their strong student government. Hence, the temptation to go outside channels is always present, particularly when it has been proven to be very effective.

Action in Crisis

The faculty should be strong enough to take action during a crisis. Occasionally at Michigan both the faculty and the administration have refused to decide the substantive issue as long as students are occupying a building, on the ground that a decision at the time would be a public display of weakness — giving in to demands backed with a show of force. I suggest that this is fallacious reasoning. The initiative to act is immediately lost and it is then in the hands of the disrupters to call the shots. There are always some of the participants who want the disruption to continue. The last thing they want is to have the issue resolved. I am persuaded that decisions should be made, that faculty and administration should have enough confidence in their own decisionmaking powers to do what they think should be done regardless of the outside pressures. The faculty and the administration must maintain the initiative, the power to act as they see fit.

Regent Power mentioned the importance of clearly defined procedures. I would agree that we need procedures but I would add a word of caution. The serious danger in making a long checklist of specifics and planning procedures for particular circumstances is the loss of flexibility. The most effective procedures in a time of crisis turn upon having people selected in advance to act in the crisis and people to serve in an advisory capacity. The people who fill these roles must have sufficient knowledge to avoid the stereotyped responses to certain basic questions: What students are involved? What is the substantive issue in this particular disruption? What has been the build-up? What is the history behind it? Are many of the participants nonstudents? One obviously needs a fair amount of student and faculty input to get that kind of information.

Every institution should encourage faculty members to be involved with students in an informal capacity. Many of the faculty, particularly the young members, spend substantial amounts of time working with student organizations of all kinds. Unfortunately, when tenure decisions are to be made, the young faculty member may find that his involvement with the students is considered a minus factor on his record. I am convinced that the informal involvement of large numbers of the Michigan faculty—their participation in many of the demonstrations on this campus—has been a positive factor in preventing the incidents from getting out of hand.

As Monitors

The faculty can fill other important roles. At this university they have been active in negotiations with students, on occasion preventing a stalemate. A more specific kind of faculty response has been tried here at Michigan and at two or three other universities—the use of faculty monitors during the actual time of crisis. We have used them in various ways at Michigan in at least five different instances in the past eighteen months. The faculty monitor can be useful in a variety of ways. Last year we had a "street liberation" in the campus area. The police did not intervene the first night. It became clear, however, that by the second night there were going to be police; in fact, there were, on the second day, three hundred or more policemen on the city streets. Our faculty group, through a telephone chain, mobilized about one hundred fifty faculty members to get out in the street and serve as faculty presence to dampen potential trouble. The faculty monitors were there to work toward two objectives: (1) to let the students and the police know that many faculty members were present, which would, hopefully, serve to cool action on both sides; and (2) to gather first-hand information—to get the facts. The latter objective is of critical importance. In most instances our faculty members are there as observers to feed back the facts to the administration and to faculty colleagues. A few times certain faculty members have played a more active role in trying to cool the situation, getting between the police and the students, trying to isolate disruptive, violent students from other students. There is no agreement among our faculty as to whether it is ever advisable for the faculty to do this. Some faculty members in their individual capacities have taken an active role, but officially, the role of faculty monitor is confined to the objectives mentioned above.

There are some risks in the use of faculty monitors: the possibility of injury; the increased potential for trouble from increasing the size of the crowd; the danger that police on the spot may not be fully aware of the presence of the faculty or may not know them. In this community we work closely with local police officials, but we have not yet worked out the procedures which are essential to this kind of operation. The basic purpose of the use of faculty monitors is to find out what is really happening and try to prevent trouble. Their effectiveness will depend on complete communication—among faculty, administration, and police—and adequate briefing on the particular incident. They must know what is happening, how it started, what issues are being pressed. We have had real problems on a few occasions because the faculty monitors did not get the essential intelligence.

The role of observer proved effective on this campus in the mass demonstration after the Kent State University affair. For that demonstration and march we had, in addition to the faculty observers, some fifty or sixty student marshals as observers. It worked very well. A very real question growing out of the use of faculty monitors is whether they are to be called as witnesses in administrative disciplinary proceedings which may arise later, or as witnesses in proceedings in criminal court. Obviously a faculty member will have to respond to a subpoena. I would suggest that you attempt to communicate with police officials and with your own internal discipline system, stressing that the function of the faculty monitor is to cool the situation, not to discipline. Faculty monitors who are used in a disciplinary capacity will quickly lose their effectiveness. Moreover, the faculty will not wish to act as monitors under those circumstances.

CHAPTER FOUR

The Students

*David Kessler**

The University Dilemma

Universities are experiencing problems today that are essentially outgrowths of their strained relationship to the larger society, which is itself strained. The university has displayed a muddled and not deeply thought out picture of its role in society. The lack of clarity in displaying that role is as extensive as the role itself. We are here today to make clear one part of that problem: the relationship of the law to that aspect of university life which we call the protest. That one should consider extending legal relationships to this and other aspects of university life is a striking indication of the nature of the present situation. It is crucial to keep in mind the limited scope of this topic. Viewing protest as isolated from the overriding problem of the whole university results in a myopic and distorted understanding. I believe that if students are credited with no other virtues over the last few years, it must be conceded that they have at least tried to keep the whole patient, the whole university, even the whole society, in view. And they have tried to develop a cure for the patient.

The Case for Reform

Students see the university as that section of society which is peculiarly theirs. By and large, they believe the university to be

---

* President, Student Government, 1970, Kalamazoo College, Kalamazoo, Michigan.

inhabited by people of intelligence for whom they feel responsible and about whom they feel guilty. Certainly this institution should be on the right side in the eternal struggle between good and evil. The students see that the last several decades of American life have tended to make the struggle qualitatively more crucial and they will accept no blame or guilt for taking that position. Increasingly, they have injected into the stuffy air of contention the interesting proposition that knowledge implies judgment which ethically requires action. This phenomenon would inspire some very interesting studies if it were not true that the crisis the activists see is, unfortunately, a real one.

The problems are not made by the students; they are the handiwork of the universities themselves in cooperation with the larger society. The universities have preached value neutrality and devotion to the humanistic tradition. Yet they have been photographed in cahoots with government military programs and have been pronounced guilty of treating their members as if they were cogs in a machine. At this point in time they are likely to be found scurrying in the shadows, engaging in subdued muttering, not preaching at all. The shield of academic freedom has turned into a villain's cloak. The university rarely makes a frank effort to achieve a thoughtful and philosophically consistent new position vis-à-vis a larger society, free from contaminating connections. When universities changed from centers of free discussion and research to technological resource pools for the government and industry to preserve the status quo, surely there had to be protest. When university practices—investment policies, attitudes towards students and employees, curriculum structure and funding policies—appear consistent with a systematic attempt to maintain existing social relationships, people who believe that the universities are not private property should insist upon a real examination of the problem.

I do not mean to say that the university should immediately switch all of its commitments and create a relationship to some other group or idea. I wish only to make the point that the university-society relationship ought to be grounded upon something other than an unseemly acceptance of the status quo. Moreover, the decision for change must be based upon open debate in the university community. The university must seek an awareness of its relationships. It must, in maintaining its independence, also give reasonable assistance to those people who wish to create a more just society. At this time, the university is helping to maintain an unjust society. It must get out of the client-management relationship and order its priorities as for a free society. It must be less than an ivory tower but more than a problem-solving factory. The university must find its own way of taking sides without taking sides. This larger problem, not the mechanism of protest, poses the real issue for concern. But the real solution lies not only in solving the problems of the university but in solving the problems of the larger society. As long as these problems exist, protest will continue.

Limitations on Student Leaders

In contrast to the monolithic educational establishments and law enforcement agencies, students are highly fragmented. The student leader has no automatic support in complex situations. The many "submovements" are quite divided. I cannot claim to speak for all student leaders, just as Julius Hoffman cannot claim to speak for the legal profession. The student leader maintains leadership only to the extent that other students choose to follow him. Nobody follows his orders. Certainly he can persuade many because of his office, but an orthodox or official position sometimes inhibits leadership in times of crisis. A student leader must decide upon his goals. Will he seek concrete changes, radicalization, persuasion, alienation, or symbolic protest, or will he try to close down the university? One rarely knows exactly which goal to aim for in advance; usually it is in the heat of events that one finds previously nonexistent forks in the road. It would be impossible, and perhaps altogether wrong, to try to predict what an individual in a given situation should do. While moral and legal sanctions do not weigh as heavily as in former years, they must, nevertheless, be considered in the decisionmaking process, along with the consequences for the students, the university, and the community at large.

I wish to suggest what I believe to be the ideal role for the student leader, with the caveat that it will not work in all situations. Moreover, it will not work at all unless school administrators are receptive to change. The student leader should attempt to function as an educator. He is in a unique position, having clear access to thoughts and pressure points of both students and administrators. He knows things about the consequences of protest that students should know. He is capable of presenting to the administrators the students' contention that radicalization, in the sense of getting to the root of the problem, is necessary. Certainly, the student government leaders can and should do everything possible to insure that all that happens during a protest is carefully planned to avoid violence and spontaneous, irrational destruction. They can and should be ever ready to talk and even compromise, but it should be emphasized that the control of the student leader is limited. He has an army of alienated individuals who have no obligation to respect or to follow him. If he fails in his initial effort to obtain from administration an understanding of the issue and substantive changes in the situation, his ability to direct the protest and keep it peaceful will necessarily diminish. His chance of succeeding as an educator is then quite slim. Too often the student leader ends up keeping the pot from boiling over without obtaining any change in the cooking arrangements, sowing the seeds of dangerous future bitterness.

The student leader can try to make all students aware of the antinomies of a situation, as well as the possible consequences of action they may wish to take. He can make the institution aware of the student view of its shortcomings. He can try to show the community that the protest may be on the side of democracy and better education for all. He cannot do this, however, unless the university is willing to take action on the strength of the knowledge he offers. This does not mean that the university must accede to every proposal or demand. It does mean that the university can no longer ignore the substance of change while rotating the trappings. While I believe that violence should be avoided at all costs, there are others who feel differently; a stolid and unchanging university will bring these people to the fore. Although the student leader may project a humanist image, the substance of power remains with the university. If that institution does not abandon its position for a new synthesis, either the student leader will be forced to shop for different tools or the students will shop for a new leader. As a student leader, I believe nothing impressed me as much as the limitations imposed on student government leader initiative. Almost every issue with which we were involved emanated from above—from President Nixon, the president of our college, or someone else. Generally, something was started to which we had to react. Perhaps this does not occur in other universities, but in our case the student leader has a limited amount of power. For the most part, his role is to react to actions of others.

If confrontation results in meaningful compromises, the alienation of students will decrease. On the other hand, if the student leader must either accept a token gesture or risk everything on all-out action, he will have less chance of managing the action. Too often the university forces the student government into such untenable positions. Too often the responses of the university make a reality of what had been only ideological rhetoric. The university should listen thoughtfully to the rhetoric, despite its sometimes inaccurate cast. It is possible to sort out the genuine. The era of consensus politics on campus is over. The university must determine how to handle adversary relationships without promoting violence or destroying itself.

CHAPTER FIVE

The Office of the Students' Attorney: A New Development

*James G. Boyle**

For some time in the late 1960s, a *Lord of the Flies* mentality pervaded many college campuses, especially large state institutions of higher learning. The University of Texas at Austin was no exception. "End the War," "Stop War Research," "End Imperialism," "Smash the Pigs," "Administrators are Repressers"—the age of slogans, the age of "them against us," and the age of paranoia seemed to be accurate statements about the mood of the Austin campus during the spring of 1970.

Perhaps those statements were not so accurate about the less vocal portion of the student body. Only a small segment of the students were ready to say that the federal, state, and local governments and university administrations would not change in the near future to become more responsive to radical prejudice, to industrial pollution, and to unwarranted military spending.

The creation of the office of the students' attorney appears to be a denial of the proposition that local governments and a university administration should be radically altered. On the contrary, the birth of such an office seems to be saying these institutions can be made more responsive to student concerns.

---

* Students' Attorney, The University of Texas at Austin.

I was extemely apprehensive about accepting the position of students' attorney at a university where students wanted to radically affect racism, war, and pollution. If my success or failure was to be measured by whether I was able to have a significant impact on these problems, I was doomed to failure. Problems of racism, war, and pollution are certainly not going to be appreciably lessened by one university, let alone one attorney.

The Office of the Students' Attorney Act[1] did not allay my fears, for it set forth the requirement that individual students were to be represented only in cases which involve the "interests of students generally."[2]

My anxiety was compounded when I learned of the regents' restriction on my office.[3] The restrictions prohibit any attorney employed in whole or in part by the Students' Association of the University of Texas at Austin from representing any student, faculty, or staff member before any administrative, disciplinary, or judicial body where the university may be in an adverse position.[4] I could not employ whatever skill I possess as a lawyer to probe, negotiate, and compromise on behalf of students in order to raise the level of student-administration contact from physical confrontation to reasoned discussion.

With all the doubts and fears about my effectiveness as an advocate on behalf of students, I accepted the students' attorney position; I felt that there was some hope that I could get the restriction removed either by legal action or by convincing the regents that an unrestricted students' attorney was in the

---

1. University of Texas Student Assembly Acts, 1969, B-75-68-69 [hereinafter cited as the Students' Attorney Act]; *see* Appendix IV.
2. On October 29, 1970, § 4(3), (4) of the Students' Attorney Act was amended so that litigation could be brought without the approval of two-thirds of those present at the student assembly. The amendment was made so that no one could interfere with the attorney-client relationship once it has been established.
3. Board of Regents, University of Texas System, Rules and Regulations, Part II, Chapter X, §§ 11.1, 11.2 (1969).
4. *Id.* §§11.11, 11.13.

best interest of the university. Despite the restrictions, however, a students' attorney can be particularly effective in dealing with consumer fraud and unscrupulous landlords.

In the time I have been the students' attorney, I have, with the invaluable assistance of nine law clerks, counseled more than six hundred students. In the consumer protection area, we found that the most common problems are automobile repairs, door-to-door sales, charter air flights, and collection agency practices.

A typical automobile repair problem develops when a student takes his car to a garage for a front-end alignment which supposedly costs $7.77. When he picks up his car, he is handed a bill for $50.00, and of course, he must pay the bill in order to get his car.

All too frequently, my attention is directed to the door-to-door sales contract which binds the student to pay over four hundred dollars to a company which promises to do research papers for the student, but in reality is only selling encyclopedias.

Charter flights to Europe, Acapulco, and other exotic spots are organized by travel agencies operating on a shoestring. Students are promised that they will be flown as members of charter-worthy organizations. Only after paying their money do the students find out that the charter organization is a sham created by the travel agency and that the Civil Aeronautics Board will not approve the flights.

Collection agencies dealt with by my office have been tenacious in their attempts to collect debts alleged to be owed by students. In one case, a collection agency made numerous and harassing attempts to collect eighteen dollars which we could prove was not even owed. The student, a quadriplegic, received fifteen calls in five hours.

In the landlord-tenant area, the most common problems are wrongful evictions, refusals to return security deposits, and refusals to rent to a student for race or ethnic reasons. Recently, I represented three Peruvian students against whom an eviction proceeding was brought because they paid their rent a few days late. The students had been told by the manager of the apartments that they could make a late payment.

I have come in contact with several landlords who as a general rule of operation will not return deposit money, even to students who leave their apartments in perfect condition and break no lease agreement. I estimate that one Austin landlord with substantial rental holdings gains thirty to forty thousand dollars each year through wrongful withholding of security deposits.

Around the university area, there is still substantial discrimination in housing. My office has not made substantial progress in breaking down that discrimination.

I have thus far directed my remarks to off-campus legal controversies. However, students have many problems within the university structure. In any university with an enrollment of more than thirty-five thousand students, there will be arbitrary, unfortunate, and unreasonable decisions made in particular cases. These decisions do not usually stem from bad faith or malice, but occur simply as a result of the pressures of administering a university of such size. I believe that most persons, including college administrators and regents, are reasonable people interested in resolution of conflicts in a rational manner.

Unfortunately, the University of Texas System Board of Regents added more restrictions on the office of students' attorney on January 29, 1971; they prohibited my office from representing student groups in any administrative, judicial, or disciplinary proceeding in which the university is an interested party.[5] The regents' restrictions in force up to that time had said nothing about limiting my representation of student groups. The additional restriction on the office came as a result of our representation of a student group known as Gay Liberation.

On October 29, 1970, the office of the dean of students

5. *Id.* §§11.1, 11.2 as amended January 29, 1971.

denied to Gay Liberation status as a registered campus organization. Without being registered, Gay Liberation could not use university facilities. Gay Liberation appealed the denial of registered status to the committee on student organizations, a student-faculty committee. On December 2, 1970, a hearing was held at which the University of Texas System Law Office represented the office of the dean of students and I represented the Gay Liberation group. On December 8, 1970, the committee on student organizations reversed the decision of the dean's office by a seven to two vote. The following day the president of the university reversed the decision of the committee on student organizations, affirming the decision of the dean's office. The president made his decision without any kind of appellate hearing, without giving any weight to evidence presented before the committee on student organizations, without receiving any of the exhibits introduced at the hearing, and without receiving a copy of the transcript of the committee on student organizations hearing. The reversal, it would seem, was simply an exercise of power without regard for fundamental fairness.

After the events surrounding the attempt of the Gay Liberation group to gain student organization status, the following steps were taken by the administration in an effort to curtail my representation of students who had disputes with the university:

(1) At the December 4, 1970, meeting of the board of regents, the chairman of the board of regents introduced a rule to prohibit me from representing student groups. The rule did not go into effect at the time because the chairman failed to comply with the Texas Open Meetings Law.

(2) On December 18, 1970, I was notified that I would have to sign a form indicating that I am a state employee. I was told that I had to sign this form or I would receive no further paychecks. The student activity fee money out of which I receive my salary is collected and disbursed by the university.

(3) On January 29, 1971, the board of regents officially amended their rules to prohibit my representation of student

organizations in cases in which the university is an interested party.

I suppose that if I had tried to select a more unpopular group with the general public than Gay Liberation, I would not have been able to find such. It was unfortunate timing that I was cast in the position of representing Gay Liberation so early in the life of this office.

Attorneys providing group legal services can avoid some of the repercussions which surrounded my office by making certain that the funds used to support such attorneys are raised by a collection process outside the control of the university.

With independent funding a student government organization can contract with an attorney to protect the rights of its members in many areas, including disputes which concern university policy. Three important Supreme Court cases[6] suggest that a university, absent a threat of disruption of the educational process, cannot limit the associational right of students to hire an attorney of their choice for the purpose of redressing grievances.[7]

The students' attorney at the University of Texas is charged with the obligation to serve the interests of the university students. A critical examination of our operation raises the question of how that interest is to be determined. In recognition of the importance of the question, the students' association has created a students' attorney advisory committee, comprised of three law professors and five students.[8] The committee is charged with the responsibility of determining what litigation is in the students' interest. Important decisions regarding the operation of the office are made only after thorough examination by the committee.

The point has been argued that state money is involved in operating the office of students' attorney and that the state

6. NAACP v. Button, 371 U.S. 415 (1963); Brotherhood of R.R. Trainmen v. Va., 377 U.S. 1 (1964); and United Mineworkers v. Ill. State Bar Ass'n, 389 U.S. 217 (1967).
7. Note, 48 TEX. L. REV., 1217-1219 (1970).
8. University of Texas Student Assembly Acts, 1970, B-13-70-71.

should not pay an attorney to represent views adverse to state interest.

I do not believe that the operation of the office of students' attorney is adverse to the interest of the state. It seems to me highly reasonable that the operations I have outlined above will be a positive benefit to the interest of the state and its university through the formation of better rules to govern students, with more student input of a very meaningful sort.

CHAPTER SIX

Questions and Answers

Moderator:
John W. Reed

Participants:
Eugene B. Power
David Kessler
Robert L. Knauss
Robert G. Zumwinkle

Trustee and Student

Reed: Mr. Power, I have a question addressed to you. As background, the questioner states that it is obvious that radical students generate polarization and the growth of reactionary response from faculty and students. He then asks whether boards of trustees plan to respond similarly to both factions, or to embrace this new backlash as a salvation.

Power: I think that depends on the board. That is why I stressed the need for variety in membership of governing boards. A board tends to be more conservative, more to the right than the faculty or the students. There is a tendency for the board, if they are led by their administration, to take a firm, somewhat reactionary stand. It is essential that a board member have contacts outside his administration and outside sources of information to help him reach a balanced decision.

Communications Gap

Reed: Mr. Power, a student asks what can be done to enable governing boards to gain more understanding of the aspirations of their students.

41

Power: There is always a barrier. And of course the administration people are usually not very happy to have trustees "going behind their backs." The average administrative officer, the average president, prefers that his trustees know what he tells them and nothing more; but an effective trustee cannot be dependent upon one point of view. Some of the Michigan regents have invited small groups of students to breakfast. Because I live in Ann Arbor, perhaps I had more access to both student and faculty points of view than most regents. A conscientious trustee must extend his range of contacts beyond the administration to be effective.

Student Members of Boards

Reed: How about allowing student members on boards, or at least allowing them to sit as nonvoting members?

Power: Many of the problems facing a board require maturity and experience. The presence of student members, while admirable in itself, does not provide for a continuity of membership. It takes about four or five years to become an effective regent. The student member will usually serve a year or two, at most. He will spend most of that time learning his job. Moreover, he has not lived long enough to have developed the necessary experience and maturity on which to base his judgments. He has not had a chance to make mistakes and see what happens when he makes them. I believe that the role of students or student groups should be limited to periodic meetings or consultation with regents.

Zumwinkle: I wonder, really, whether the presence of one student is going to contaminate a board to that extent . . .

Power: Not a bit.

Zumwinkle: . . . and I would think a nonvoting student member, for starters, would be good for a board in many cases.

Power: It certainly would give the board another point of view.

Kessler: I think occasional meetings have not served the function quite so well as having a student member on the board. I think a student member would be very useful. There are enough members of the board, aside from the students, to provide all of the maturity and experience necessary. I believe the students can provide some insight that maturity and experience cannot provide. If we blend the two, we might have a very excellent balance of opinion. I see nothing at all pernicious in having an occasional student member on a board.

The Administration and Ad Hoc Groups

Reed: I have a question here that seems appropriately headed for Mr. Kessler or Mr. Zumwinkle. When the relationship is good between the student government group on campus and the administration, does the administration undermine the student government by dealing with ad hoc student groups that make demands? Do you believe that the administration ought to insist that representations be made through the student government group?

Kessler: Generally, the ad hoc group is a black student group. I find absolutely nothing wrong with their direct approach. I would not expect them to go through student government channels.

Reed: Do you have any comment, Mr. Zumwinkle? Have you had any experience with ad hoc groups?

Zumwinkle: In general, I would agree with Mr. Kessler. Perhaps such demands should be routed through student government or at least through a more representative body than certain ad hoc groups, but we have to have flexibility.

Kessler: The more serious complaint we have is that we get undermined because there is no real bargaining. The other side is not willing to put the chips on the table or to make any real compromises. A general who doesn't want any battles soon loses his troops. Then you see an increase in the number of ad hoc groups.

The Faculty Role

As Dormitory Residents during Disruption

Reed: May I have your opinion, Professor Knauss, of faculty residents in student dormitories during a campus disorder? The questioner mentions an experience at the University of South Carolina where faculty residents in dormitories had a calming effect and served to "educate the faculty as to the student problems." Have you tried that? Do you know anything about it?

Knauss: We have not done that at Michigan. Some time ago the ROTC building on this campus was "liberated" and turned into a child care center for a few days. Some of our faculty members spent time in the building, scheduled on a twenty-four hour basis. I would agree that the incident provided a very educational experience for those faculty members who were involved. It also gave support to the majority of the students involved, who did not want violence or destruction of property.

Use of Faculty Monitors

Reed: Several people have asked about the role conflict in the use of faculty as monitors. You mentioned the conflict that would arise if the faculty who were monitoring the street situation, for example, are then called upon to give evidence. Somebody described this as a "cop-out"—that you ask them to take some responsibility but then give them no accountability. Have you any comment about that?

Knauss: The responsibility I was referring to is that of cooling the existing situation. It is similar to bringing in police specifically to protect individuals and property rather than to arrest wrongdoers. There are many situations when police—small numbers of police—can be used effectively in a protecting situation. If you want to arrest, you need large numbers of policemen. I look on the faculty monitoring role as being a positive one at this stage. If they are used later to give evidence in disciplinary proceedings, their effectiveness as faculty monitors will soon be lost.

Reed: Did you instruct your monitors as to what they were to do if violence occurred? If so, could you tell us what you asked them to do?

Knauss: Our specific advice was to leave the scene as rapidly as possible. As I indicated, the official capacity of the monitors was as observers and to provide a visibility. They were not to attempt to thrust themselves between police or students or to take an active role. In fact, some of our faculty people did take an active role despite the official policy.

Faculty as Mediators

Reed: I have a question for Mr. Kessler. In what situations, if any, do you believe that students would agree to allow a faculty member to assume the role of third-party mediator between students and administration?

Kessler: The faculty can almost always act as effective mediators. They can help establish communication, attempting to understand what the students are talking about and telling the students what the administrators are talking about. But I cannot place too much reliance on the possibility of success. They cannot always smooth things out and cool the protest. The faculty members have to be willing to accept new ideas. Obviously this will be difficult. In effect, students seem to be saying, "You have to give in to our way of thinking before you can play a useful role." But if faculty can exercise a certain amount of tact and willingness to compromise, I think they can play a very useful role. I am certainly happy to see them involved on our campus when things happen. They are part of the community and they may as well get into the fray.

Black Protest and the Faculty

Reed: Several questions relate to use of the faculty in one way or another to help cool the situation. I had thought that administrators were the prime targets until fairly recently. Now it appears that students in some schools have begun to see that the faculties have resisted change and development and the target has changed.

A question to Professor Knauss, from a Kent State student, asks what methods the faculty should employ to scale down the conflict when violence begins to develop. What can the faculty do? Bob, would you expand a little on the faculty's role here? The specific question states: The role of faculty involvement in crisis management seems desirable, yet the orientation of this conference is essentially directed toward disruption or crisis initiated by white, militant radicals. How can a white, middle class faculty member help in a crisis involving large numbers of black militants? In other words, do we need to make a distinction in our responses to white radical protests and black protests? Could you respond to this general line of questioning?

Knauss: There are two aspects. One is the role of the faculty in mediation; the other, its role in attempting to solve the underlying substantive problem. On this campus, the substantive issue in the Black Action Movement strike was the question of financing a vast increase in black student enrollment. A strike developed — an attempt to close down at least a portion of the university — some violence, some classroom disruption. What is the faculty role at that stage? I accept the fact that the faculty cannot do too much on substantive issues. People should not be overly optimistic simply because the faculty is involved. However, I believe their involvement in the issue is essential and should occur quickly. I believe that the faculty at Michigan missed the boat, in some ways, on the matter of black student admission. We should have started six months earlier. No one suggested that we be brought into it, but we should have done it on our own. We should have seen it as an issue. We should have started operating. We should have had some committee work. We should have had an independent viewpoint to present to the administration in advance, instead of trying to respond quickly in the face of the strike. Obviously, the black faculty should be involved. It was difficult at Michigan, because there had not been sufficient advance contact with black faculty. However, they did provide a very good bridge of communication. The white faculty also provided some help.

Reed: Mr. Kessler, do you wish to comment?

Kessler: I believe that faculty members can really be helpful before a crisis. Mr. Knauss' statement is entirely valid. If people of some authority are willing to go through the proper channels and really make a systematic effort to understand the issues and forge ahead, offering solutions for problems, it should be most beneficial.

Stopping Faculty Salaries in Shutdown

Reed: I have a question for Professor Knauss. If a university is closed down, would reopening be expedited if faculty salaries were stopped during the shutdown period? I mention this because such a proposal was made at the time of the BAM strike on the Michigan campus.

Knauss: It has been suggested by some people that Michigan faculty members who did not meet their classes during the Michigan strike should give up a portion of their salaries. As you know, this proposal was a reaction to the fact that some of our faculty members were involved in the strike. Once this process is begun, and I see it as a real possibility, it is the first step toward the formation of a faculty union. How do you define a faculty member's job? How do you write a job description? Many Michigan faculty people who were on strike insisted that striking was a part of their job of making Michigan a better educational institution—that they were providing as much as the person doing research or other public service work. Whether or not you accept that philosophy, you should recognize that you are immediately faced with writing job descriptions. Once you do that, you are quickly thrust into a collective bargaining situation and a faculty union.

Law Faculty as Advisers

Reed: I have a question for Professor Knauss: Would it be advisable for proximal schools of law to work out mutual arrangements to advise small schools on control of disruptive protest and solutions to related problems?

Knauss: I doubt that just the presence of a school of law is, in itself, beneficial. Individual faculty people certainly can advise smaller schools on the legal problems they may have. The matters which schools must deal with today are outside the normal range of problems which the general counsel of a school is prepared to handle. A different kind of experience is essential.

Reed: If you were president of a university seeking counsel in these matters, would you, knowing how these things operate, prefer to have a fully informed special legal assistant as your counselor, or would you rather choose your people out of a resident law school?

Knauss: I would rather have the special counselor, even on a part-time basis, who would become very familiar with the field. I could rely on him for help with specific kinds of problems. For example, a special assistant could collect information from the fifty schools who are working to develop a new kind of internal judicial system. Much more could be done to make that kind of information readily available.

Reed: I trust that nearly everyone here knows that there is a National Association of College and University Attorneys who do exchange information, providing some of the clearinghouse functions you mentioned.

PART II

ADMINISTRATIVE DISCIPLINE

CHAPTER SEVEN

The Administrative Tribunal

*Theodore J. St. Antoine**

Introduction

I need go back no more than a decade to give you a histori-
cal curiosity concerning the responsibility for the maintenance
of discipline on an American university campus. There was in
existence during the past ten years, and for all I know there
may still be in existence, a two-paragraph, two-section procedure for the resolution of campus disciplinary problems. I find
it quaintly charming in its pristine simplicity. I shall paraphrase it, out of regard for those kind people everywhere who
sent us information for our study of other campus disciplinary
procedures:

Section I. There shall be a Dean of Men, and he shall be
responsible for the governance of the male students in this
university.

Section II. There shall be a Dean of Women, and she
shall be responsible for the governance of the female
students in this university.

Things are obviously changing. De Tocqueville is again
being proven right about the American reaction to societal
problems. Eventually, nearly all our problems become problems for lawyers. The strained relations between faculty and
administrators and students, now one of the major concerns of
American society, have brought out the lawyers in full force.

---

* Professor of Law, The University of Michigan Law School, Ann Arbor,
Michigan.

During the past summer I have had the good fortune to join with colleagues of the university community from the administration and from the student body in two separate but related endeavors: first, to draw up a body of substantive rules for nonacademic conduct on the campus and, second, to establish a judicial body to enforce those rules. The latter problem, the composition of a university judiciary, is the subject of this discussion. The views I shall present about structuring a university judiciary are drawn in large part from the discussions of the committees to which I belong. In addition, I shall draw upon our examination of the procedures in use at some twenty different campuses across the United States, and three helpful statements of concerned organizations — statements that have dealt with the problem of disciplinary procedures on campuses over the past three or four years. One is the *Statement of the Rights and Responsibilities of College and University Students*,[1] drafted in 1970 by the Section of Individual Rights and Responsibilities of the American Bar Association. Another is the *Joint Statement on Rights and Freedoms of Students*,[2] formulated in 1967 by representatives of the American Association of University Professors, the United States National Student Association, the Association of American Colleges, and other interested organizations. The third document we found helpful is the *Model Code for Student Rights, Responsibilities and Conduct*[3] prepared by the Law Student Division of the American Bar Association.

Because I am currently involved in deliberations with two different committees, I shall not emphasize my personal opinions about these matters, but shall attempt to set forth the different views and opposing arguments of the various groups concerned with the creation of an effective campus judiciary. I shall enumerate what I would describe as a checklist of factors for your consideration, raising certain key questions and then

1. *See* Appendix I.
2. 54 A.A.U.P. BULL. 258 (1968); STUDENT PROTEST AND THE LAW at 181 (Institute of Continuing Legal Education, 1969).
3. *See* STUDENT PROTEST AND THE LAW at 371.

indulging in the law professor's ploy of failing to provide the answers.

Criteria of Campus Judiciaries

There are five different criteria that must be met by an all-campus judiciary capable of handling the kinds of problems we find in universities today. First, the tribunal must be competent and qualified to do its job. Such competence presupposes knowledge of the particular mores of the university community. Second, it must be fair and impartial. It must have the capacity to weigh opposing positions in a highly emotional situation, yielding neither to prejudice nor to outside pressure. Third, the tribunal must be acceptable; that is, it must seem to be fair to the different factions whose interests it will protect — both the persons who are charged with violations and the persons who are victims of those violations. It goes without saying that the appearance of fairness must spring from the fact that it is fair and just. It must not be counterproductive; that is to say, it must not, by the simple fact of its presence on campus, add to the difficulty of maintaining order.

Most persons would readily concede the validity of the three criteria enumerated above — competence, impartiality, and acceptability. The next two criteria, though a bit more subtle, are also of critical importance. Fourth, the judiciary must be suitable for doing the particular job entrusted to it. It may have a narrow or a broad jurisdiction. It may deal only with maintaining order on the campus; it may be analogous to a police court. On the other hand, it may have a very broad jurisdiction to deal with the kinds of problems lawyers would call civil problems, including disputes between individual members of the university community or disputes between students and their organizations. The type of tribunal to be constructed will be determined to a considerable extent by the particular function it is to perform. Fifth, the tribunal must be consistent with the traditions of the particular institution where it is established. This important requirement is frequently overlooked in the search for the one ideal tribunal for all situations. I suspect there is no such thing. A school that has maintained an authoritarian control in the past may be able to construct an administration-dominated tribunal acceptable to that school community, while the same kind of tribunal would be entirely unacceptable at The University of Michigan or any other school where a student judiciary has been a long and respected tradition.

Types of Tribunals

I shall now examine some of the principal kinds of tribunals in existence and proposed at various campuses across the country. In general, it may safely be concluded that the solution is not the creation of an all-administration tribunal or an all-faculty tribunal, if the accused are to be students. I think one can simply set aside the model I mentioned at the opening of my remarks. The stark statement that "[t]here shall be a Dean of Men and he shall be responsible for the governance of the conduct of the male students of this university . . ." is an anachronism in today's world.

The extent to which there shall be student participation in any such tribunal is always a critical question. The growing sentiment of various professional groups that have considered the matter favors student participation. The American Bar Association *Statement* drafted by the Section of Individual Rights and Responsibilities of that body states flatly that students should be entitled to participate in any all-campus judiciary. *The Joint Statement on Rights and Freedoms of Students*,[4] drawn up in 1967, suggested the advisability of student participation. It is not surprising that the third study, the *Model Code*[5] prepared by the Law Student Division of the American Bar Association, plumps firmly for an all-student judiciary.

Our committee studied a relatively good cross section of American colleges and universities, examining the judiciary systems, actual and proposed, of some twenty schools. By and

4. *Supra* n. 2.
5. *Supra* n. 3.

large, they break down into three types of campus judiciaries—mixed faculty-student tribunals, all-student judiciaries,
and systems using individual hearing officers. Over half of the
twenty systems we looked at are mixed tribunals, with both
faculty members and students participating. The precise ratios
vary rather widely. Some are evenly balanced, but frequently
the student members exceed the faculty members by one, or
conversely, the number of faculty members is greater by one.
Some four or five of the systems we examined have all-student
judiciaries. Significantly, we found that at least two of these
systems provide for a faculty adviser. This person does not
have a vote but is responsible for providing professional counsel in the handling of the procedures of the tribunal. Finally,
about five of our sampling of twenty or more schools have
tribunals involving hearing officers. These systems make no
provision for student participation. A case is heard by a hearing officer, either a faculty member or an outsider. Three
schools use outsiders — independent hearing officers not con-
nected with the school in any capacity. The hearing officer
system is used in three schools under what might be described
as emergency conditions, a significant and troublesome point
which I shall discuss later. The unhappy fact is that some
long-standing internal judicial systems have broken down in
the last two years when the crunch came and there were
serious, campus-wide disturbances. Three of the Big Ten
schools, including The University of Michigan, resorted to
outside hearing officers in aggravated cases.[6]

Critique of Tribunal Systems

Let me now attempt to apply to the three general patterns
of judiciaries—the mixed tribunal, the all-student tribunal, and
the hearing officer—some criticisms based upon the criteria
listed earlier. At this point in time, these five factors—
competence, fairness, acceptability, suitability for the assignment, and consistency with a given school's traditions—guide

6. *See* M. Sowell, Chapter 8.

my thinking about the desirability of any particular kind of tribunal.

I shall deal first with the all-student judiciary, a body composed entirely of students, possibly with a professional to offer guidance and counsel, especially regarding procedural matters. The counselor may be an outsider or a faculty member. What are the points in favor of this system? One can be sure that such a tribunal will be knowledgeable, that it will understand the mores of the university community, and that it will be acceptable to the students. In most cases, students will have the most confidence in a tribunal composed of members drawn from their own constituency. As the students are wont to say, they believe a person should be tried by a jury of his peers.

There are valid objections to an all-student judiciary. If it is really intended that the tribunal deal with campus-wide problems of a major nature—the kind of massive disturbances experienced within the past two years—serious questions arise. Can the members of such an all-student tribunal withstand the inevitable political pressures? Can they be counted on to find persons guilty of disruptive conduct when they may sympathize with the aims of the persons engaging in such conduct? Another question of critical importance is whether such a tribunal will be acceptable to the faculty and the administration of the university community. Faculty members or administrators, after all, are likely to be the principal victims of major disruptions. It is understandable that students who are the accused have a special concern about who will judge them; at the same time, the faculty and the administration have a legitimate concern about who will judge the persons who have allegedly victimized them. There are possible compromises to minimize these conflicts. Certainly an all-student judiciary will not present the difficulties I have indicated as long as its jurisdiction is confined to dealing with problems between students or problems between students and their organizations. Moreover, if an essentially all-student tribunal is to be entrusted with the responsibility for dealing even with major cases of disruption, the insertion of some outside voice such as a professional counselor or law officer to provide procedural guidance for the students may help to ensure an orderly hearing and heighten faculty confidence in the soundness of the system.

The hearing officer—the single individual entrusted with responsibility for handling cases—has some distinct advantages. The hearing officer is thought by many to be the most likely to guarantee impartial treatment for all parties. An outside person will not be subject to the special pressures imposed upon a member of the university community. His impartiality should be assured if care is taken in the selection process; he should not, for example, be the unilateral appointee of the president of the university.

Students constantly stress two problems about a judiciary employing a hearing officer. The first is in the nature of a philosophical objection, and I apologize if my phrasing fails to convey its full flavor: he who sits in judgment should be a member of the same community that is governed by the laws the judge is administering. In other words, with the practical implications now emphasized, one who applies a rule or regulation should act with the realization that one day that rule or regulation might be applied against him. The second objection students lodge against the individual hearing officer from outside is even more practical: they are skeptical that he has a sufficient understanding of, or sympathy with, the peculiar mores of the university community. They doubt whether he can properly assess the significance of acts of dissent, especially in a time of great social change. They question whether he can assess the impact of sanctions, if he is the person who is going to impose sanctions.

The third type of tribunal, the mixed student-faculty judiciary, is by far the most common among the cross section of campus systems we have examined. The advantage of a mixed tribunal is the capability of providing a breadth of views, a characteristic not always found in the all-student tribunal.

A possible serious defect in a mixed tribunal is that it may promote factionalism, dividing the members along political lines. Thus, a student member of a mixed tribunal may actually find it much harder to vote to convict an accused student, joining those faculty members voting for conviction, than he would if he were sitting as a member of an all-student tribunal. Traditionally, students have been hard judges of fellow students. It is only in the last few years, since political problems have become central campus issues, that skepticism has developed about the objectivity of student judgment of their peers. There is a risk that in serious cases where feelings run high a mixed tribunal may have trouble avoiding splits along party lines. That would, of course, destroy the acceptability of the final result, either to the accused or to the charging party.

Variables Affecting Tribunal Composition

I would suggest that three variables are vitally significant in determining the right kind of campus tribunal—one that is adequate for the task and acceptable to the different persons affected by the decisions of that tribunal. These variables may ultimately control the decision as to the best kind of tribunal for a particular institution. The first variable is the method of selecting the members of the tribunal. Regardless of who they are, how are they to be selected? The second consideration is the scope of the jurisdiction of the tribunal. What kinds of offenses will it deal with? What kinds of problems will confront it? Thirdly, is there any appeal from decisions of the tribunal? If so, to whom or to what body? I shall deal with each of these factors in turn, relating them to the three general types of tribunals we have examined.

Selection of Members

The objections customarily lodged against the hearing officer—that he is likely to be the unilateral appointee of the university president or another administrative official, and that he will not really know the campus situation—can be greatly diminished if the students have a hand in his selection. Similarly, much of the sting can be removed from the arguments against an all-student tribunal if there is some arrangement for joint selection by faculty and students. Of course, the joint selection process immediately calls up the specter of other problems. Will diverse groups ever agree on appointees? How do you handle the situation where one faction refuses to act? Such pitfalls surely exist. Nevertheless, one might work out a system to establish a predetermined pool of candidates. If the hearing officer system is used, for example, the pool might be a group of professional arbitrators. From that pool, one constituency could choose a panel of a prescribed number, and the second constituency could choose half of that panel to form the actual roster of hearing officers. If you can get agreement on some predetermined group as the initial pool, I am persuaded it would be easy to work out a quick, simple method for joint selection.

A novel way of choosing students for an all-student judiciary has been suggested by the Section of Individual Rights and Responsibilities of the American Bar Association. To my knowledge, it is not in use in any of the schools surveyed by our committee, although we at Michigan are now considering it seriously. This method is a random selection of students in a process similar to that employed to draw jurors for the civil courts from the general community. Many persons object to an all-student judiciary, especially one in which persons petition for appointment and then are screened by a student government body, on the ground that such a tribunal is too likely to be ideologically oriented. The detractors claim that the judiciary becomes a self-selected group of political activists of the university community, who are not typical of the vast majority of students. The objectivity of the activists is suspect in the eyes of many faculty members. A random selection can avoid that particular problem by providing a genuine cross section of students. I suppose that most faculty members would concede that if we cannot rely upon the good judgment of the mass of our student body, then the future is pretty bleak no matter what we do.

One difficulty with a randomly selected tribunal, especially if it is to serve on an ad hoc basis, is that it cannot acquire professional competence—experience in interpreting either the substantive or the procedural rules that it must apply. Any kind of ad hoc body would need the guidance of a law officer or some kind of professional counselor to a far greater degree than would a permanent student judiciary.

Scope of Jurisdiction

As I have said earlier, the scope of the jurisdiction of a campus judiciary will have a significant bearing upon the kind of tribunal that is needed. "Civil" disputes among members of the university community, or even individual cases of disorder, disruption, or violence, may well be handled competently by a student tribunal. But what about the major disruptions?

The critical questions involved in attempting to establish a campus judiciary must ultimately be faced. To what extent should cases of group violence on the campus be left to the civil authorities? To what extent should a campus judiciary limit its jurisdiction to cases involving peculiarly institutional problems—relations between students or their organizations, for example—leaving the massive disruption case entirely in the hands of the public prosecutor and the civil courts? There are benefits to be derived from this kind of approach. It places much less strain on the internal system. Students would not have to worry about the prejudices of faculty members on the tribunal influencing judgments, destroying or gravely impairing a student's academic career by applying the heavy sanctions of suspension or expulsion. Faculty members would not have to worry about excessive leniency on the part of student judges. It would be strictly a matter for the civil authorities.

The notion that the university is like a private club, in which honorable gentlemen alone are to be admitted, may very well be an anachronism. In today's world, the great state university may be more akin to a public utility. If the civil authorities conclude that a man is sufficiently safe to be allowed to walk free in society, why should the university complain about his attending a lecture? On the other hand, I do not believe that simply turning the whole business over to the civil authorities is the proper course to take. I have a deep concern that students do not fully appreciate the damage that may be done to their future careers and even, perhaps, to their psyches in the present, by a tangle with the criminal process. A felony or a substantial misdemeanor on their records and a month or two in jail are deadly serious matters. Moreover, the heavy costs of bail and attorneys' fees cannot be treated casually. From the faculty's and administration's perspective, I think experience indicates that there is always a risk to academic freedom and autonomy in inviting courts and legislators to become involved in university governance. So I am not happy about a wholesale transfer of campus discipline to external bodies.

There may be an acceptable middle position with regard to the second variable—the scope of jurisdiction of the campus tribunal. Perhaps we could adopt the approach that the university system should grapple with cases having a peculiar institutional flavor, or cases in which the magnitude of the offense is not really assessable by general community standards, leaving all others to the civil authorities. Let me give you an example of each kind of case. One can validly argue that a private quarrel between two students or between a faculty member and a student, with resulting violence, does not involve the university as an institution and should be left to the civil authorities—to the parties to resolve between themselves outside the university system. On the other hand, there are certain kinds of offenses that the civil authorities will recognize, but will fail to comprehend fully the seriousness within the university context. For instance, I presume most courts would regard the deliberate misappropriation of a five or ten-dollar book for two or three days as a very minor offense, punishable, perhaps, by a fine of ten dollars. If, however, that book were one of only two library copies urgently needed by a large class two days before an examination, the university community might feel that a ten-dollar fine did not adequately reflect the gravity of the offense.

The distinction I have just outlined would leave most major campus disruptions — those directed against the university itself — within the jurisdiction of some campus judiciary. At this point in the development of a campus jurisprudence, I think that necessitates some substantial involvement by the faculty and administration in the selection and manning of the tribunal dealing with such cases. Faculty involvement need not be total. For example, the faculty might have a hand in the selection process, or at the appellate level, and leave fact finding to the students.

Appeal Procedures

The third important variable affecting the adequacy and acceptability of any trial judiciary is the process of appeal from its decisions. All of the tribunals I am familiar with that have all-student trial bodies provide for some kind of an appeal. Generally, provision is made for an appeal to an all-faculty or mixed faculty-student tribunal. More informally, the accused has the right to request clemency from the president of the university. Student judiciaries have traditionally made harsh judgments and some form of appellate review has always been included as a protection against such harshness. The most pressing issue today is whether complainants should have the right of appeal. What happens, for example, if there is an acquittal by a student tribunal in a significant disruption case, where political issues are at stake? Should the prosecution be allowed to appeal? A prosecution appeal grounded upon alleged erroneous rulings of law or allegations that findings of fact are clearly at variance with the evidence is certainly no denial of due process, in the strict sense. But it is contrary to the American tradition in the criminal process, and I can assure you from my experience that the students will vigorously oppose prosecution appeals. At the same time, however, an individual complainant may justifiably feel incensed if he is unfairly denied redress, and then has no opportunity for appeal. Again, it may be possible to find an acceptable middle position. In cases which involve a "civil" rather than "criminal" controversy, that is, where it is not the institution against an accused student, but rather a faculty member against a student, or a student against another student, and the plaintiff feels that he is entitled to some personal relief or restitution, it may be that the complainant should be allowed to appeal in what is essentially a private action. On the other hand, the prosecutor acting on behalf of the university in quasi-criminal proceedings could be denied an appeal.

Tribunal Procedures

I have been asked to go a bit beyond my discussion of the structure of a campus judiciary and say a few words about the procedures of such a body. My experience suggests that procedures do not present problems as difficult as those involved in the composition of the tribunal and the method of selecting its members. Of course, the courts require that before a student can be deprived of his status within an educational institution, he must be accorded due process. By and large, the due process required in university administrative proceedings is a relaxed kind of due process. There must be a fair hearing before an impartial judge. There may be need to have witnesses present and to afford the right of cross-examination. The accused is entitled to some kind of counsel, but not necessarily a lawyer. This kind of elementary due process, I assume, will be considered sufficient by the courts. Helpful analogies can probably be found in the very large body of law concerning the due process requirements in disciplinary proceedings of labor organizations against their members.

There are a few difficult problems. First, if the university has a paid attorney serving, in effect, as public prosecutor, will the student be left to his own devices, having to hire a lawyer or find a law student to defend him? Or should we provide for some kind of public defender for students? I do not suggest that this issue rises to the level of due process, but I do think it presents a substantial policy question for any institution with a fairly formal procedure, including a public prosecutor—a university lawyer who will be presenting the case on behalf of the institution.

The courts have clearly indicated that double jeopardy is not technically applicable to university procedures; thus, it is not a defense against university discipline that a person has already been tried for the same act by the civil courts. Yet surely there is some kind of problem, at least in terms of the spirit of fairness, about prosecuting a man twice for a single offense. Again, I think some distinctions may be in order. There are certain kinds of offenses that are so obviously off-campus offenses that it really makes no difference whether they are committed by a student or a nonstudent. I would regard a traffic offense as the classic example of this type. If a man has served his time for illegal driving (under some kind of influence—alcohol does not seem to be the problem so much these days), why should a university try him all over again? Probably such offenses are inappropriate bases for campus discipline anyway, but at least let me suggest that we consider a rule whereby the university as an institution is given a choice: either it will proceed against a person within the university system or, if a case is so serious that internal discipline is inadequate, it must go outside. Having chosen the latter course, the institution may not turn back to the campus tribunal and invoke its processes. I recognize that some offenses may have both university and nonuniversity implications, and thus justify in theory two separate trials and penalties. It is so difficult to draw a line here, however, that I don't think the exercise is worth the effort.

Many of the judicial systems in schools around the country now provide for the suspension of any university proceedings as long as a criminal charge is pending at the trial level against a student. This approach avoids problems of self-incrimination. It also allows the campus judiciary to take into account the court decision on the charge against the student, in its deliberations and especially in its sanction.

Conclusion

I shall conclude with one or two personal comments. I have worked extensively with the students on two committees—one committee attempting to establish an all-campus judiciary, the other seeking to write a substantive code of conduct. I learned many lessons, but one I would put near the top was confirmation of my feeling that many students view us—faculty and administrative personnel—with a great deal of distrust and suspicion. We, of course, feel that is unjustified. We can remind them of all the good things their elders have given them—opportunity for an education and an easy affluence, among other advantages unknown to earlier generations. And yet, from their perspective, why should they trust us? They hear our generation talk everlastingly of peace, while sending them off to be killed in a war they regard as morally reprehensible. Right here on the university campuses, they hear professors speak glowingly of the life of the mind, while struggling mightily for academic status and the material rewards it brings. They hear administrators praise the concept of student participation in decisionmaking, while all too often proffering the form and denying the substance. Indeed, I am satisfied that the creation of an effective university judiciary through joint faculty-student efforts may mean much more than the maintenance of campus discipline. It might be the first long step toward bridging differences between faculty members and students, and restoring a sense of trust and common endeavor.

Another important lesson I learned from my committee work was more comforting. There is a feeling in some academic circles these days that the current crop of students has abandoned the pursuit of truth through reasoning, and relies instead on blind leaps of intuition. I am convinced this is not true. The students' premises are not always our premises, of course, nor their values our values, but in a time of accelerating horizons such as ours, the advantage in those variations may lie with the young. At any rate, during our deliberations I saw the students again and again confront the faculty and administration representatives with closely reasoned, well-articulated, and often compelling arguments for their positions. And on occasion they even recognized the merits of their elders' analyses. I should like to think that augurs well for the ultimate success of our enterprise.

CHAPTER EIGHT

The Independent
Hearing Examiner:
A Case History

*Myzell Sowell**

The Black Action Movement (BAM) strike at The University of Michigan occurred in March, 1970. There was a considerable amount of disruptive activity on the campus. After the crisis, and as a result of negotiations between BAM representatives and the administration of the university, it was decided that those Michigan students who were charged with disruptive activities would be given an alternative to having the charges heard by routine university disciplinary channels and procedures. The alternative procedure requested by BAM was to have charges heard by independent hearing officers who should be black. Consequently, four independent hearing officers were retained by The University of Michigan to serve in that capacity. I was one of the four. The others were James Baker, of Bay City, Michigan, and Charles S. Brown and Aubrey McCutcheon, both of Detroit. All of these gentlemen shared with me a firm belief and commitment to the fact that their responsibilities as hearing officers were not to the university, not to any student, but to the causes of justice and truth.

I want to share with you a brief history of one of the cases which grew out of the BAM strike. A charge was brought by a law professor against an individual we shall refer to as John Doe. The specific charge against John Doe was that on March

* Chief Defender, Legal Aid & Defender Association of Detroit, Michigan.

26, 1970, sometime between the hours of 1:45 P.M. and 2:15 P.M., John Doe did disrupt a law school class. The specific provision or university regulation that John Doe was accused of violating provides that any student who intentionally interferes with a member of the academic community and any of his activities or endeavors that are sponsored by or under the auspices of the university, who does not cease and desist when asked by a member of the academic community to stop disruptive activities, shall be subject to disciplinary action. Not only must the student be involved in activities that are disruptive of university sponsored activities — including, of course, offices, libraries, classrooms, or laboratories — but there is the additional requirement that the student must be asked to cease and desist and must refuse to do so.

In the hearing on the charge made by the law school professor, he testified, as I recall, that he commenced a class on commercial transactions in a rather small auditorium which has two doors. One row of seats at the back of the room was unoccupied. He testified that at about 1:45 P.M. his class was disturbed by a lot of yelling and screaming and clanging. The doors were closed. He did not know who was committing the disturbance or the reason for it. He testified that he tried to continue his instruction. In about five minutes the noise increased in intensity and suddenly both doors at the rear of the classroom opened and perhaps one hundred fifty or two hundred students streamed through the doors into the classroom, banging sticks on ashtrays and metal containers, picking up chairs and banging them against the desks or the floor and generally creating havoc. There is no question that the class was thoroughly disrupted. The professor said that the noise was so intense that he had to scream at a person standing beside him in order to be heard. Out of fear, he stated, he stepped into a well immediately adjacent to the podium, seeking refuge. The clamor continued for about thirty minutes. At some point, John Doe, amid all the clamor, noise, and hullaballoo, came ambling down the aisle, apparently with nothing in his hand and making no noise. John Doe was about ten or fifteen feet from the podium when the professor first noticed him. The professor knew John Doe's real name, because he had been his prelaw adviser. The professor said he wanted to talk to John Doe and ask him what was going on, but before he could attract John Doe's attention, Doe walked in front of the podium, made a right turn in the next aisle and started toward the exit. This, in essence, is the sum total of the law professor's case against John Doe. Two other witnesses — law students — gave the same account of the incident. They corroborated substantially everything that the law school professor said, except that they stated they did not know any of the one hundred fifty or two hundred people who came into the classroom.

The hearing examiner in this case made the following findings of fact: (1) The law professor was conducting his class between the hours of 1:15 P.M. and 2:15 P.M. on March 26, 1970, and the disrupters left the classroom about 2:15 P.M. (2) At approximately 1:45 P.M. the law professor heard noises in the hall, the sources of which he did not know or was not aware of at the time. (3) Sometime between 1:50 P.M. and 2:15 P.M., and at some time after the class had been thoroughly disrupted, the professor saw his former prelaw student walk in front of the podium without anything in his hands and without making any utterances, to the knowledge of the professor, and then walk toward the exit door. The hearing examiner's findings of fact were fully corroborated by the testimony of the two law students.

The examiner stated his conclusion that the charges brought against John Doe were not sustained by the evidence adduced by the university community: (1) The class had been thoroughly disrupted some five, ten, or fifteen minutes before the professor observed John Doe. (2) At the time he saw John Doe, that student was not carrying anything, was not making any noise, orally or otherwise, and had no instruments of destruction on or about him. The examiner concluded that the conduct of John Doe, particularly at the time that it can be pinpointed, was as consistent with that of the casual interloper or curiosity seeker as with that of an actual disrupter.

While the hearing officer also admitted that he suspected

that John Doe was actively involved in the disruption, he came to the firm conclusion that such suspicion was not sustained by the evidence adduced by the university community. He felt, therefore, that the charges against John Doe should be dismissed and they were.

I stated earlier that the university rule which John Doe was charged with violating would permit a finding of guilt only if it was found that John Doe, as a student, did knowingly interfere with the activities sponsored by the university and under the auspices of the university, and that John Doe was asked by a member of the university community to cease and desist and he did in fact refuse.

While there were a few minor problems in connection with the experimental use of independent hearing officers by the university to resolve the problems of the BAM strike, I believe it was a very educational experience for those of us who acted as hearing officers. I would like to think it was of equal value to the student attorneys who participated, and to those members of the private bar who sought to assist the university in resolving its problems at that given moment.

CHAPTER NINE

On Civilizing University Discipline

Paul D. Carrington*

Introduction

Academic discipline used to be a cozy, family affair. The benign dean played the firm, fair father; his students, like good children everywhere, never questioned his integrity or his wisdom. Is there today, anywhere in the western world, an institution so remote to the winds of change that the romantic fancy of the fatherly dean still abides? I doubt it. There are many vestiges yet, but the idea is dead. Parental authority was always an awkward partner to the university's responsibility for promoting maturity and independence; this may have contributed to its demise. Also, our institutions became so large and impersonal that it was impossible to preserve the resemblance to a family. But, above all, it died because parents lost or surrendered their power to control mature offspring. The substitute parent can hardly maintain greater authority than the real one.

These times have brought a new idea about university discipline. Unfortunately, the idea whose time has come is not a very good idea. The idea seems to be that we should use the traditional sanctions of suspension and expulsion, after the model of the criminal law, as society's, or the university community's, response to disapproved student conduct. This im-

---

* Professor of Law, The University of Michigan Law School, Ann Arbor, Michigan.

plies a considerable procedural apparatus or ritual not too
different from that customary in criminal proceedings. In my
opinion, the whole movement in the direction of identifying
university discipline with criminal punishment is unlikely to
produce anything but frustration, misunderstanding, and related commodities similarly in oversupply.

Why the alternative uses of university discipline are so
difficult for us to see is not certain. There are abundant examples of alternatives to be seen in the operation of civil courts
and other administrative agencies. Somehow, we seem to share
a primitive instinct for the punitive response to trouble. I
recall a remarkable example of this impulse which is exhibited
in the legislation of a western state which imposed criminal
sanctions on any chattel mortgagee who failed to record his
property interest. A curious myopia, which we all share to
some degree, apparently blinded that legislature to the alternative of making the mortgagee's despicable neglect an
occasion for impairing his property rights. We now suffer the
same disability.

Failures of the Criminal Law

At some risk of departing from my assigned subject to cover
familiar ground, let me treat briefly the failures of the criminal
law, because I believe that such a treatment may point toward
some of the difficulties to be encountered along the road on
which we now proceed. If we can keep the problems of criminal punishment in mind, we are better equipped to identify
and evaluate the prospective failures of universities as arms of
the criminal law.

First, let me briefly note that the theoretical model of the
system of criminal law serves multiple goals. It serves first as a
kind of vent or lightning rod by relieving or absorbing hard
feelings which might otherwise cause continuing disorder.
This is socialized vengeance, if you like, and it is related to the
objective of giving expression to the public mores, reinforcing
the shared morality, and celebrating our agreement about
proper standards of behavior. These goals relate, in turn, to

that of deterring disapproved conduct, partly by means of the social pressure generated by the expression of common disapproval, and partly by making the misconduct a bad bargain for the premeditating miscreant. All of these shade into the objective of rehabilitating the wrongdoer by teaching him to behave acceptably. Such rehabilitation involves a rebuilding of the social fabric which was damaged by the misconduct; this is partly accomplished by the process of venting the odium which otherwise blocks the reformation of a suitable relation between the offender and the offended. Thus, we are back to the point of origin. Wherever you start on this wheel, all the goals interconnect to justify and shape the design.

For some people, the design has worked pretty well. We must reflect with admiration on the engine of social control designed by the Cheyenne and described for us by Llewellyn and Hoebel. Partly to emphasize the romantic nature of our instinctive assumptions, let me describe it briefly. The major social problem for the Cheyenne was to prevent cheating on the communal buffalo hunt. It was always very tempting for the lone hunter to take the easy first shot before his fellows were in line for a common charge, but this would rouse the herd and thus greatly reduce the common take. How did the Cheyenne deal with the cheater? Tradition required that he be promptly and severely beaten, his pony destroyed, and his goods forfeited. But this was followed by a healing ritual in which his pony and goods were replaced with slightly less desirable substitutes, at public expense. In this way, the public odium was spent, the standard of conduct was reinforced, misconduct was deterred, and the offender was rehabilitated. It was a remarkable system, a significant cultural achievement.

The virtues of such a system are, however, best enjoyed by members of primitive societies like the Cheyenne. The model of social punishment just does not work very well in a large, impersonal society, and especially one which shares some of our ideals. In short, no society has found an effective way to punish strangers in large numbers, especially not in a way consistent with the ideals of humanism, individual dignity, and freedom. Without belaboring the point, let me list several respects in which the simple model of retributive punishment fails us.

One troublesome feature which results almost inevitably from size and technology is the separation of the functions of policymaking, enforcement, and administration. Those who express our moral standards, especially in a democratic legislative tradition, are almost inevitably isolated from the rest of the process of enforcing them. This means that the rules are formulated and the penalties prescribed absent the humanizing presence of a real wrongdoer. At this level, the miscreant is never seen as a friend, relative, or neighbor, but as a dehumanized abstraction. The result is that we do not express our real morals, or ones that we would apply to ourselves or acquaintances, but only those we apply in judging the conduct of unseen strangers. That is to say, they are harsh. We tend not to use punishment to express our best instincts, but our worst. Not only does this impair its value as an expression, but it profoundly obstructs the deterrent and rehabilitory effects of punishment.

Our laws, inadequate as they are to express our morals, must be put in the hands of police and judges whose purpose is to enforce them. Because policymaking can never be complete, and is often very crude, much discretion is left with both police and judges. This means that officials impart some of their own values to the process as it operates on each possible wrongdoer. Insofar as the punitive law is too harsh, they may be prone to overlook some transgressions. But this makes the process less social and more arbitrary, even as it adds an element of humanity. Often, it works the other way. Because we depend on professionals who must harden themselves in order to do their work, they are prone to disregard whatever humane sensitivity is reflected in the law. Thus, the punitive system becomes still less effective as an expression of our ideals, and simultaneously, less effective as an instrument of rehabilitation, or, ultimately, of deterrence, because those punished are more deeply alienated from the system.

Partly because we know this is so, we are forced to try to constrain our officials with a variety of procedural requirements intended to assure fair enforcement. The Marquis of Queensberry Rules we apply to police and prosecutors, and the rules of evidence we apply to judges and jurors, manifest a deep distrust of such officials and, indeed, a deep-seated uncertainty about the worth of social punishment. Some of these inhibiting rules may well be appropriate subjects of disagreement, but most of them we could not do without, despite the fact that they obstruct the system by producing substantial delay which, in turn, destroys the prospects for both deterrence and rehabilitation.

Finally, when we do get to the punishment, it is a poor substitute for vengeance. The most common characteristic of civilized punishment is the absence of any participation by those who were offended. The opportunity to exult in the shared experience of not being punished, of being thus rewarded for right behavior, is minimized by the remoteness of the punishment administered. In order to make it remote, we find it necessary to destroy the social roots which may be the instrument of rehabilitation, without knowing or caring enough to provide an alternative. The result often is that our punishment tends to reinforce antisocial tendencies, not to change them. The most that can generally be claimed is that we sometimes get wrongdoers out of harm's way.

I am not making these points, I ask you to recall, for the purpose of suggesting that the criminal law should be repealed, but only for the much more limited purpose of suggesting that it is an inappropriate model for university discipline. All of these failures of the criminal law are repeated on a larger scale when it is used as a model for university discipline.

The Criminal Law as a Model:
Socialized Punishment in University Life

Presumably, the goals of a system analogous to the criminal law should be to express the university community's moral standards, to invigorate those standards by giving reinforcement to those members of the community who abide by those standards, to deter bad conduct, and to rehabilitate the alienated students. Described abstractly, these goals are surely unobjectionable. But are they effectively served? Rarely, if ever. If there are obstacles to making effective use of socialized punishment in our society, the problems are compounded when we try to adapt the instrument for use in such a sub-society.

One pervasive cause of the ineffectiveness of socialized punishment in the university is that there is no satisfactory sanction. The only significant punishment known to tradition is that of exclusion, by means of suspension or expulsion. Exclusion is likely to be on the one hand too mild, and on the other too harsh, to support a system which effectively serves the goals prescribed. Expulsion is obviously too mild to deal with very serious misconduct such as real violence to persons or arson; such serious matters must be handled by other officials in other ways. It may be too mild, also, in that it fails to interrupt the unwanted behavior. While imprisonment at least puts the wrongdoer out of reach, exclusion does not have that effect because the excluded student is free to remain in the vicinity and is likely to do so if he is really bent on further mischief. Indeed, by relieving the wrongdoer of academic responsibility, the university can be giving him more time and energy to devote to his harmful activities.

Exclusion may also be too harsh in several respects. First, just as it fails to sever the relations which encourage the unwelcome behavior, it does sever those which might operate to engage the wrongdoer in useful activity and end his truancy. All our experience indicates that young people who continue with their academic efforts will probably find some useful occupation in the end. But what is to become of the expelled or suspended student who is cut off from progress toward utility? Is it reasonable to suppose that he will find a steel mill where he can perform day labor and repent his sins? Or will he join the street people? In dealing with prisoners or parolees, our public institutions make every effort to interest convicts in study as a means of rehabilitation. A judge who sentenced a criminal for a term and then suspended the sentence on condition that the convict abandon his studies and spend some time in the streets would rightly be thought mad and impeached. Yet that is precisely what a university must do when it resorts to exclusion as a means of punishment.

Second, exclusionary sanctions may be too harsh if and when there are long-term or unseen consequences. Indeed, in the eyes of some students, exclusion is seen as an academic parallel to capital punishment, or at least to outlawry, which was abandoned as a punishment in England many centuries ago. To some extent this view is related to the war, because expelled students are somehow presumed to go to Viet Nam and be killed in the muck. This is pretty emotional, but it should be remembered that students have been told since early childhood how bad it is to become a dropout. Every year, the competition for academic credentials becomes more critical to career success. It is true that we do not know what we are doing to a student when we subject him to exclusion, and the consequences can be, in some cases, quite grave, with the gravity bearing no relation to degrees of guilt or to any measure of the harm caused by the wrongdoer's misconduct.

Of course, we are free to hope that the excluded student will find another school or a job and work out his salvation, but we are poorly equipped to supervise or help his efforts to do so, and, if he does so, the punishment may seem too mild and perhaps superfluous.

The fact that the exclusionary sanction is so crude and counter-productive is of pervasive consequence because the widely shared doubts about its utility make it very difficult to marshal intramural community support for the application of such punishment. This can be seen at a variety of different stages and levels in the disciplinary process.

First, it would be true in any event that the process could not be expected to reflect real community standards unless those expected to adhere to the standards were consulted in their formulation. But such consultation is made more critical in light of the suspicion of the punishment to be applied. While there is no legally enforceable right involved, both the *Joint Statement*[1] and the American Bar Association Section *Statement*[2] (which has now been published in the first issue of the Section's new periodical, *Human Rights*) have endorsed the right of students to participate in the formulation of rules of conduct.

Second, doubts about the efficacy of the punishment must heighten our interest in the question of what kind of behavior standards are appropriate for a university to administer. There are some ill-defined legal limits on what kind of behavior can be proscribed, at least by public institutions. Rules or bylaws must have an "educational purpose," a term which may be subject to increasingly narrow interpretation. But beyond that legal constraint, and far more crucial to the success of punishment, are the limits imposed by the university community's willingness to lend moral support and acceptance. Those limits may, indeed, be very narrow. Universities are staffed and organized to stimulate students, not to inhibit their action. The abandonment of the parental role and relation leaves relatively little of a student's conduct that is not his private concern rather than the legitimate concern of the university. In addition, some relatively passive forms of conduct may be defended as expressions of ideas; the line between thought and action is becoming increasingly blurred, and it especially behooves a university to be very scrupulous in not stepping over that line. A university which exceeds any of these limitations on what is properly punishable conduct, even if it is supported by a few student representatives, is risking serious discredit and loss of moral force to its whole system of punishment.

Third, we must have heightened concern for the clarity with which university conduct rules are expressed. Even if students

1. STUDENT PROTEST AND THE LAW (Institute of Continuing Legal Education, 1969), Appendix A.
2. Reprinted as Appendix I.

participate in formulating a rule against behavior which is within the appropriate limits of university concern, the application of the rule must be quite clear if it is to carry the necessary moral force to sustain a dubious punishment. This concern also has a legal basis. A recent decision of the Seventh Circuit affirmed the *Soglin* case,[3] which held a university rule against "misconduct" unconstitutionally vague. Insofar as first amendment-type activities are concerned, the principle applied rests on firm ground, as does the companion principle of overbreadth, which invalidates rules that are too inclusive and have a chilling effect on constitutionally protected activity. It may be doubted that the court of appeals decision would really prevent a university from administering punishment in a grave case because of bad drafting. But, at the least, the decision gives added emphasis to the need to draft clearly in order to make the enforcement proceeding creditable.

Fourth, effective punishment requires student participation in the process of fact determination. Again, there is no legally enforceable right involved, although both the *Joint Statement* and the ABA *Statement* endorse the proposition of student participation. But the dubious quality of the punishment administered reinforces the compelling need for it. Once participation is established, however, we must recognize the possiblity of debilitating the process through jury nullification, or, worse, nullification by a student government which appoints the student members and which also controls the behavior of the wrongdoers.

Fifth, the dubious character of the punishment reinforces the need for a variety of procedural safeguards which are quickly finding a place in university disciplinary systems. It is clear that many of these safeguards are now imbedded in the due process requirements of the Constitution, at least in cases involving the application of a major sanction such as extended exclusion. It is still early to say which safeguards have constitutional status, or how far the constitutional requirements

---

3. Soglin v. Kauffman, 418 F.2d 163 (7th Cir. 1969).

are applicable to private institutions. But even without legal compulsion, it is simply good sense to recognize the right to counsel, the right to confrontation of hostile witnesses, and the right to a transcript of the proceedings. Expelling students who have been denied access to professional help, or on the basis of evidence untested by public scrutiny, or without a complete and official record, is not effective in serving any useful purpose. In making this assertion, I have the support of the draftsmen of the *Joint Statement,* the ABA Section, and a scattered lot of judicial decisions.

Sixth, we are forced to give consideration to the possible application of exclusionary rules to control the investigative activities of university prosecutors. While it is still fatuous to suggest that every interview between a dean and a student should begin with a *Miranda* warning, it is not premature to suggest the need to face up to the challenge of a university proceeding to consider whether certain evidence obtained by a dean was gained through improper fraud or harassment. The writing is also on the wall, if it does not yet have the force of legal authority, that such activities as dormitory searches will be open to challenge if they are viewed from the setting of such a disciplinary proceeding.

Seventh, we must be more concerned about the quality of the evidence of guilt. Not only is the need for good evidence increased by recognition of the shortcomings of the punishment to be imposed, but also access to the evidence is obstructed by widespread student reluctance to speak up. Universities have no subpoena power; more importantly, universities are short on investigative staff. And the general hostility on the part of students and faculty toward the process discourages witnesses and complainants from coming forward.

Eighth, doubts about the punishment increase its urgency. If it is a failing of the criminal law that offenders are not imprisoned, and rehabilitation commenced, for months or years after the act, it is even more absurd to think of an expulsion or suspension delayed over a year. There is a substantial turnover in a university community in a four-year period; with the lapse of even one year, the community that administers and supports the punishment is a different one from that which was offended by the misconduct. The youthful offenders have also grown and changed. Disciplinary proceedings, it seems fair to say, are hopelessly stale after a year, and nearly so within a semester. It might be thought appropriate to solve this problem with a provisional, temporary suspension pending a hearing. Such action is of dubious legality, at least in a public institution, in the absence of a continuous threat to the public order which might be thus relieved.

But in any case serious enough to merit this much attention, substantial delay is very likely. Time must be allowed for counsel to prepare. Moreover, great delay may result from the overlapping jurisdiction of the criminal courts, which requires us to take precaution not to prejudice his right not to incriminate himself. The university proceeding is technically "civil" in the sense that the student has no right to remain silent in order to protect against an adverse outcome. But a student is justified in silence if his answers might be used in a criminal proceeding. It is very doubtful that a student could be lawfully punished for exercising his privilege in that way in the discipline proceeding, although if he were coerced to yield, he might succeed in suppressing the use of any evidence thus disclosed. As a practical matter, if the student is to be expected to testify, or if he is to be given a fully protected opportunity to do so, the only alternative is to delay the disciplinary proceeding until the criminal case is decided.

Ninth, there is heightened concern about what students perceive as double jeopardy. There is no legal basis for this problem, because one who violates two sets of rules created by different authorities is subject to punishment at the hands of each. But it is legitimately questionable whether it is fair that students should be punished more severely than nonstudents. Given the dubious quality of the university punishment, many are especially reluctant to apply it in addition to the sanction imposed by the criminal law.

Tenth, we must be increasingly troubled by the flourishing

technicality which all these developments bring to the disciplinary process. Dissatisfaction and concern for the punishment tends to stimulate students, who if nothing else are always energetic, to devote massive energies to the exploitation of all of the foregoing rights, issues, and problems. The criminal bar could profit from the example of exuberance provided by student participants. University tribunals tend to be very querulous and contentious. This tends to produce a carnival effect, with much histrionic haggling, which amateur factfinders find difficult to control. Many universities have already demonstrated the need for a bylaw to control conduct in contempt of the institutional judiciary. All the horseplay further increases the difficulty of maintaining any moral force to the proceeding.

Eleventh, doubts about the punishment must reduce our tolerance for its expense. How much is it worth in administrative time and energy to obtain a single suspension? If it is necessary to crank up all this machinery, prudent men will often judge that it is not worth the cost. The threshold of irritation which must be attained before punishment is commenced is raised. As it is raised, it approaches the level at which resort to ordinary criminal punishment is more appropriate, anyway, and narrows by yet another dimension the range of misconduct properly subject to university discipline.

Indeed, when all these problems are taken into account at once, when at last we survey the field, are we not forced to the conclusion that the case for socialized punishment in the university is wholly lost? In order to gain the kind of support which is needed if the goals of punishment are to be effectively served, we must so confine its application that it is not clear what, if any, application it has, and we must so burden the process with dilatory safeguards, collateral inquiries, risks of miscarriage, and expenses to both institution and student, that it is simply an impossible venture. Universities are just no good at the job. If this makes them seem inferior to the Cheyenne, it should be reflected that the Cheyenne were not much good at running universities.

Perhaps the emerging institutions and processes of socialized punishment in universities should be preserved for the amusement and diversion they create. In today's world, amusement and diversion are not easy to find. But it is folly to suppose that any of the theoretical goals of punishment can be effectively served by such a monstrous device so unthinkingly appended to the body of an institution to which it is almost perfectly unsuited.

University Punishment as an Arm of the Criminal Law

Into this laughably grotesque situation now comes the voice of those who urge that the university should be using this machinery, not merely to serve the narrow interests of the university, but to express the public's idea of right conduct, as an arm of the criminal law. In the halls of Congress and the state legislatures, in meeting rooms of alumni and trustees, in editorial pages and in the speeches of the vice president, in opinion polls and election returns, the word is coming through quite clearly that ungrateful students who offend their parents' neighbors, the voters and taxpayers, with their disruptive conduct should be rewarded with a forfeiture of their rights to further enjoyment of relationships with universities. In the public's name, let the universities damn their troublesome students!

Why are universities so slow to respond to this mandate? As we have seen, universities are not really up to condemning their students to outer darkness in their own interest; much less are they able to do so effectively in response to the external pressure. The external pressure does almost nothing to solve any of the problems I have just described; it is still a cumbersome, ineffective enterprise. And new problems are added.

It becomes a new and pervasive difficulty that a university tribunal cannot effectively express and enforce the morality of a larger constituency. University autonomy is more than a political theory, it is a largely inevitable fact. Institutions serving special constituencies are ultimately dominated by them. The tendency of the criminal law to fail in its purpose because of the discrepancy in standards between the legislative policymakers and the enforcers is greatly increased when the two sets of officials serve different constituencies. University institutions, however autocratic in structure, cannot fail to respond to the values of the university community. To expect a university tribunal to play the role of a hanging judge to enforce the public's opinion about student conduct is little more realistic than to expect a Mississippi governor to serve as chief prosecutor of the campaign for school desegregation.

The difference in moral standards applied to student misconduct by the general public and by the university community is substantial. The generation gap needs no elaboration. Moreover, the inadequacies of exclusionary penalties are much more keenly felt by the university community than by the general public. The university community is generally more tolerant of rebellious expression, although less comfortable about violence. But, above all, the university community and its institutions, which the general public seeks to press into service, are far more likely to view offenders as fellow humans rather than as abstractions lacking in redemptive worth. The general tendency of the public and its policymakers to be overly harsh is nowhere more apparent than in their response to recent student misconduct.

In fact, I believe that the student values are much closer to the operative morality of the American people than is the rhetorical morality which serves as the basis for the criminal law. Relatively few members of our society would actually apply a forfeiture morality on their friends, neighbors, and relations. The outcry expresses the morality used only in our utterances about the behavior of unseen strangers.

If the public's indignation must be vindicated, the proper place to achieve that result is in the public's own courts. A university administration which feels too much heat should deflect it to the public prosecutor who is in business to absorb it. The parental responsibility of a university to protect its children from law enforcement is as dead as the university's parental authority. Students are in every respect subject to the criminal law. There is little excuse for imposing different penalties on students than other offenders by imposing university punishment in the form of exclusionary sanctions, at least insofar as the purpose is to vindicate public indignation.

I pause here to note the difference between the use of prosecutors, as I am suggesting, and the use of police in a crisis situation. The latter is a much more delicate question, which can only be answered in the light of a detailed understanding of a particular situation.

Here I also wish to note with emphasis that the public morality can be enforced in civil courts as well as criminal. We are now familiar with the use of injunctions, but why does no one seek civil damages? Building seizures, class disruptions, and recruiting incidents are all torts; the offenders are liable for compensatory and, in some cases, punitive damages. True, many students have no resources with which to pay large civil judgments, but many do, and most plan to acquire them. This approach offers the very important advantages of using the public's own judges and jurors, of dramatizing the harm by presenting a real plaintiff as well as a real defendant, of providing personal as well as public satisfaction to those harmed, and of providing a more hospitable procedure than the criminal court.

It is true that the civil courts can become entangled in cumbersome, dilatory, and expensive procedures. In some communities, they may be quite unsatisfactory for small claims. But for all their shortcomings, they can be far superior to anything that the university can provide as a response to troublesome behavior. Increasingly, private law remedies are gaining recognition as instruments for influencing conduct.

The Private Law Model: Compensation for Academic Harms

Indeed, if we could perhaps overcome our primitive instinct for retributive punishment, we could fashion a quite different system of university discipline which would follow the pattern of private civil remedies, rather than the criminal law pattern which is so rapidly becoming traditional. I have tried my hand at drafting a bylaw on such a model.[4] As I view it, the model gives substantial promise. I believe that it is not subject, to the same degree as the conventional criminal model, to all the problems which I have described. Indeed, I would expect such a model to give better service to the goals of punishment than the punishment model itself.

Let me describe my model. The primary response of the university to acts of misconduct would be to require appropriate compensation or restitution. Wrongdoers would be required to repair damaged or misappropriated property, the common law of trover or conversion being used as a model for harms to tangible personal property. Harms to intangible interests of the university community would be compensated. They would be liquidated the same way they are liquidated in ordinary tort litigation where persons are compensated for pain and suffering, or loss of reputation or prospective advantage—except that the university tribunal would be assisted in making the computation by some standard formulas which would place a roughly computed value on the harm resulting from interruption of instruction or interference with the ongoing operation of the institution. These formulas would be intended to reduce the amount of discretion vested in the university's trier of fact.

Provision would also be made for an analogue to punitive damages. As I have it, the judiciary would be authorized to impose what I have called a deterrence obligation in any case in which restitution is deemed inadequate. The amount of the deterrence obligation would generally be limited to treble damages, a concept borrowed from antitrust law. In fixing the size of the deterrent, the judiciary would be authorized to consider the financial means of the offender, his motives, and any other factors bearing on the need for a deterrent. A

---

4. *See* Appendix VI.

properly drafted bylaw should preclude the possibility of duplicating criminal punishment or punitive damages imposed by a civil court. All obligations imposed for the purpose of compensating the university community for intangible harm, or for the purpose of deterrence, would be payable to the scholarship fund.

Unlike a civil court, my judiciary would be authorized to allow the wrongdoer to spread his payments over a year. The university would be obligated to provide employment for offenders needing an extra work opportunity, but an offender who failed to perform adequately could be fired with very little judicial review. The jurisdiction of my university judiciary would be limited to claims of one thousand dollars or less; for larger claims, it would be necessary to use the civil courts. Exclusionary sanctions would be imposed only on students who are in default of their obligations as fixed by the judiciary.

Now, let us recount the problems faced by traditional discipline based on the criminal law model, and see how we fare as a result of the proposed changes. It would still be appropriate to consult student representatives in the formulation of the standards of conduct, but there is much less reason for concern about refinements in drafting such rules. There is no reason to suggest that a university judiciary should be a common law court making its substantive rules of whole cloth, but the possibility suggests the appropriateness of some leeway for the judiciary. There would be no "void for vagueness" problem.

It would remain appropriate to include students on the judiciary, but the risk of jury nullification is greatly reduced. If the worst that can happen to the offender is that he will have to pay for a harm, or forgo the fruits of a few weeks' work, there is much less incentive to participating students to obstruct the process of enforcement. This change in perspective will operate even more importantly on the problem of inducing witnesses to come forward. The morality of informing on a colleague is greatly changed by the shift to the civil model; there is much less reason for a student to refuse to involve himself when the complainant is seeking compensation rather than seeking to harm a fellow student by exclusion.

Moreover, the problem of constitutional due process is put in an altogether different light. It is very unlikely, at least at present, that the paraphernalia of right to counsel, right of confrontation, and right to a formal record would be imposed on a proceeding with such limited consequences. While it would doubtless be unwise to exclude counsel from such a proceeding, it would be a very rare case in which counsel and client thought it worthwhile to professionalize the proceeding. The one procedural right which I would consider it appropriate to abandon completely would be the right to a formal record. Appellate review, if any, would have to be de novo. This would allow the taking of the offender's testimony privately, and would alleviate the concern for the protection of his right to refuse to give testimony which could be used against him in a criminal proceeding. The exclusion of evidence rules and other trappings associated with the control of criminal investigations would be made completely irrelevant to a university disciplinary proceeding. Among the collateral consequences of all of these changes would be a substantial reduction in the probability of prolonged delay in the disciplinary proceeding. Likewise, the prospects for a carnival of contentious bickering is much reduced because the very aggressive tactics which produce the carnivals are so manifestly out of place in a proceeding leading to such minor consequences. Finally, the problem of double jeopardy is completely eliminated. Considering these factors, there is no room for debate that a system designed to follow a model of civil remedies rather than criminal punishment will function much more smoothly in the university setting.

What purposes would be served by converting university discipline into such a small claims court? Foremost is the goal of deterrence. The consequences of misconduct would be much swifter and more sure. In order to dissuade a premeditating miscreant that he should not engage in the kind of misconduct which is the subject of disciplinary proceedings, big penalties are not needed. Who would think it worth a hundred dollars to disrupt this meeting?

Likewise, the cause of rehabilitation is advanced because the student's useful activities and development are not disturbed; he is provided with a suitable means for making amends and is restored to the community, just as the punished Cheyenne who violated the rules of the hunt.

With respect to the need to express the moral code of the community, the civil remedies are far more humane and expressive of our common ideals. Some listeners may be attracted to the thought that monetary remedies are crass and unfair to impecunious students. But this is a mistaken thought. It is important to keep in mind that money is liquid power or freedom which entitles the holder to make some choices for himself; such a rearrangement of monetary resources is a limitation on freedom not different in its essential nature from sanctions in kind, such as imprisonment and exclusion. The critical characteristic of the monetary sanction is that it respects the individual's freedom to make his own choice about what he will forgo as a consequence of his misconduct. Millenia of western history teach us that monetary sanctions are the cheapest, most effective, and most civilized way to cope with misconduct.

Finally, we must ask whether civil sanctions serve the need to vent community anger and forestall private retribution. There are surely some vocal members of the public and some of its elected representatives who would be offended by the thought that a class disrupter, for example, got off with paying only one hundred fifty dollars to the university scholarship fund. But, to the extent that civil sanctions are inadequate as deterrents, they are less inadequate than the criminal-type exclusionary punishments which must be administered slowly, awkwardly, and erratically.

I would imagine that many of you must share my sense that something is lost or missing in the civil model. So far as I can tell, the only thing that is lost is satisfaction to the harsh and primitive instinct that causes us to believe that a forfeiture should be imposed on other people's ungrateful children. For reasons that I have already disclosed throughout the course of these remarks, that instinct leads us astray. The instinct may be basic and normal; but, like fear of crowds, noise, airplanes, or a distaste for all change, it is an instinct which operates against self-interest. It is a part of the instinctive dislike of strangers which civilized men must learn to suppress if the fruits of civilization are to be harvested in full.

Are there any new legal problems raised by the proposed conversion to a civil model? None that I can see. There is a long-standing rule that the power to impose criminal punishment cannot be delegated to administrative agencies. This has been invoked to invalidate provisions for agency fines, but only, in recent years, for agency fines which are collectible by the ultimate sanction of imprisonment. It seems clear that monetary sanctions collected by the ultimate sanction of suspension would not be a criminal fine within the meaning of the old rule.

Perhaps the most serious objection to the proposal is that it may appear to some to be novel. I find that objection difficult to evaluate. As one who has devoted some years to an effort to initiate students into the mysteries of the forms of action, I am stunned by the suggestion of novelty in a proposal which embraces, almost in whole, the old law of trespass, trespass on the case, and trover. All that I can say is that ancient ways are sometimes best. If they do not fill the expectations of those who wait for universities to curse the darkness more loudly by uttering grievous but vain threats at our troublemakers, they would be nonetheless more suitable to the needs of those who seek illumination for the path toward a more humane and peaceable society.

CHAPTER TEN

Questions and Answers

Moderator:
John W. Reed

Participants:
Karl J. Bemesderfer
John P. Holloway
John Holt Myers
Myzell Sowell
Robert G. Zumwinkle

The Problem of Identification

Reed: There is always a problem of identifying the participants in disruptive incidents. Mr. Sowell, you stated in your speech that the reason a particular student was charged in the case before you at The University of Michigan was that he was the only one anybody could identify. Is that correct?

Sowell: That is correct.

Reed: From your vantage point as one who listened to proofs, was there anything that could have been proved that the attorney for the university failed to prove?

Sowell: No. I think the problem was just one of those that arise in a big city or on a large campus with a multitude of people. Many other cases were decided in which there was both corroboration by other witnesses and positive identification. In those cases the hearing officers made determinations that there were in fact violations of university rules and regulations, and they imposed those sanctions which they deemed proper under the existing circumstances.

Independent Hearing Examiners

Reed: Questions for Bob Zumwinkle: Have you had any experience with the independent hearing examiner? Did you observe at all closely the Michigan experience? Do you intend to use the method?

Zumwinkle: Kentucky is moving in this direction, but modifying the Michigan approach. The hearing examiner will serve as chairman of the judicial board, which is a student board. Another hearing officer will serve as chairman of the appellate board. I think this is certainly worth trying. On the other hand, my feeling is that on issues as serious as expulsion or suspension, two or more heads are better than one, even though the one may be an experienced legal person. The idea makes me nervous. In my past role as dean of students, and now as vice president of student affairs, I have refused and will refuse to be put in the position of sole judge on such a serious matter. And I question whether an outsider, even a legally trained person, really ought to be the sole judge.

Reed: What about using an outside person as a factfinder, leaving the imposition of penalty to other agencies within the academic community?

Zumwinkle: I would be more comfortable with that.

Holloway: We have had one such experience at Colorado. A troublesome political case involved the so-called disaffiliation of the SDS. The discipline body at that time was composed of faculty members and administrators, none of whom had any legal experience at all. The SDS showed up with five or so lawyers, several law students, and two people from the ACLU, about nine legally trained people. I recommended to the regents that we would have a carnival if the faculty committee were not provided with someone to preside at the hearing. The regents authorized the president to appoint a retired justice of the supreme court to preside, without the power to vote. The hearing was very well handled. I think this approach is a promising one and should be seriously considered by the academic community. In other words, let the faculty, or faculty and students, handle the discipline, with the power of adjudication; but provide them with a professional to conduct the hearings.

We have now shifted all the way from the totally informal hearing in the in loco parentis situation to a sophisticated, highly structured, adversary type of hearing. An adversary hearing cannot be maintained in an informal manner. You have to play the game all the way.

The other approach is to give the total responsibility to hearing officers with full powers of adjudication, as was done at Michigan. Ultimately, we may have to come to this. The fantastically complex pieces of disciplinary machinery we have devised to comply with due process requirements simply are not moving anywhere. I have recommended the use of independent hearing officers with full powers to the Board of Regents at the University of Colorado.

Zumwinkle: I think this kind of independent legal expertise is extremely helpful, but I am uncomfortable at the prospect of totally replacing the established judicial body on the campus.

Myers: The University of Illinois also, as you may know, has used hearing officers. They have used a very distinguished lawyer from Chicago, Albert Jenner, as hearing officer. He has presided at some thirty cases there. I believe he has factfinding powers only, rather than full adjudicatory powers. A number of institutions across the country are going to this system.

Bemesderfer: There is another very compelling reason for using outside hearing officers. If you have a large scale disruption, as we did two years ago, administration and faculty people simply cannot handle the cases. We had over two hundred separate cases that had to be heard. We tried to rely on our law faculty to provide us with legal advice. Although they did it, afterwards they were terribly angry about it, for two reasons. First, it was a tremendous drain on their resources—they lost the faculty time of several people for an entire quarter. Second, it tended both to divide the law school internally, faculty members against one another, and to separate it from the rest of the university. The law professors who helped were regarded as hardliners by some other people.

Myers: I think it is a mistake to cast the law faculty into this role. They get badly polarized in such a situation.

Reed: I'm not sure that they are good people for it, anyway. Most are law teachers rather than practicing lawyers. They tend not to be good judges in some of these matters.

PART III

LAW ENFORCEMENT
IN CRISIS

CHAPTER ELEVEN

Intelligence Gathering
on the Campus

*Paul A. Brest**

Introduction

Intelligence gathering by law enforcement agencies on the university campus has played a controversial role in the control of campus disorder.

"Intelligence" is a formidable word, summoning up, to quote a colleague, "frightening pictures of snooping and infiltrating and spying; of disguised members of the bomb squad peddling dynamite; of Mata Hario in jeans and sandals; of electronically bugged crash pads." These visions and similar real-life incidents, though fortunately infrequent, have helped give "intelligence" its bad name. There is no doubt that it in fact encompasses some surreptitious and murky activities; but it also covers a variety of rather pedestrian, overt activities—equally important to law enforcement and somewhat less menacing to libertarian values. I shall touch upon intelligence-gathering activities of both sorts, raising the question of their proper limits. This is an issue which an increasing number of universities are now facing.

The courts are only now beginning to address themselves directly to the constitutional and other legal questions presented by intelligence activities and it is too early to say which way the winds are blowing. At the moment they are still "light and

---

* Assistant Professor of Law, Stanford University School of Law, Stanford, California.

variable," although the Weathermen may help determine their course. I am, in any event, more concerned with the underlying questions of policy presented by these issues than with the construction of arguments from case analyses. Conscientious administrators and policemen will not necessarily go to the constitutional limit where they believe that something less intrusive and antagonizing will suffice. Moreover, the law at its best appraises, weighs, and resolves the questions of competing policies. Our own resolutions of these questions, although they cannot predict or determine the outcome in the courts, may at least help sharpen the issues that the courts must resolve.

Let me make explicit two assumptions that underlie the remainder of this talk. The first, which will not provoke serious disagreement, is that the university serves a unique role in society which requires special sensitivity in the gathering of police intelligence on campus. The university is in the first amendment business, and freedom of inquiry is its fundamental institutional norm. To fulfill its functions, the university must provide an atmosphere in which all members of the academic community are not only unhampered in expressing themselves, but are affirmatively encouraged to express themselves on all matters, in and out of the classroom. At the same time, freedom of inquiry presupposes the freedom to communicate privately, to one, two, or a handful of persons. New ideas and one's commitments to old ideas often make their first appearances in private communication, where they are stated tentatively and in confidence. Thus, the educational process also requires a high degree of trust among the community's members. "Scholarship," as the Supreme Court has said, "cannot flourish in an atmosphere of suspicion and distrust."

My second assumption is that the university is not a sanctuary from the laws of civil society. The National Commission on the Causes and Prevention of Violence has said that members of the university community cannot argue that of all Americans they are uniquely beyond the reach of the law. This assumption is ahistorical to some degree, and it does not reflect a clear consensus of university members. For present purposes, however, we may leave aside such debated areas as the enforcement of drug laws, and confine the assumption to cases of violence and disruption. I think it is beyond argument that the university has a right and a duty to defend itself, its members, and society at large against such acts. And it has become increasingly evident that universities cannot do this without the assistance of public law enforcement agencies.

It is the conflict between these two principles, of course, that makes intelligence gathering on campus the difficult problem it is. Virtually any gathering of intelligence pollutes to some degree the atmosphere necessary for free inquiry. Yet effective protection of the university requires some level of intelligence activity.

Methods of Intelligence Gathering

Overt Activities

The most innocuous means of intelligence gathering on the campus are also the most generally used and useful: keeping current about campus activities through student newspapers and leaflets, through consultation with administrative personnel of the university, and in a variety of other overt ways, including unsolicited reports and complaints from students and others.

In these ways, law enforcement authorities can keep abreast of issues brewing on the campus; they can discover some criminal conduct; and they can learn of planned mass meetings and demonstrations, which may require the allocation of police resources and manpower.

The Police Presence

The presence of law enforcement officers at a large public rally or demonstration has not been the subject of any serious controversy. The police are obligated to protect the participants and to protect others from the possible misconduct of the participants. Mass assemblies have, on more than a few occasions, erupted into spontaneous or planned (but not previously announced) disruptions or building occupations. Police observers at such meetings can convey to their superiors on-the-spot information respecting disruptive activity — information essential to an appropriate and measured response by the police.

Police presence at even a large public meeting may deter attendance and inhibit speech. A massive display of force may, of course, arouse fears that the police are all too ready to employ that force. But even an unobtrusive police presence may deter, if it appears that the police are identifying people or recording what is being said.

In general, there is no justification for photographing or otherwise attempting to identify those present at a large meeting, or for maintaining a record of what was said at the meeting. The likelihood that photographs or recordings made before a disturbance will identify those who engage in the disturbance is simply too small to outweigh the students' fear and resentment that their pictures and words will go into an official file for a later, and possibly improper, use.

Once an assembly or demonstration has become criminally disruptive, or is very clearly about to become so, recording and photographing seem clearly appropriate and may be essential for prosecution of the offenders.

Informers and Undercover Agents

A far more controversial issue is presented by the use of informers and undercover agents on campus. Informers typically are students, paid or unpaid, who provide information to the police on a continuing basis; undercover agents typically are police officers who pass themselves off as students, and who may actually be registered as students. These agents may serve useful functions, both before and during disruptive incidents.

Many campuses harbor small groups of persons who are

experienced in techniques for transforming a peaceful assemblage into a disruptive or violent mob. Moreover, there are small numbers of persons willing to engage in specific violent and destructive acts, including arson, malicious destruction, bombing, and physical assault. I do not mean to suggest that the woods are full of these types, or that much of the disruption that has occurred on our campuses has not been spontaneous. One must recognize, however, that such persons and groups exist; that they have been responsible for serious harm; and that some disorders that pass as spontaneous have, in fact, been carefully engineered.

Conduct of this sort is almost always done in concert. By infiltrating clandestine groups, the police can learn in advance of their intended activities. In some cases, a group plan to engage in unlawful conduct will be sufficiently specific so as to be unlawful in itself—a criminal conspiracy. In that event the infiltrator's information may lead to arrests before any harm is done. In a much larger number of cases, the informant can provide information to alert the police to potential disorders. Such intelligence may not enable police to prevent the disturbance, but at the least it gives them time to prepare to cope with it.

An informant can be valuable during a mass disruption. He may be able to identify active participants—rock-throwers, for example—for use in prosecution of the offenders. Identification is particularly useful in a sit-in or building occupation. There are situations in which a university will be wise to wait out a sit-in instead of forcibly dispersing it: the presence of police agents or informers among the protesters allows identification of offenders so that they may be prosecuted after the affair has ended.

Difficulties and Dangers in Their Use

The use of informers or undercover agents creates serious difficulties which must be recognized and balanced against their apparent value. Although it is obviously an abuse for an infiltrator to act as agent provocateur, his credibility may well depend on his willingness to participate in unlawful activity. This is a problem endemic to the practice, and it is hard to draw very clear lines. It is of no great moment if an agent is merely the passive participant in a peaceful sit-in; it is deeply troublesome when he begins hurling rocks; and it is certainly intolerable when he urges others to do so.

This problem pales beside the much more serious one created by the very presence in the university of persons who pretend to be what they are not. I have emphasized that every aspect of the educational process requires freedom of members of the academic community to express ideas and exchange information without constraint. Such freedom depends upon a condition of mutual trust, and to a degree upon confidentiality. The perceived presence of police agents on the campus—in a classroom, in a dormitory bull session, in a meeting of a student organization—undermines these preconditions of academic freedom. To be sure, anyone who expresses himself always takes the risk that his listener will misuse the information or not respect his confidence. But this is a very different matter from the systematic disingenuousness of an undercover agent.

It would be nice to be able to recommend that police informers and undercover agents be prohibited altogether from university campuses, but I fear that this is impractical. There is some reason to believe that the incidence of unlawful conduct on campuses—especially concerted, violent conduct—will increase. Thus, as Chief Jerry Wilson of the District of Columbia Police responded to the Scranton Commission when queried about the wisdom and ethics of infiltrating student groups: "I will admit that an undercover operator is in a somewhat questionable position in regard to ethics, [but] it is a necessary evil." Some compromise with the ideal of the university appears necessary to assure that the institution remains standing at all.

I would caution that the use of informers and undercover agents must be exceedingly sparing and closely circumscribed. Generally, I think, they should not be used at all in the absence of some independent reason to believe that seriously dangerous activities are brewing on the campus; members of the university community must be secure in the belief that secret agents are not engaged in massive, widespread fishing expeditions. When they are employed, such agents must limit both the scope of the information they seek and that which they pass on to their police superiors. In particular, they must observe scrupulously the distinction between the expression of political views and opinions—matters which must be none of their business—and the planning and pursuit of unlawful conduct, which is the legitimate concern of the police. That the line between these areas may be imprecise is no excuse for obscuring the very large areas in which there is no conceivable overlap.

Police Dossiers on Students

Finally, I shall discuss the matter of maintaining police dossiers or files on members of the university community. I begin with the obvious proposition that the maintenance of dossiers can be justified only for the purposes of preventing and detecting crimes. Dossiers ought to contain only information that is directly and narrowly relevant. Again, the distinction between criminal conduct and political views must be sharply drawn, and the latter must be treated rigorously as off-limits. That information regarding political views may come from public sources—student newspapers or pamphlets, for example—is no justification for including it in a dossier. The very collection of information about a person constitutes an invasion of his privacy, to which this age of computer technology should make us especially sensitive. Whatever the motivation or means, the collection of data of this sort contains more than the seeds of political repression.

With this caveat, we should recognize that dossiers are essential law enforcement aids for dealing with persons who engage in repeated misconduct, alone or in concert with others. Descriptive information, including photographs, will aid police in determining the participation of such persons in disorders; information concerning their whereabouts will help locate them for questioning or arrest; and information concerning their associates is essential for coping with concerted misconduct—conspiratorial crimes.

The last category is obviously troublesome. We have had enough experience with the evils of guilt by association to be wary of drawing inferences from the mere fact of association. But associates are what conspiracies are made of, and in the process of discovering actual or potential conspirators, the police will come across others ultimately found to be entirely innocent of any criminality. The best one can do is to obliterate any file references to them once it appears that they are not implicated in anything unlawful. In any case, it is absolutely essential that dossiers be kept under closest security, accessible only to those few senior personnel with a clear need to know.

Conclusion

It may seem that my remarks are more appropriately addressed to police officers than to university administrators; the matters touched on certainly are, or should be, central concerns of the police. Administrators should be equally concerned, however, because they, too, are required to make decisions concerning the permissible limits of intelligence gathering on campus.

The police frequently enlist the cooperation of the university administration in carrying on intelligence functions. Even in areas where cooperation is not essential, the university may often be in a position where it can, if it wishes, impede covert intelligence activities of law enforcement agencies. Every institution should, after discussions within the university community and with relevant law enforcement agencies, determine its general policies respecting the gathering of intelligence, and act accordingly. This much the university owes itself and its members.

Some university security forces are themselves engaged in intelligence-gathering activities. A university must decide whether, and to what extent, this is desirable. It may reasonably decide to prohibit its own police from performing functions which are legitimately performed by the local law enforcement agency. Duplication may simply be an inefficient allocation of resources. Moreover, a university may wish its own police to gain a degree of trust and respect which, as a practical matter, cannot be achieved if they are engaging in covert and unpopular activities. Most important, the vast majority of campus security forces simply lack the professionalism and competence to undertake these complex and sensitive tasks. Bungling the job of intelligence gathering is more than a waste of time and money. The potential for repression, real and apparent, and for invasions of privacy, is simply too great to allow the job to be left in the hands of amateurs.

Finally, let me emphasize that the questions I have raised — and not pretended to resolve — should be considered openly within the university community. Intelligence activities affect all members of that community and it is essential that all views be given full consideration. Although too great specificity may defeat some sorts of intelligence activities, the university should make as explicit as possible the types of activities it permits and the circumstances under which they are permitted. I suspect that in many more cases than not, such disclosure will allay unfounded fears of many students and faculties.

CHAPTER TWELVE

The Police

*Walter W. Stevens**

Perspectives of Law Enforcement

I wish to clarify two basic points so that my remarks will not be misinterpreted but will fairly present the general position of law enforcement agencies concerning educational institutions in times of civil disorder. First, my frame of reference is that of a professional policeman who has devoted the last twenty-nine years to the practice of his craft. I make no apologies for the many failures of my craft in the past. We are working to cure our deficiencies and looking to the future with hope and enthusiasm. Second, we in law enforcement are probably far more aware of the continuing social changes than most persons attending this conference. After all, the initial impact of the changed attitude toward civil liberties was directed toward the system of criminal justice. We have been involved in social justice changes since 1958. I believe our involvement provides us with a unique perspective and considerable insight into the current problems which have grown out of rapid social change. Police responsibility dictates the expenditure of every effort to minimize violence. The main concern of law enforcement is the protection of the lives and property of all persons and the prevention of crime and violence.

---

* Captain, Michigan State Police, and District Commander, 2d District of Michigan, Detroit, Michigan.

The Police Role

Basic Concepts

Some basic concepts involving the role of law enforcement in educational institutions require expression:

(1) The educational institution historically has been the focal point of dissent in this country and throughout the world. This dissent has been the foundation for many of the improvements in the democratic process. Great leaders to guide our country through the perils and triumphs of its history have developed out of such dissent and the consequent evolution of ideas. This dissent must not be stifled. Rather, youth must be encouraged to seek out truths, to challenge and to improve society.

(2) The educational institution no longer stands in loco parentis. The child has obviously outgrown the parent. Educators and law enforcement people need to accept this fact. That is not to say that the control and operation of the educational institution should be handed over to the student dissident nor surrendered to students for the creation of militant revolutionary centers. Such a course would violate the civil liberties of all other students who wish to attend classes and pursue their education without interruption. I must reaffirm the principle that the primary concern of police is with the total concept of prevention of crime and protection for all.

The Contradiction

Student unrest, racial discrimination and the attitude toward the Vietnamese conflict are some of the issues which affect that total concern. The police officer cannot bargain the right and the wrong of issues. He has taken an oath to uphold the right of all citizens to a peaceful pursuit of life and happiness. The law does not permit him to tolerate injury to citizens and destruction of property. If we direct him to look the other way when violent acts are committed, we are endangering our first line of defense necessary to a peaceful and orderly community, state, or nation. A policeman cannot passively and blindly watch mayhem, property destruction, and drug abuse taking place on the university side of the street, then suddenly regain his vision and act against those on the other side of the street for the same offenses. His position today is untenable—chastised by some for overreaction and damned by others for failing to take stronger action. We preach freedom of speech, freedom of expression, freedom to dissent. We all support these freedoms, but I suggest that we cannot afford complete blindness, condoning the wanton destruction being carried out by university and school militants bent on forming a new coalition of control. The coddling and the blindness must stop.

Law enforcement people recognize the thin line they must walk in order to preserve the balance between the academic community and society as a whole. We find our role to be that of peacemaker, very similar to the situation we face when we respond to a call to settle a family fight. There are charges and counter-charges, emotion is escalated to its highest pitch, physical violence often follows verbal abuse, and once again the policeman is in the middle. He risks injury if he fails to take positive action; if he takes positive action he is accused of police brutality.

We must be tolerant but firm; fair but objective; willing to stand and be counted but not recalcitrant and spiteful. Reasonableness and understanding are necessary ingredients in solving campus disorders, but we cannot interpret those qualities to mean complete abjection and submission. The police can and will help if given the opportunity to understand the problem and become a part of the planning team, and if then afforded proper support in recognized and accepted techniques for calming the troubled area.

Planning for Police Intervention

A discussion of all aspects of police handling of campus or civil disturbances is beyond the time allotted to me in this seminar. I shall confine my observations to some basic principles. The most important initial step is advance planning, always mindful of the need for keeping plans flexible and open to innovation. New problems nearly always arise. The dissidents may use new techniques to achieve their goals; they may suddenly become violent and more destructive; or they may decide to become more vocal, interrupting orderly procedures in order to provoke the institution or the police into a confrontation to gain sympathy from the public and the press.

It is extremely important to have a continuing plan for gathering intelligence to be quickly relayed to top police command and to field police command. There must be an open and free exchange of intelligence between responsible administrators of the school and the law enforcement officials. The insignificant piece of information may well turn out to be the most important. The lines of communication must remain open and easily accessible. Responsibility should be determined, procedures worked out, and opinions freely exchanged. Quelling civil disorder requires unity and a bona fide team effort to stop the hostilities with a minimum of direct conflict.

Specific Concerns

All concerned parties need to be given any advance information about meetings which may indicate possible disruptions. The academic community must understand and accept the proper role of the police in preventing or controlling disorders. There is a great need for an expression of mutual confidence and a willingness to exchange ideas and information. I believe that meetings of school administrators to plan for the handling of disorders should always include a police representative. If dissidents make demands and meetings with administration are held, law enforcement people should be informed and included in the meeting, if possible. In other words, overall advance planning should include responsible representation from all the agencies that might be involved: campus and security police, city, state and county law enforcement, the national guard, the mayor's office, the prosecuting attorney's office, and certainly the fire department. These agencies need to know the administration's plans. Such planning sessions should answer a number of specific questions:

(1) At what point will police assistance be requested? Should police be mobilized the moment trouble is indicated or only after an overt disruptive act?

(2) Will police be called as soon as a building is illegally occupied or only after violence or destruction occurs?

(3) What kinds of police action will the school administration support? Will they support arrests and, if so, under what circumstances? Is protection of buildings all that is desired? Administration should make clear in advance what stand they take on such specifics.

(4) Are faculty or staff members of the university likely to be involved in the action? If so, what procedures with regard to them are acceptable to the institution?

(5) What will be done about removing those sitting-in or lying-in? If they are to be removed, adequate transportation and manpower must be planned in advance.

(6) Does administration want video taping, movies, still photographs, or tape recorders to record advisements or threats?

(7) What are the plans to handle situations involving drugs, alcohol, or obscene or immoral behavior? Consider that it may be better to identify and arrest later, to avoid escalating the conflict.

Trying to make "on-street" decisions in the midst of trouble — decisions which will be acceptable to both the academic community and law enforcement people — simply compounds the difficulties and leads to further chaos. It is critical that administration decide in advance how far they will go toward meeting the known demands of disrupters. If no advance thinking is done on this problem, there is always the danger of the sell-out under extreme pressure, agreeing to unreasonable demands. Recognize these for what they are. When you surrender to unreasonable and harmful demands, or when you close down your school, you have possibly violated the civil rights of the majority of your students. Academic freedom is always a two-way street. At some point in your course of action you must take a firm position and articulate it clearly or you will lose control of your institution and may ultimately have to close it down. Moreover, positive, planned, and articulated action allows police to move with the minimum force and in a precise manner.

Frequently it is possible to use the services of dissidents to control their own group. If this can be done it promotes a better atmosphere for control.

When the situation requires that a curfew be imposed, be prepared to determine the area of coverage, identify boundaries, and establish time limits and rules to allow necessary movements. Establish an information center located within the curfew boundaries, as it may become necessary to seal off the campus or the city. A curfew and road blocks protect against outside interference and will ease the situation. It may be wise to keep the police out of an area of off-campus housing if destruction is not occurring. If the situation is reasonably calm, the police may become the only targets in such areas.

Conclusions

I have emphasized that briefing of the police is an essential factor in planning. Top command should be informed at the outset. Responsible university representatives should explain the university position, who has authority to speak for administration, whether they will support arrests, who will sign complaints, the area controlled by the university, and related matters. Later briefing meetings should ideally include all officers from all agencies at one time. As this is seldom possible, briefing will need to be done by individual group or squad leaders.

Planning the technique and equipment to be used by the police should be done with administration leaders and the goal should be mutual agreement on all operation procedures.

Proper planning and cooperation gives police more of a chance to use the lowest possible level of operating technique and equipment to restore peace and make an early withdrawal of forces.

I have described the role of a police officer during civil disorder at educational institutions as that of a peacemaker. There is another, critical dimension to his role: he reflects the larger society and its desires and needs. In that dimension, he reflects society's demand for a cessation of disruptions involving educational institutions.

CHAPTER THIRTEEN

Injunctive Orders

John P. Holloway*

Introduction

Recently I discovered what is probably the earliest statement of principles with respect to discipline for students and faculty. It is an order issued by St. Benedict at the Abbey on Monte Cassino, circa 528 A.D.:

Statement on Procedural Standards in
Dismissal Proceedings

If any pilgrim monk come from distant parts if with wish as a guest to dwell in the monastery, and will be content with the customs which he finds in the place, and do not perchance by his lavishness disturb the monastery, but is simply content with what he finds, he shall be received for as long a time as he desires.

If, indeed, he find fault with anything, or expose it, reasonably, and with the humility of charity, the Abbot shall discuss it prudently, lest perchance God had sent him for this very thing.

But, if he have been found gossipy and contumacious in the time of his sojourn as guest, not only ought he not to be joined to the body of the monastery, but also it shall be said to him, honestly, that he must depart.

If he does not go, let two stout monks, in the name of God, explain the matter to him.

Perhaps our need today is for a few stout monks.

* Resident Legal Counsel, University of Colorado, Boulder, Colorado.

Injunctive relief is one of the tools available to a university to deal with campus disorder. I am not recommending that injunctions or any other form of sanction be employed against legitimate protest in the exercise of free speech. My remarks are limited to the use of this remedy only in cases of actual or threatened disruption, the destruction of property, or injuries to persons on campuses.

The Injunction Defined

What is an injunction? An injunction is an order of court commanding persons named therein to do or to refrain from doing certain acts which the order directs them to do or prohibits them from doing, as the case may be. Injunctions may be affirmative, referred to as mandatory injunctions, or they may be negative. Generally speaking, injunctions as they have been used in this country are negative. They direct that people refrain from doing certain things. They are frequently used in divorce cases, and in the 1930s through the 1950s they were used in labor disputes. However, their use in the latter area has been definitely limited to certain circumstances. They have also been used in school and religious cases.

Obtaining an Injunction

How is an injunction obtained? I fear that a great many people who are not lawyers think that all one does is drop down to the courthouse and say, "I would like an injunction," somewhat in the same way one would order a chocolate soda. Let me emphasize that injunctions are not obtained that easily. The law regards an injunction as an extraordinary writ. It is applied for on the equity side of the court and certain conditions precedent must be met before the court will issue an injunction. Application to the court is made in the form of a complaint or a petition.

The complaint or petition is against named defendants or respondents, as they are frequently called, and their agents, servants, employees, and attorneys, and any other person acting or threatening to act in active concert or participation with them. All of you have read newspaper accounts stating that an injunction was obtained against John Doe or Jane Doe. This terminology of persons in a court order is intended to identify persons the applicant believes should be brought within the purview of the order, but whose identity is unknown to him.

The restraining order or temporary restraining order, which lawyers refer to as TRO, is usually the first step. It may be obtained with or without notice but, as will be discussed later, the latter course is not recommended. The second step, i.e., the more permanent writ, is an injunction. It may be either a preliminary or a permanent injunctive order. The generic term for all of the above procedural steps is "the injunctive process."

The Bases for Injunctive Relief

Certain basic showings are required of the plaintiff seeking injunctive relief. First, he must show that there has occurred, or that there is a threatened occurrence of, some injury to the plaintiff which is irreparable. In the case of damage to university property, there seems to me to be no doubt about the irreparability of the injury that has occurred or could occur on many campuses. This showing has not been troublesome to the courts, but I would emphasize that you must show an irreparable injury.

Second, if the order is going to issue without notice to the other side—the legal term is ex parte—you must also show that the injury will be immediate and that you cannot possibly, under any circumstances, contact the other side and therefore an ex parte issuance is justified.

Third, you must show that you have no plain, speedy, and adequate remedy at law. The key word of this description is "adequate." Certainly there are remedies for disruptive and destructive behavior. There are, among others, trespass remedies, criminal statutory remedies, assault and battery, and

actions to recover damages, provided, of course, that you
know who caused the injury. The essential showing to obtain
injunctive relief is that there is no other adequate remedy.

Fourth, courts are beginning to impose a requirement that
you must have exhausted your internal remedies, within the
institution. Technically, this limitation is not a condition precedent for equitable relief, but it is, nevertheless, being imposed
more and more by courts. I encountered this trend in judicial
thinking when I recently made an application for a temporary
restraining order without notice. Ultimately, we obtained the
order, but one of the things that disturbed the court was the
failure of the university to employ the internal remedies available to it when the building had been occupied the night
before. The specific remedy which the court had in mind was
summary suspension. While the school might not have been
able to identify all seven hundred persons occupying the
building, it certainly could identify eight or nine and suspend
them. The judge, from the bench, made the following remarks:*

> I am inclined to the belief based on the inferences to be
> drawn reasonably from the verified complaint and the
> affidavits, that it was not a lack of adequate remedy, but an
> unwillingness to use those remedies. I wish to indicate
> quite strongly that in the future this Court will want to
> have a complete explanation of the reasons why available
> remedies are not utilized to control students identified as
> such at the University of Colorado on the campus. As to
> nonstudents, such persons are licensees. Someone on the
> public walkways on the University grounds is a licensee.
> Students, perhaps, have greater rights than the public
> generally who are there as licensees. However, even as to
> students, if summary suspension occurs, they become li-
> censees and that license, it would seem to me, can be
> terminated at will, at which time they become trespassers.

As a judge of this Court I am not too pleased with the

---

* Edited for sentence structure.

idea that time, energy and efforts are resorted to before the University officials face up to the necessity of enforcing their own laws and rules and regulations through whatever means are available to them. If the plaintiffs in this action [the Regents] were the *only* parties in interest, I think the failure to at least attempt to enforce their own laws with the powers that were at their disposal the preceding night would preclude them from relief; however, the interests of many other persons the following morning were involved and at that point when the matter was presented to the Court for a temporary restraining order, I believe the action taken by the Court in granting the temporary restraining order ex parte was proper.

Subject to editorial corrections, the language above is directly from the transcript of a minute-order ruling; it is not from the formal written ruling which followed. I believe this order may signal a coming trend. The courts are not only going to require a showing of irreparable and immediate injury, and a showing that there is no plain, speedy, and adequate remedy at law, but that the school also has attempted to use its own internal remedies before it can apply to the courts for relief.

If the injunctive order is obtained ex parte—without notice to the adverse party or his attorney—additional findings have to be made. The pertinent portion of the Colorado rule applicable to injunctions (Rule 65, Colorado Rules of Civil Procedure) is very similar to rules in other jurisdictions. It provides:

(b) *Temporary Restraining Order; Notice; Hearing; Duration.* A temporary restraining order may be granted without written or oral notice to the adverse party or his attorney only if:

(1) It clearly appears from specific facts shown by affidavit or by the verified complaint or by testimony that immediate and irreparable injury, loss or damage will result to the applicant before the adverse party or his attorney can be heard in opposition, and

(2) the applicant's attorney certifies to the court in writing

or on the record the efforts, if any, which have been made to give the notice and the reasons supporting his claim that notice should not be required.

Let me impose two caveats. The United States Supreme Court, in a 1968 case entitled *Carroll v. President and Commissioners of Princess Anne*[1] stated the limitations on temporary restraining orders without notice. In the *Carroll* case, an ex parte restraining order had been issued prohibiting a white supremacy group from holding any meeting at any place in the county. The Court said the following:

> There is a place in our jurisprudence for *ex parte* issuance, without notice, of temporary restraining orders of short duration; but there is no place within the area of basic freedoms guaranteed by the First Amendment for such orders where no showing is made that it is impossible to serve or to notify the opposing parties and to give them an opportunity to participate.[2]

In seeking the ex parte order to prevent the further occupation of the building at Colorado, I had less than three hours in which to get the temporary restraining order. I did not give notice and I insisted that the court enter a minute order, which the court agreed to do. The order said:

> As a basis for his request Mr. Holloway relates to the Court the events of the night of April 13, 1970 relating to the wrongful occupation of Regent Hall. The Court is advised that the building was occupied wrongfully and contra to express orders to vacate it until 2:30 a.m. on April 14, 1970; that in order to restore the building to the control of the University, it was necessary to assemble over 100 reserve police and law enforcement units of the City of Boulder, Boulder County Sheriffs Office and the Colorado State Patrol; and that, based upon statements of the students who so occupied the building that "We will be back tomorrow," verified by such reports in the Colorado Daily, counsel had reason to believe a reoccupation would occur

---

1. 393 U.S. 175 (1968).
2. *Id.* at 180.

and that the time remaining, i.e., less than three hours, made the giving of notice impractical.

Motion for temporary restraining order is therefore granted.

Temporary restraining orders without notice have other limitations. The most severe restriction on their use is the limited time for which they can be issued. Rules setting the time for which an ex parte order may remain in force exist in all jurisdictions. In Colorado, for example, an order obtained without notice is controlled and limited by the following provision of Rule 65 of the Rules of Civil Procedure:

Every temporary restraining order granted without notice shall be indorsed with the date and hour of issuance; shall be filed forthwith in the clerk's office and entered of record; shall define the injury and state why it is irreparable and why the order was granted without notice; and shall expire by its terms within such time after entry not to exceed 10 days, as the court fixes, unless within the time so fixed, the order, for good cause shown, is extended for a like period or unless the party against whom the order is directed consents that it may be extended for a longer period.

The lesson which may be distilled from the foregoing discussion is clear: If there is any way that you can give notice, give it. Give it by telephone. Give it by sending somebody out to contact the student leaders and tell them, "Mr. Holloway is going to be in court at nine-thirty in the morning," or, "Mr. Holloway is going to be in court in two hours." Send witnesses along to hear the statement made. That notice, however short, should meet the test imposed in the *Carroll* case.

Evaluating the Injunctive Remedy

What are the characteristics of the remedy itself? Injunctive relief has advantages but it also has disadvantages. On the positive side is the fact that it introduces into the controversy the judiciary and the public, third parties who are not in a position to grant demands and who can be impartial. Moreover, the injunction gives students a chance to back off, to obey without losing face in the particular controversy. If the remedy of arrest for criminal trespass is used, the effect is immediate and there is no chance to back off.

Another advantage of an injunctive order is that punishment for its violation is by order of the court that the violator is in contempt. Usually this punishment is summarily administered without a jury and is not bondable. Appeals are limited, and contempt hearings are moved up on the docket, avoiding the long delays almost always associated with criminal cases.

The most serious disadvantage of injunctive relief is that it is not self-executing. The procedure to enforce punishment for violation of the order is complex, cumbersome, and time-consuming. In order to enforce an injunction which has been violated, you must go back to the court and advise the court, by affidavit or other testimony, that students *A, B,* and *C* violated the order by doing specific acts related in the affidavit or testimony. The court then issues an order to *A, B,* and *C* to appear at a time certain to show cause why they should not be held in contempt for the violation. The order, motion, citation, and affidavit then have to be served on *A, B,* and *C* by police officers or by sheriffs or by private process servers. If *A, B,* and *C* do not appear in court at the time designated, a bench warrant for their arrest is issued. The warrant must be served by police or the sheriff. I suggest that you reflect on the practicality of this remedy in the case of a mass demonstration.

There are other disadvantages of the injunction: (1) If the order is drawn too broadly, it may be an unconstitutional restraint of first amendment rights; (2) Once you start the process, you must pursue it to the ultimate, or you give the students good cause to lose respect for the law and the whole process; (3) It is always difficult to identify violators and you must rely on the "persons in active concert" phrase, thereby creating a burden of proof problem as to their identity and the fact that they had notice of the existence of the injunction and the general context thereof.

The "Self-executing" Injunction

In an effort to eliminate the problems surrounding feasible enforcement of an injunctive order, I recently engaged in some legal innovation, and included within a temporary restraining order a "self-executing clause." Although the rules of civil procedure do not specifically authorize such a clause, they do not seem to prohibit it. I cannot cite any cases directly in point which approve self-executing clauses in this context. I can cite two cases[3] which we felt were closely related. They arose out of the bloody coal mine strike in Ohio in 1952. In the *United Mine Workers* case the court held that the sheriff and his deputies, acting under the direct and explicit order of the court to exact compliance with its injunction decree, represented the presence of the court; and any commission of violation in their presence was constructively in the court's presence and might and would thereafter be dealt with and punished summarily.

The court in the *Compton* case held that the deputies appointed by virtue of a court order for the purpose of enforcing an injunction were officers of the court, and violation of the injunction in the presence of these deputies, while they were cruising the district, was constructively in the presence of the court. They would have been justified in making arrests for a violation of the order on the spot.

You will note that the language of the self-executing injunctive order[4] which we obtained in Colorado stated:

... that if any of the Defendants, or any person acting in concert or participation with them, shall willfully disobey this Order, any peace officer be and is hereby authorized and directed to forthwith apprehend and arrest such person or persons and take said person or persons into custo-

---

3. State *ex rel.* Bruns Coal Co. v. United Mine Workers of America, 63 Ohio L. Abs. 531 (Common Pleas), 110 N.E.2d 162 (1952); State v. Compton, 96 Ohio App. 541, 123 N.E.2d 43 (1953).
4. *See* Appendix VII.

dy and forthwith bring such person or persons before this Court to show cause why he or they should not be punished therefor and a fine or imprisonment imposed to vindicate the dignity of this Court. . . .

In the particular incident we served the order on three or four of the leaders. Their names were on file in the Office of Student Relations because they were officers of the Student Mobilization Committee. We made service upon them personally as they were marching back to Regent Hall to reoccupy the building. They were somewhat intrigued by this new process and when they reached the building they decided to read and discuss it on the steps of the Hall. I could never have had a better opportunity for service of notice of the order. They read it word for word, debated it, elected not to have their confrontation with the court, and walked away. The effect was startling, to say the least.

After the students left, the injunction was obeyed and we had several days of peace. Several days later, however, the resistance to the ROTC, one of the targets of the Student Mobilization Committee, had reached explosive proportions. It was decided by the SMC that the ROTC drill should be disrupted. Once again the university security people, using bull horns, announced the terms of the restraining order as the students were marching to the drill field. This time the terms of the order did not stop the action. Some of them immediately attacked to break up the drill. In the melee that followed, nine of their number were arrested, handcuffed if necessary, and taken before the district court for violation of the temporary restraining order. Additionally, they were charged with violation of the Campus Disorder Act, a misdemeanor. At our university, security officers are deputized as city and county peace officers with full powers of arrest.

Colorado has a special section in Rule 107 of the Rules of Civil Procedure, the Rule covering civil contempts. I believe similar rules provisions exist in other states, but perhaps lawyers have not studied them carefully enough to discover their possibilities. The pertinent sections of Rule 107 are as follows — note particularly the italicized portion of the text:

(c) *Out of Presence of Court.* When it appears to the court by motion supported by affidavit that a contempt has been committed out of the presence of the court, it may ex parte order a citation to issue to the person so charged to appear and show cause at a time designated why he should not be punished therefor. The citation and a copy of the motion and affidavit shall be served upon such person a reasonable time before the time designated. If such person fails to appear at the time so designated, *or if the court so orders when the citation is issued or thereafter,* a warrant for his arrest may issue to the sheriff. Such warrant shall fix the time for the production of such person in the court. The court shall direct by endorsement thereon the amount of bail required, and such person shall be discharged upon delivery to and approval by the sheriff or clerk of a written undertaking executed by two or more sufficient sureties or a corporate surety company, to the effect that he will appear at the time designated in the warrant, and at any time thereafter to which the hearing may be continued, or pay the sum specified. If such person fails to appear at the time designated in the warrant, or at any time to which the hearing may be continued, the undertaking may be forfeited, and the amount thereof, to the extent of the damages suffered by the contempt, shall be paid to the aggrieved party. If he fails to make bond, the sheriff shall keep him in custody subject to the order of the court. [Emphasis added]

(d) *Trial and Punishment.* The court shall hear the evidence for and against the person charged and it may find him guilty of contempt and by order prescribe the punishment therefor. A fine may be imposed not exceeding the damages suffered by the contempt, plus costs of the contempt proceeding, plus reasonable attorney's fees in connection with the contempt proceeding, payable to the person damaged thereby. If the contempt consists of the failure to perform an act in the power of the person to perform he may be imprisoned until its performance. In addition thereto, to vindicate the dignity of the court, if the citation so states, a fine or imprisonment may be imposed. If any such fine is not paid the court may order the contemner imprisoned until payment thereof.

We judged that in this rule we had the machinery to handle the situation. We took the nine students to court to have a warrant issued for their arrest. The warrant would permit the court to fix bond as in a criminal situation. When the Boulder Nine, as they called themselves, were brought before the court about eight o'clock that night, they had been run through the criminal booking process. They were dressed in jail coveralls and white sneakers. I observed an entirely different attitude from that exhibited on the drill field earlier in the day. Because of the lateness of the hour, the court continued the matter overnight and the "Nine" were held in custody in the county jail—another event they had not contemplated. The following morning we filed our motion, supported by police officer affidavits stating that a contempt had been committed out of the presence of the court and presented some oral testimony to support the affidavits. Thereupon the court issued an order, citations, and warrants for arrest, and fixed bond at $2,500 each. A number of the respondents were unable to make bond and spent at least two more days in jail. All were later charged with violation of the Campus Disorder Act and a $500 bond was required by the court. Total amounts fixed for bonds amounted to $3,000 for each person in the group, or more than $300 in premium costs for each one. I would emphasize that this procedure resulted in a higher expenditure than has been imposed as a fine in many criminal trespass cases, and it was not refundable. Moreover, all had spent some time in jail, a rather sobering experience. When the cases were ultimately tried, all were found in contempt and jail sentences ranging from 2 days to 180 days were imposed. Portions of the jail sentences were suspended on stiff probationary terms. Six of the nine were represented by counsel so will also have attorney fees to pay. I am persuaded that the Boulder Nine entertain some misgivings about their behavior. There were no further disruptive outbreaks, and the student body rejected any attempts by the Student Mobilization Committee for amnesty. The university referred the pleas for amnesty to the district court and the district attorney. A preliminary injunction containing the self-executing clause was later issued. In its memorandum opinion the court again upheld the clause.

The self-executing clause of our injunction was attacked in another division of the state district court, in a separate suit in the federal district court, and in a proceeding in the nature of prohibition initiated in the Colorado Supreme Court. In every instance the clause was upheld. Unfortunately, the supreme court did not write an opinion. They simply refused to prohibit the trial court from proceeding.

Related Problems

There are some legal problems in these simultaneous proceedings, but double jeopardy is not one of them. At least two courts have squarely met the issue of double jeopardy and campus discipline. Both found the student to be in danger of losing a benefit, but in no danger of losing "life or limb."[5] There are problems of self-incrimination, since the students are testifying in three proceedings going on at once—criminal, university discipline, and contempt. However, courts recognize that university discipline would be ineffective if it were to await the outcome of proceedings in courts of law. Comparing the discipline committee to a motor vehicles commissioner, a federal court thought it obvious the university could proceed notwithstanding the pendency of other proceedings:

> It ought to be obvious that a motor vehicles commissioner, authorized to suspend a driver's license for speeding without more, need not wait for the months or years of a

---

5. "For, while the expelled student may suffer damaging effects, sometimes irreparable, to his educational, social, and economic future, he or she may not be imprisoned, fined, disenfranchised, or subjected to probationary supervision." Esteban v. Central Missouri State College, 290 F.Supp. 622, 628 (W.D. Mo. 1968). *Accord:* Goldberg v. Regents of the University of California, 248 Cal. App. 2d 867, 57 Cal. Rptr. 463 (1957).

negligent homicide prosecution before considering such administrative action. It is not less obvious that the University need not refrain in every case even from learning whether disciplinary charges are admitted or denied until criminal proceedings, which may or may not implicate the same events, have been brought to their conclusion.[6]

Another federal court applied *Garrity v. New Jersey*[7] to disciplinary proceedings. In *Garrity,* the Supreme Court said evidence found in an attorney general's investigative hearing could not later be used at a trial growing out of the same action. Applying this to a campus discipline case, a federal court found no threat of self-incrimination:

> If at such hearings they are forced to incriminate themselves to avoid expulsion and if that testimony is offered against them in subsequent criminal proceedings, they can invoke *Garrity* in opposition to the offer. Therefore, expedited college disciplinary hearings pose no threat to Fifth Amendment rights.[8]

These cases reflect the awareness of the judiciary of the need for speedy campus discipline, if that discipline is to be effective at all. And the above cases made it clear that the fifth amendment is not an obstacle when minimal due process and fairness are followed.

Adequacy of Injunctive Relief

Lastly, let me pose the question: Is injunctive relief really an adequate remedy? My answer is yes, but only in those cases where the university has exhausted its internal remedies, having separated the student from the institution by suspension or expulsion, where the same student or students remain on campus or return to it. This is a continuing trespass which equity will enjoin. In those circumstances, the remedy is not

6. Grossner v. Trustees of Columbia University in City of New York, 287 F.Supp. 535, 551 (S.D.N.Y. 1968).
7. 385 U.S. 493 (1967).
8. Furutani v. Ewigleben, 297 F.Supp. 1163, 1165 (N.D.Cal. 1968).

only adequate, but probably the best available. In all other cases, I suggest that injunctive relief is really a secondary line of defense — all too often a substitute for internal discipline and hence a retreat from institutional responsibility. Nathan Glazer, Professor of Education and Social Structure at Harvard Graduate School of Education, hit the nail on the head, in my opinion, in an article in *The American Scholar:*[9]

> I do not believe for an instant that universities need any special assistance or legislation from government to deal with student disorders. It would only be damaging by encouraging the false opinion of student radicals that universities are not autonomous but simply arms of American imperialism and the military-industrial complex. The chief task in the defense of the universities must fall on the faculties and on the administrations, which so largely reflect faculty views. Thus, when students engage in attacks on other students and prevent them from attending class, or professors from teaching them; when they destroy books and notes and research materials, the *universities* should deal with them quite independently from the state. It is an unpardonable withdrawal from responsibility for universities to leave all questions of discipline and punishment to the civil authorities. Universities may have to call on the police to defend students, faculty and property from militant students. Beyond that, however, they themselves must determine proper standards of conduct that make it possible for a university to continue. They must find ways to assert and maintain these standards without turning the university into a police state or into a parody of the court system. If they cannot, if they fail to reach and educate enough students and faculty so that a university can be maintained without these conditions, then I think the proper response is to close the university and to set up a new one with faculty and students who do

9. Glazer, *Campus Rights and Responsibilities: A Role for Lawyers?*, 39 THE AMERICAN SCHOLAR 445 (1970).

accept the common code of conduct required in an academic research and teaching institution.

If universities do not assume the responsibility of maintaining their own internal discipline systems, the state legislatures and Congress will do it for them — a highly undesirable state of affairs.

CHAPTER FOURTEEN

Questions and Answers

Moderator:
John W. Reed

Participants:
John P. Holloway
David Kessler
Walter W. Stevens
Robert G. Zumwinkle

The Police Role

Advance Planning

Reed: How much input is the academic community allowed in the formation of law enforcement procedures? You spoke of conferences with local police, with prosecutors, with academic personnel; I assume that you are not there to issue orders, but that you ask for their counsel in this matter.

Stevens: Very true. By the exchange of ideas and opinions, defining our goal and recognizing the responsibility of the academic community, I believe we can arrive at a collective opinion on the proper procedure and technique to put down disorders.

Police Access to University Intelligence

Reed: A member of our audience has said that there appeared to be some conflict between Zumwinkle and Stevens over the matter of intelligence on campus and the means to obtain it. Do we need intelligence? If so, what should be the role of the university? I will ask Mr. Zumwinkle first: To what extent do you think the university's intelligence—the information it gets from within the campus situation—should be made available to the police?

Zumwinkle: I find myself torn on this question. Although I probably would not have been two or three years ago, I am now in agreement with Mr. Stevens on the need for advance planning, sharing of information, and sharing of the planning process. I base this feeling on the belief that careful planning will insure against overreaction, keeping the action to the minimal amount necessary for effective control. At the same time, I worry very much about the effect of sharing certain kinds of information with external police agencies, particularly when that information concerns a belief, thought or expression. These are central to the mission of the university and I think we must guard against making our universities miniature police states. I know this is not what Captain Stevens is recommending, but I sense a danger here.

Reed: Would you like to respond to that, Captain Stevens?

Stevens: Mr. Zumwinkle makes a point, but I would emphasize that my concern is that we plan together to act in concert to accomplish cessation of hostilities with the least amount of difficulty. We can accomplish this only if we have freedom of exchange of basic information, ideas, and opinions. As police officials, we are not interested in the inner workings of the university. Our concern is handling the immediate situation.

Arrest by Campus Security Officers

Reed: I have several questions for you, Captain Stevens, if I may present them in series here. What is your view of university security forces having the power of arrest, either by creation of a separate police district or the fuller deputization of present campus security forces?

Stevens: An answer which would fit all school problems is most difficult. It would be a mistake in some areas. I cannot give a clear-cut answer. Generally speaking, security police probably should not have police powers.

Use of Plainclothes Police

Reed: Do you use plainclothes squads to deal with student disruption?

Stevens: We do to a limited degree. The specific situation would determine whether or not plainclothesmen would be effective.

Reed: To avoid the reaction that a uniform sometimes evokes . . .

Stevens: Yes. We use them to filter through the crowd, to try to get the temperature of the crowd and discover what the crowd may intend to do. With a little lead time, perhaps we can take action to head off some potential conflict, or at least minimize the destruction.

Kessler: I think we should keep in mind that it may be necessary to ask for the use of warrants. It takes only a few plainclothesmen to turn a university from a center of free discussion into a place of fear. Using them may do more harm than an occasional protest that gets out of hand.

Stevens: It is necessary to look at both sides of the question in dealing with campus disruptions and disorders. We must not quickly assume that police are doing undercover work for a dubious purpose. The police are trying hard to solve the problem with the least amount of conflict. Their objectivity should not be called into question at the outset.

We can then make decisions together, acting under general guidelines set by the top command. We should be able to arrive at amiable decisions. The university people on the scene can voice their thinking. The police people are going to be receptive to these opinions, if the university people are objective and impartial in their expressions.

Kessler: The point I would make is that just the presence of policemen on campus, whatever the purpose, causes students and faculty to be afraid to speak out.

Who Calls the Shots?

Reed: The next question has to do with some of the mechanical arrangements by which police get called in. In the team effort you spoke of, where you have police agencies and the university people working together, who calls the shots? If state police or National Guard troops are called, where does the university stand on the team? Who from the police department has power to make decisions on the site? Could you describe, by specific example, where the responsibility lies once everything is mobilized?

Stevens: Again, it is difficult to give a single answer to such a question. There are several factors to consider: Is a state of emergency declared by the governor of the state? If so, he may delegate or designate a person to be in charge. In that case, the question is answered. If there is no declared emergency, field command posts can be set up on the scene, with the top level of department command back in the office running things.

Injunctive Orders

Reed: I have a question sent up for John Holloway. It says, "The new look in injunctions appears to include the following elements: the use of police to enforce a civil order; the imposition of court costs and bond premiums as penalties; the substitution of a process originated in the civil context and lacking the safeguards for defendants found in criminal cases; the use of punishment before conviction." At the bottom of the page, the question: "How can you sleep at night? To what level of appeal have any of the injunctions you have obtained been challenged?"

Holloway: Let me say that I sleep very well at night. As for the four elements named, they are not new. They have always been a part of the civil law in the area of injunctions. As to the levels of appeal, let me repeat that I have obtained only one injunction with the self-executing clause. It was taken to the Colorado Supreme Court on writ of prohibition and the writ was denied. I won in that the court did not prohibit the trial court from proceeding further, but it did not write an opinion. We do not, therefore, have any reported case law.

Multiple Punishment

Reed: We have several questions asking that you discuss the so-called double jeopardy contention that students can be subject to contempt of court, criminal action, and college disciplinary action for one act.

Holloway: The correct term is multiple punishment, not double jeopardy. Let me say emphatically that while it is not double jeopardy to employ all three remedies, it is double or triple punishment in many cases. I do not sanction multiple punishment, except in those extreme cases where personal injury or damage to property is involved and where ample notice has been given. I would much prefer to see institutions take steps to administer their own discipline systems rather than fall back on a secondary line of defense, asking the courts to act through civil contempt or criminal prosecution. I suggest that most lawyers who represent colleges and universities must feel the same way. However, colleges and universities are not administering discipline internally, whatever the reason may be. Their administrations are turning to their lawyers and asking them to get the courts into the fray. It should not be necessary, in my opinion, except in extreme cases such as arson and other clear violations of criminal law, to utilize any of the other sanctions.

PART IV

THE AFTERMATH
OF CRISIS

CHAPTER FIFTEEN

Political Reactions

John Holt Myers*

The Anatomy of Legislative Response

Legislative responses to campus disruption and to political activities on campus at the federal level and within the states are remarkably similar. The first reaction of the legislative body is to bring pressure on school administrators to enforce the laws already in existence. The second general reaction is to conduct an investigation. A number of state legislatures have had investigative bodies. The United States Congress has investigated various aspects of student unrest, as well as other aspects of campus activity. For example, the Internal Security Committee of the House of Representatives recently sent a questionnaire to schools and universities, inquiring how fees are paid to public speakers on campuses. It is difficult to believe that an investigation would grow out of this kind of query, but the questionnaire may be characterized as one kind of response. The third and most important response available to Congress and the state legislatures has to do with appropriations, either directly to the institutions or indirectly to students who attend them. The fourth kind of response, one which is largely within the prerogative of state legislatures and has been frequently employed by them, is the enactment of criminal and civil laws to deal with disruption on campus or to control the use of campus facilities.

---

* Williams, Myers and Quiggle, Washington, D.C. General Counsel, American Council on Education and Association of State Universities and Land Grant Colleges.

The federal reaction is expressed primarily through limitation on the use of federal funds. In general, this restriction
affects public and private institutions with equal force, because
both receive federal money either directly or through aid to
students. The state reaction may be expressed through limitations on appropriations, but the states have usually responded
by enacting criminal or quasi-criminal statutes. The first wave
of state legislation was largely confined to state institutions,
creating special problems for the public colleges and universities. Later statutes, however, have been made applicable to
both public and private institutions. Such state laws, proposed
and enacted, range from extremely restrictive provisions, with
severe and drastic penalties imposed upon both student and
institution, to joint resolutions expressing an opinion or a view.
Many of the most restrictive proposals have fortunately been
bottled up in committee procedures. Unhappily, numerous
intemperate and unfortunate provisions have been enacted
into law or may well become law in the near future. Some are
clearly subject to constitutional challenges; some are simply
unfair. Many are unworkable and will not accomplish the
results that the legislature had in mind.

The Federal Response

The initial federal response, as I have indicated, has been
and will continue to be in the form of investigations. These will
continue as long as unrest exists. But the federal government
can and does employ effective methods to pressure administrators to take action under the existing laws. The threat of
losing the tax-exempt status has caused many schools, particularly private ones, to reexamine their policies concerning the
allowance of political activities on campus. Although such a
response is clearly administrative, it originates with Congress.

One direct federal legislative response was provided in the
Tax Reform Act of 1969. The specific restrictions against
participation or intervention by exempt institutions in campaigns of candidates for public office, already set out in the tax
exemption provision, were included in the estate and gift tax
provisions of the 1969 Act. A similar kind of legislative re-

sponse was reflected in a suggestion by the Department of
Justice that colleges and universities might be violating the
Corrupt Practices Act by providing space for, or supporting,
political activities on campus. The Corrupt Practices Act,
which has been in existence since the time of President Theodore Roosevelt, applies to corporations, banks, and labor
unions. It has been very narrowly construed by the Supreme
Court of the United States. Only in the last several years has it
been applied against corporations. Basic federal appropriations statutes allocating funds for facilities at colleges and
universities have for a number of years included limitations on
the use of such funds for publicity or propaganda purposes.
One example of such restriction is found in the Department of
Defense Appropriation Act for 1969 and 1970.

The most effective response of the Congress to campus
disruption or campus political activity has been through the
denial or threatened denial of funds appropriated for use by
students and, more recently, for teachers and research per
sons. Now the threat of denial of funds has, in some statutes,
been extended to funds provided directly to the schools or
universities. The two most recent NASA authorization acts, for
example, have required denial of funds to an educational
institution which bars armed forces recruiters from its campus.
Moreover, the Department of Defense is directed to make
periodic reports on those institutions which have not allowed
recruiters on campus.

The Higher Education Amendments of 1968[1] provide that
subsidized institutions must refuse scholarships to individuals
under specific circumstances. The institution must deny funds
to one convicted of a crime involving the use of force, disruption, or the seizure of school property, and which results in
a serious disruption of the school; or to an individual who has
willfully disobeyed a lawful regulation or order of the institution, if the refusal contributed to campus disruption or
interfered with the administration.

Despite the growing trend in federal legislation to impose

1. *See* Appendix VIII.

the penalty of denial of funds directly upon the institution, the majority of the statutes provide that the individual who commits certain offenses is to be denied grants of money from federal subsidies. While federal statutory provisions in this area are not consistent, they do follow a general pattern. A substantial number of such restrictions are included in appropriations acts, although some are contained in the authorization acts.

Statutes requiring the institution to deny funds to a person who has disobeyed a lawful regulation of the institution but has not been convicted of a crime may or may not specify that denial of funds must be preceded by a hearing. Where the statute is silent on this point, presumably due process requirements will compel a hearing before denial of funds.

Some statutes require outside certification of compliance of the institution, similar to the directive that the Department of Defense make a report on institutions banning armed forces recruiters. Others impose no requirement for reporting compliance, or provide for report by the institution as to its own compliance.

The kinds of bills discussed above have already been enacted into law. Proposed legislation, however, is more extreme. One proposal would make it a federal crime to be involved in a disruption on the campus of any federally-assisted college or university — virtually every college or university in the country. Another would suspend federal aid to institutions failing to take appropriate corrective action in the case of disruptions. Still another would make interference in the operation of a federally-supported college or university a criminal offense and would make the carrying of firearms on such a campus a federal crime. On the other side of the coin, it is heartening to note that a bill to provide a federal conciliation service to deal with campus disorders has been introduced in Congress, as well as a bill simply providing for a study of campus unrest.

Many of the proposals now in the federal hopper will die in committees. But the simple fact is that major appropriation and authorization bills involving grants to colleges and universities are at this time* being held up in committee because of fear that some of these extreme provisions may be added on the floor of the House or the Senate. This is a serious matter. I would suggest that the bottleneck will be broken after the November election, when it will be easier to get the major bills through without burdensome restrictions such as those described above.

The State Response

Criminal Statutes

Many state legislatures have reacted to campus disruption and violence by passing new criminal laws. The statutory offenses thus created take varying forms. Nearly half of the states have enacted into law some kind of provision that interfering with the lawful administration of the school is a crime. Some of these provisions may speak in terms of interference with lawful "ingress to and egress from" the campus buildings and facilities, but many others forbid interference with the full and lawful use of the campus. The statutory offense of interference is usually labeled a misdemeanor or a gross misdemeanor. The states of California[2] and Washington[3] have enacted statutes which provide that a threat of bodily harm to an administrator or other duly constituted person in authority on a campus is a misdemeanor. I would characterize the latter provisions as concomitant to the basic interference statutes.

Apparently there has been some doubt as to what is trespass on a college campus. Trespass statutes have now been enacted in a number of states to deal with what must be considered something of a gap in the law. About half of the states have enacted laws making it a misdemeanor for a nonstudent, or

---

* August 1970.
2. CALIF. PENAL CODE § 71.
3. REV. CODE WASH. § 28B.10.571.

one who is not a member of the academic community, to refuse to leave the campus after he has been ordered to do so by someone lawfully constituted to act in an administrative capacity on campus. Some states have enacted into law a provision that an expelled student is guilty of a misdemeanor if he returns to the campus without express permission. Finally, a growing number of states are enacting statutes which permit the administrator, in unusual circumstances, to withdraw the implied consent to a student to remain on campus; or, a statute may specifically authorize administrative authorities to close the campus in times of disorder.

Laws prohibiting the carrying of firearms on campus have become quite popular in state legislatures in the past two or three years. Sometimes such laws also prohibit the manufacture or possession of incendiary materials on campus. These laws undoubtedly had their origin in the Cornell campus confrontation with firearms in April 1969.

In addition to the three principal kinds of criminal statutes described above—interference, trespass, and prohibition against firearms—special kinds of misdemeanors have been created in some states; e.g., damaging state property, or the broader provision against wrongfully entering a public facility for the purpose of destroying property. Some state statutes ban unlawful assembly on a state college or university campus. The state of Wisconsin has enacted a provision that it is a misdemeanor to take a bull horn onto a state campus without permission. California has considered such a provision and may have enacted it into law. Obviously, such provisions are direct responses to specific situations in those states, where the use of the bull horn was such an important factor in generating campus disorder.

At least one state has passed a law requiring that a student must, upon enrollment, sign an agreement to abide by the rules and regulations of the school, with the condition that any failure to do so makes him subject to expulsion. One state has provided that a teacher who advocates civil disobedience is guilty of a felony. Such extreme measures have not yet been enacted into federal law.

Denial of Financial Support

No one can measure the extent of state legislative reduction of general appropriations to colleges and universities because of campus disorders. In a number of states, however, administrators of state schools are convinced it has been substantial. But states have also passed specific laws which require the withdrawal of all kinds of financial assistance to students who are convicted of crimes involving campus disruption. In some states financial assistance must be withdrawn if a student is found guilty of a narcotics violation. A Florida statute provides that a student who is found, after hearing, to have been arrested for a narcotics violation must be expelled for two years. This is rather an extreme penalty.

A second category of state statutes requires the denial or withdrawal of financial support to students, and in many cases to employees, teachers and the like, who violate campus rules and regulations in such a way as to contribute to or cause substantial disorder. Some of these statutes are carefully drafted, while others are very, very bad. One statute requires the denial of financial assistance to any student who participates in a demonstration. I suggest that this sweeping provision may be open to challenge.

Miscellaneous Statutory Responses

States have adopted miscellaneous statutes which do not impose criminal penalties or involve the specific withdrawal of financial support. One or two states have provided for the dismissal of or the bringing of dismissal proceedings against students who have been involved in substantial disruptions. This is a requirement of expulsion, not a criminal penalty. Other states require, in general terms, that the administrators penalize disruptive students or bring actions under the governing rules of the institution to deal with violations. One or two states have provided for specific injunctive relief in the case of disorders. At least one state provides for revoking financial aid to any school which fails to curb a disorder on campus. The Connecticut legislature, interestingly enough, simply increased out-of-state tuition, presumably on the theory that disruption on campus is caused by out-of-state students. The Wisconsin legislature made a similar response by limiting the number of out-of-state students. I believe a proposal was made in Wisconsin to charge out-of-state students at least five times the cost to residents. On the local level, the city of Waltham, Massachusetts, has sought to withdraw the real estate tax exemption from Brandeis University because of political activities on the Brandeis campus. We do not know how far these expressions of dissatisfaction will go.

One state requires the dismissal of faculty members involved in disorders, regardless of their tenure. Several states have enacted laws purporting to control public speakers on campuses. One state has authorized the use of the state police with or without the approval of the campus authorities. Several other states have enacted specific provisions which permit the use of campus police under the direction of the president or similarly constituted person in authority. One state has assigned peace officer status to the campus police, which may or may not be desirable. Several states have enacted laws or passed resolutions which deal with the problem of alleged obscenity in campus publications.

One response which has been frequently used is a statute requiring state schools, and sometimes all schools, public and private, to adopt rules with respect to the management or administration of a college or university. Many institutions have not had proper rules to govern disciplinary procedures and maintain order on campus, giving full notice to the students as to what was and what was not a violation. Other states specifically require that the college or university adopt rules with respect to the handling of disorders or disruptions on campus.

Some state legislatures have appointed special committees to investigate certain campus disorders. This is a normal and usual legislative response to such problems.

The attitude of Americans toward laws reveals a basic conflict in our thinking. On the one hand, we place great reliance on the passage of a statute to cure any kind of ill, particularly a social ill. At the same time we are notorious scofflaws, disobeying statutes which we consider unreasonable or unfair. The enactment of numerous statutes in this area, many of them subject to constitutional challenge, or obviously unfair, is particularly unfortunate. The students involved in disrupting the campuses have already stated that they are not going to obey certain laws. The passage of more laws will simply encourage disobedience on a broader scale. Many of these laws will be challenged in the courts. Some are unworkable. Moreover, the courts are already intolerably crowded and more litigation will simply multiply our problems. Certainly some of these laws, the trespass statutes, for example, are necessary. It is important that students and faculty know they are violating a statute when they take a certain action. Many of the housekeeping laws, requiring proper notice of what is and what is not a violation, are important and should be encouraged. I would hope that it might be possible to get some kind of drafting committee together, perhaps under the auspices of the National Association of College and University Attorneys, in cooperation with the Association of State Universities or the American Council, to draft workable statutes to accomplish useful purposes.

I would like to call your attention to two publications which give substantial information concerning the legislative response in 1969. Mr. Joseph Gonzales[4] has prepared a summary entitled *State Laws of 1969 Dealing With Student Unrest.* This may be obtained from the Office of Institutional Research of the National Association of State Universities and Land Grant Colleges.[5] At least eight states added new laws in 1970. These laws were not innovative; basically, they fit into the patterns which I have described. The second publication I would recommend is *Legislative Response to Student Protest,* published by the Urban Research Corporation.[6]

I think we must all agree that the real problem cannot be

4. Special Assistant for Legislative Relations at Rutgers, The State University, New Jersey.
5. One DuPont Circle, N.W., Washington, D.C. 20036.
6. 5464 South Shore Drive, Chicago, Illinois.

solved by the legislatures. On the other hand, legislative bodies have to respond to a situation which is of such serious concern to the public. The real solution lies with the institution itself. Each college or university must develop a sound system for accommodating, dealing with, and reacting to the student's interest in his rights within the school, particularly his rights with respect to discipline. The abandonment of in loco parentis requires the student to play a major role in his own disciplinary process.

CHAPTER SIXTEEN

The Legislators
Strike Back

*Karl J. Bemesderfer**

In May of this year the Gallup Poll reported that a plurality of their sample cross section of American adults regarded campus unrest as the single most pressing problem facing the United States. These respondents ranked campus unrest ahead of the war in Southeast Asia, poverty, racism, and violent crime on their imagined scale of seriousness. I cite this survey not to deplore the values or the judgment of the respondents but as evidence which helps to explain the rash of new legislation aimed at controlling campus unrest which has broken out in one state after another. *The New York Times* carried an article on June 28, 1970, in which the Associated Press reported the results of a survey of state legislation regarding campus disruption. According to the *Times* story, thirty-two states had recently passed such laws.

A measure of the intensity of feeling on this issue among state legislators is the number of bills introduced this year. In California alone, according to a survey published in March in the *Student Lawyer Journal*,[1] more than eighty separate campus disruption bills were introduced; in Illinois, more than twenty. If one counts multiple laws within a single state and adds revisions of existing statutes aimed at such offenses as disorderly conduct, mob action, and rioting, the total number of

---

* Assistant to the President, The University of Chicago, Chicago, Illinois.
1. Johnson, *State Legislation on Campus Disorders*, 15 STUDENT LAWYER J., March, 1970, pp. 24–27.

state laws passed in response to campus unrest in the last two years may be more than a hundred. When the multiple new federal restrictions in various educational appropriation bills are added, the picture which emerges is of a sudden, radical, and sweeping change in the legal environment in which colleges and universities have operated.

I speak today in a minor key: The bills passed and pending will not, in my opinion, have the desired effect of quieting campus disorder. They will hamper, in some cases seriously, the ability of colleges and universities to carry out their educational programs; and they will undermine academic freedom.

Consider Ohio's new education law,[2] passed June 6 of 1970, following the killings at Kent State. The Ohio legislature was in recess at the time of the Kent State incidents. They were preparing to come back to handle routine business and adjourn. After the killings, the legislators received a volume of mail greater than anyone could remember on one issue within the past twenty or twenty-five years. Legislators who usually received one letter a month from their constituents were getting three hundred letters a week. The letters ran 90 percent against the students; on three occasions armed individuals showed up in towns near college campuses and volunteered to help keep order. Faced with this kind of pressure, the Ohio legislators could hardly fail to respond with new punitive legislation if they wanted to remain in office.

The new Ohio law permits the president or the board of trustees of a college or university receiving state funds to declare a state of emergency when there is a clear and present danger of disruption of the orderly conduct of lawful activities at the institution and to impose what amounts to academic martial law thereafter.

The law also requires the immediate dismissal of a student or faculty member convicted of an offense arising out of a campus disruption and bars the individual from attending or being rehired by any state-supported educational institution in

2. OHIO REV. CODE ANN. §§ 3345.22–3345.26 (Eff. 9/16/70).

Ohio for one year. The automatic dismissal section[3] can be triggered for conviction of any one of thirty-five enumerated sections of the Ohio criminal code, ranging from arson and felonious assault at one extreme to creating a commotion in a campus building at the other. The triggering offenses include both felonies and misdemeanors, serious offenses, and what, for lack of a better term, may be called "deportment offenses." Aside from the obvious unwisdom of assigning a uniform civil penalty to all these actions, a penalty which in the case of the felonies is superfluous and in the case of the misdemeanors harsh, there is also the very great likelihood that this statute will worsen the situation and make the detection and punishment of offenders more difficult. Student and nonstudent dissidents will take steps to conceal their identities from school officials. Even when identity has been established, college officials may be reluctant to press charges, since convictions may now carry with them consequences far more serious than the disorder itself would warrant. School officials no longer have the freedom to make the kinds of discriminations with respect to individual involvement and culpability which are part of a rational system of rules, for there is one punishment for all offenders, from the soft fringe to the hard core, provided only that the button marked "conviction" has been pushed.

Hence the dilemma arises: cooperate with the state in the administration of a harsh and inflexible law or abandon recourse to civil authority except in the most extreme situations.

Of course it is possible that the existence of the law on Ohio's books will deter students and others from engaging in protest, especially violent protest, but I think it is more likely to provoke resistance. Student activists often are romantic rebels longing for concrete evils to fight. This law will be to them as a dragon to St. George; having been passed in reaction against the incident at Kent State, it appears both to threaten the living and slander the dead.

---

3. Ohio Rev. Code Ann. § 3345.23 (Eff. 9/16/70).

In general, the new state statutes are of two kinds. One is similar to the riders attached to many recent federal appropriation bills. Laws of this kind usually enumerate certain types of bad conduct and then state that anyone found to have engaged in such conduct, either by a court of law or, after notice and hearing, by the institution, loses his entitlement to certain benefits from the state. The Ohio law is an extreme example of this kind. The other kind of new statute is an addition to the state criminal code. Such an addition generally does not create new offenses but adds a gloss to some existing offense. The gloss is to specify certain conduct on campus which will thereafter qualify as an instance of the main offense. For example, the definition of criminal trespass has been reworked in many states to include sit-ins and other similar behavior. In 1969, the Indiana legislature added chapter 179 to its criminal code, making it a misdemeanor for any person

> ... to go upon or remain upon any part of the real property of any institution established for the purpose of the education of students enrolled therein in violation of any rule or regulation of any such institution for the purpose of interfering with the lawful use of such property by others or in such manner as to have the effect of denying or interfering with the lawful use of such property by others.[4]

This same statute also makes it a misdemeanor for a person to refuse to leave the premises of an educational institution when asked to do so, regardless of the reason, by the officials of the institution; or to enter or remain within a public building for the purpose of interfering with the lawful use of such building by other persons, if his actions have that effect.

Similar legislation dealing with such offenses as "unlawful assembly," "disorderly conduct," "rioting," and others have been added to the laws of several states. The Oklahoma Riot Control and Prevention Act of 1968[5] makes it a felony punishable by five years in prison and a $10,000 fine to advocate

---

4. Ch. 179, § 2, [1969] Indiana Acts 457.
5. Ch. 125, [1968] Okla. Sess. Laws 191.

unlawfulness, criminal syndicalism, or sabotage on public school grounds; and a felony punishable by ten years in prison to advocate or teach sedition or treason on public school grounds. Arkansas has also enacted antiriot legislation with particular application to college campuses. The Arkansas statute imposes a penalty of $200 and six months imprisonment for disrupting campus activities, in addition to any penalty the school may impose.

It is interesting to contrast the Oklahoma and Arkansas statutes. In Oklahoma, advocating treason on campus is a felony and apparently to be punished more seriously than the same offense committed off campus. In Arkansas what would be a "riot"—and a felony—if committed off campus is a "disturbance"—and therefore a misdemeanor—when committed on campus. In Oklahoma the focus of legislative concern is seditious teaching; in Arkansas it is unruly behavior. One can only speculate about the reasons for these different perceptions; they may have something to do with the well-known history of repeated communist attempts to overthrow the government of Oklahoma.

One might well ask what is added to the power of the state to control the behavior of unruly persons by particularizing unruliness on campus. And one might ask further on what grounds more serious penalties for some variety of behavior may be assessed if the behavior occurs on campus rather than on the grounds of a state hospital, courthouse, or other public building.

To avoid misunderstanding, let me say that I recognize the power of a state to impose different penalties for the same behavior under different circumstances. In Illinois, for example, simple battery becomes aggravated battery when committed on a school teacher or park official at his place of employment.[6] It was thought by the legislature, on the basis of experience, that these categories of people needed greater protection than ordinary citizens. Whether a higher penalty provides greater protection is another question. What is im-

---

6. Ch. 38, § 12-4, [1964] Ill. Ann. Stat. 711.

portant is the existence of a rational relationship between the group being protected and the attachment of a more serious penalty. It is precisely this kind of rational relationship which is lacking in the Oklahoma statute and others like it. One can imagine statutes making it a crime to do damage to state property and increasing the penalty with respect to property which is very likely to be damaged, such as college buildings. But such a precise approach is quite opposite to the sweeping embrace of the campus sedition statute.

The present situation is reminiscent of the loyalty oath craze which swept through the states in the early 1950s. College and university teachers were singled out as persons whose attestations of loyalty it was particularly important to collect, even though no compelling case could be made for the proposition that teachers were more disloyal than lawyers or that their subversiveness was more dangerous than that of corporation presidents or union leaders.

With respect to both kinds of statute, I would like to ask two questions. First, will they help achieve peace on campus? Second, what harmful effects do they have?

My personal judgment is that neither the denial-of-benefit type statute nor the new criminal provisions will do much to bring order to college campuses. It is well known that students by the thousands risk the harsh penalties of the drug and draft laws, acting from motives compounded of righteous indignation, guilt, and naive moral courage. Why should it be supposed that they will be less willing to risk the penalties contained in these statutes? Further, at least insofar as the leaders of demonstrations are concerned, denial-of-benefit statutes will largely miss the target, for many of the leaders are either nonstudents or former students; many do not need funds; many are not eligible. In this last category are the out-of-state students who attend the better state universities despite high out-of-state tuition and the unavailability of scholarships. Finally, they will not work because they require the school administration to act as the state's investigative agent, a role most administrative officers will find uncomfortable; the harsher the statute, the greater the discomfort.

The real perniciousness of these statutes is apparent when one looks at the harms they are likely to cause. For instance, the newly amended Pennsylvania Higher Education Assistance Act[7] denies student aid to any Pennsylvania resident attending an institution which fails to certify to the state at periodic intervals that none of the state's money is being spent by a student who has engaged in disruptive activities. If, to protect its own freedom from government supervision, an institution refuses to make such certifications, students whose only offense is that they reside in Pennsylvania and attend that institution become ineligible to receive any aid from the state. To date only a handful of the more than eight hundred institutions to which Pennsylvania residents carry their state scholarships and loans have indicated that they will comply; another handful have indicated that they will not; most remain undecided, caught between the desire to protect themselves from being called on to investigate and report upon student conduct to a government agency and the desire to continue to provide education to those of their students who happen to be from Pennsylvania.

Some people regard as a hopeful sign in this situation the conclusion of an agreement between the state of Pennsylvania and Haverford College which represents an apparent compromise by the state on the issue of certification. Under this arrangement, the responsibility for certifying his compliance rests with the student. The school then states officially that to the best knowledge of its responsible officers, the student is telling the truth. This scheme is either a fraud or a nullity. If the school officials routinely execute certifications for all students, then the requirement of official certification is meaningless, serving only to add a spurious authenticity to the student's assertions. On the other hand, if the school actually undertakes to determine the truth or falsehood of each student's submission, the situation is the same as if the school itself were the only certifying body. Finally, if the school only comments on those submissions it knows to be false, the ques-

---

7. P.L. 1546 (1966), *as amended by* P.L. 169, *approved* December 18, 1969.

tion is: how can the school know this? If the student has been disciplined for a disruptive offense, this fact should appear on his transcript and no other form of certification is necessary. If he has not been so disciplined, a statement by the school that he should have been is improper. Under the circumstances, I should think many colleges would still be reluctant to comply, even though this plan seems at first glance to offer a face-saving way to do so.

The greatest harm of these statutes, in my judgment, is that they will undermine academic freedom. The threat to freedom in sedition statutes is evident. They touch directly on questions of free speech and, although they are probably unconstitutional in whole or in part, until they are struck down they represent a very real threat to the intellectual freedom of all students and teachers. The denial-of-benefit statutes can also be expected to exert pressure toward ideological conformity in some students even while rousing others to anger and further protest. They, too, will be tested in courts and some, no doubt, will be found wanting. But the greatest threat to academic freedom does not lie in the direct prohibitions upon persons. It lies in the corrosive effect such statutes have upon institutions. The freedom of individuals in the academy is a direct function of the freedom and independence of the schools themselves. This is a point often forgotten and easy to overlook. It was the universities, not the courts, which protected faculty members from Senator Joseph McCarthy. In particular, it was the presidents and trustees of a few great schools, acting in the tradition of institutional freedom, who provided leadership during that period of stress.

The new statutes share a common skepticism about the ability of institutions to govern themselves. They reveal a ready willingness on the part of politicians to transform institutions of higher education from places with special responsibilities and special traditions into bureaus of state government undifferentiated in structure from other parts of the bureaucracy. In this respect, we may perhaps look to California to read the nation's future. Not only has the California legislature this year passed one of the most sweeping of the recent denial-of-benefit statutes, but the Regents of the University of California, acting in the spirit of the times, have moved to reassert their ultimate authority over faculty hiring. In the exercise of this authority they have recently denied continued employment to an admittedly qualified teacher on grounds of political affiliation. In less than twenty years the wheel has come full circle. Those who sought to protect universities from attacks on their freedom now restrict that freedom themselves in the name of order. Whether this will be the direction taken in other states remains to be seen. I am not hopeful.

CHAPTER SEVENTEEN

The Litigator's Response

*Robert M. O'Neil**

Major national events have a way of generating concentric waves of litigation. Anyone who has studied first year contract law—or watched the Forsyte Saga closely for that matter—knows of the "Coronation Cases"—a rash of suits brought in the British courts at the turn of the century when a palace tragedy threw the royal family into mourning and destroyed the value of viewing sites along the route of Edward VII's coronation procession for which hundreds of pounds had been paid. Within the past six months the American courts have experienced a wave of litigation that may come to be known as the "Cambodia Closing Cases." The resemblance between the two episodes is more than superficial. Last May† a sudden and wholly unforeseen pair of tragic events—the invasion of Cambodia and the death of four students at Kent State—drastically altered the relations between American universities and their students, much as the shrouding of the British royal carriages in 1920 sharply impaired relations between those who owned and those who rented choice locations along the coronation route. And in the current context, as in Edwardian Britain, the anger and bitterness bred by these frustrations have been channeled into the courts. Yet the implications and hazards of the Cambodia closing cases are vastly greater than those of the coronation cases.

---

* Professor of Law, University of California School of Law, Berkeley, California.
† May 1970.

An Overview of the Litigation

We might profitably begin with the ordeal of New York University (NYU)—a microcosm of the problems bred by last spring's events. There have already been at least three major NYU cases growing out of the relaxation of academic requirements and the redirection of many courses after May 4. The cycle began when the New York Court of Appeals told the law faculty of NYU (and all other schools preparing candidates for New York practice) they must give final examinations in a form acceptable to the court. Despite a fervent plea for reconsideration mounted by law students and professors, the state's high court insisted that no applicant could take the summer bar examination "unless he has first taken and been tested by an authentic written examination in each of his courses of study in accordance with previous practice in the school." That is to say, if the course usually required an examination for completion, that practice apparently could not be varied even to the extent of allowing a paper or an oral examination as a substitute. Thus the NYU Law School, which initially left to individual arrangement the matter and manner of completion, called its students back to Washington Square to take the examinations that the court of appeals, not the faculty, deemed essential to certification of professional competence.

The university won the second round in the courts. Shortly after the May closing, a group of students brought a suit to compel the administration to reopen the campus for one week to make up classes that had been cancelled or missed during the May turmoil. The claim was that the university had breached its contractual obligations set forth in its bulletin by failing to provide the specified number of weeks of instruction and course hours. The judge was sympathetic to the administration's plea of extenuation; he ruled that "under the conditions and circumstances prevailing, it may not be said that the exercise of discretion in favor of suspending formal classes was arbitrary, capricious, or improvident." The court added that even if there had been a breach of the university's contract, equity would not compel specific performance, especially after the end of the regular semester.

The worst was yet to come. Round three brought a serious setback for university autonomy and discretion—and at the hands, ironically, of the New York City Small Claims Court. A disgruntled NYU parent—a Queens fireman named Roger Paynter—filed suit for a refund of the tuition and fees he had paid for education he claimed his son had never received because of the May events. Though recognizing that "the faculty continued in attendance, available for consultation," the small claims judge concluded that the university had defaulted on its legal obligation to the plaintiff in the amount of $277.40—a pro rata share of the payments covering nine days of foregone instruction. The opinion ranged broadly over issues of law, morality, and campus disorder—quoting Learned Hand, Lord Russell, and Sidney Hook at appropriate points—but ended by calling this a simple, ordinary case of broken contract—a breach unexcused either by the extraordinary nature of the "Seven Days in May" or by the "subject to change without notice" provision in the catalogue.

If NYU has been the institution most beset by litigation, the stakes have been far higher elsewhere. Since last May, at least four other cases have been filed that deserve note. The administration of Washington University in St. Louis has been sued for $7 million by students claiming a denial of their educational and political rights during the troubles of last May. A number of students, faculty members, and student organizations have been sued by another student group at Ohio State for $1 million in damages for similar reasons. A parallel case is pending against the president and regents of the University of Minnesota, though without a money damage claim. And most recently the state of Indiana, through the attorney general, has sued the administration officers, the governing board, and a group of students at Indiana State in Terre Haute to recover some ten thousand dollars (plus fifty thousand dollars punitive damages) for damage done to state property on the campus during a disturbance last April.

Both the Washington and Ohio State suits, like those at NYU, focus upon reconstitution of classes last spring. The former attacks the chancellor for having made a speech opposing the Cambodia invasion on the day of the Kent State deaths and later in the week having urged departments to relax or revise their academic requirements to accommodate student concern. The Ohio complaint originally named a senior faculty member (who has since left Columbus and has been dropped from the suit); his offense was giving a speech on the day of the Cambodia invasion attacking the student conduct rules. Several teaching assistants remain among the defendants, charged with the same transgressions which allegedly disrupted the normal operation of the institution.

These cases have another thrust in common. Both the Washington University and Indiana complaints charge the administration with failing to call the police in time to prevent damage to property. The Minnesota suit claims the administration unlawfully allowed the use of campus facilities by groups advocating such crimes as fornication and sodomy, while failing to protect campus access of such other groups as the FBI, ROTC, and Army and Navy Intelligence. Plaintiffs in both the Minnesota and Terre Haute cases directly attack the hiring policies of the institutions, charging that irresponsible administators either deliberately employed troublemakers or failed to hire personnel capable of maintaining order.

Two premises underlie most of these suits. The first is quite naive — that the courts can somehow restore or maintain order on a deeply divided and troubled campus when the administration and even the police have failed. The other premise — not the least bit naive — is that the president or chancellor may have to pay heavy damages for his inability to achieve the impossible. Thus the plaintiffs seek to have it both ways.

The Sources of Litigation

There are now enough cases pending against universities to speculate why they have emerged in such large volume at this time. Several factors appear to explain the sudden resort to the courts for decision of a range of novel issues. First, the events of 1970 brought two disheartening realizations to many who kept hoping for an early peace—the one, that campus disorder may be a permanent or at least a long-term condition; the other, that internal resources are increasingly inadequate to maintain or restore order. An inability to solve internal problems has always brought people to the courthouse, often in anger and frustration—as witness the usually fruitless efforts to litigate the internal problems of religious organizations, fraternal societies, and, most obviously, of tense and divided families. Thus it is hardly surprising that campus conflicts have come eventually to the courts.

Second, during the 1960s the courts have appeared increasingly as protectors of interests adverse to campus order and stability. Hundreds of suits have been brought for the reinstatement of students dismissed or suspended on disciplinary charges since the 1961 decisions opening the doors of the federal courts to such pleas. In a high percentage of these cases the plaintiffs have prevailed—often where the guilt was clear, but because of doubt about the fairness of the procedures or the clarity of substantive regulations. In much the way white supremacist groups have wondered since 1954 why "we can't have courts too," conservative campus groups seem to have felt increasingly since 1961 that courts intervene only to help agitators and troublemakers to the detriment of the silent majority.

Third, conservative groups have only recently organized to the extent that litigation appears a viable form of redress. The Minnesota case, for example, was sponsored by the campus chapter of Young Americans for Freedom. The plaintiffs' attorney in the Washington University case is a member of the Board of Directors of the newly organized and conservative faculty group, University Centers for Rational Alternatives, Inc. It would, of course, be an oversimplification to attribute all such litigation to such organizations; the Indiana suit was brought by an apparently politically ambitious attorney general; the Ohio State case by a seemingly spontaneous student group claiming to be fed up with campus violence; and the NYU tuition-refund suit was simply the plea of an angry fireman who had worked hard and saved to send his son to an expensive private university and wanted his money's worth.

Fourth, there is undoubtedly a conviction that courts can solve problems even when all other agencies have failed. De Tocqueville's famous observation that most divisive political questions in the United States eventually reach the courts seems quite apposite. Today campus conflicts are perhaps the most deeply divisive questions of our society, and they have vast political implications, as the wave of repressive legislation and the continued use of campus unrest as a campaign issue suggest. Thus it would be surprising if the courts had not been asked to decide questions that others cannot resolve. Moreover, the courts have powers that other agencies lack for the enforcement of their judgments, and are thus seen as far more effective in the settlement of disputes.

Finally, there may be an element of self-infliction in the wounds recently suffered by the academic body. Beginning in the early spring of 1969, many colleges and universities sought court injunctions to restrain demonstrations they felt powerless to check by enforcing campus rules, and for which they fervently wished not to call the local police. Although much uncertainty exists among lawyers about the propriety of such equitable intervention, courts have almost without exception granted injunctions when asked by campus administrators to do so. Ironically, New York University apparently went farthest in this regard, seeking last November a permanent injunction forbidding violence on its campuses by specified groups and unspecified "John and Mary Does."

Thus it should not have come as complete surprise to university officials that equity cuts both ways—so that in the very same week a trial judge in Ohio could order the Kent State campus permanently closed, while a trial judge in Florida could order the University of Miami campus permanently reopened. Perhaps it is unfair and simplistic to charge university officials with reaping the bitter fruits of a harvest they sowed a year earlier. But it is true, to paraphrase the maxim, that many who had equity done to them had also been seekers of equity.

Theories of Litigation

The factual issues involved in this rash of lawsuits are quite novel. But the complaints do purport to invoke settled legal principles as the basis for recovery. In the NYU tuition case, of course, the father's claim was simply for the return of money paid the university for the unperformed portion of a contract to educate his son. Other cases appear to sound in tort, suggesting that university administrators, faculty, and students may be liable for the wrongful breach of a duty to maintain order on the campus and protect university property. At least one complaint, brought by a group of Queens College students against their administration, charges a violation of a New York City Board of Higher Education resolution requiring that the campus remain open for regular instruction during May.

What is the probability of recovery under these several theories? The courts do not appear to have recognized a general student right to an uninterrupted higher education. Whatever contractual claim there may be would ordinarily be qualified by cautionary language in the catalog or bulletin or on the registration card, although the small claims judge rejected NYU's reliance on that exception. Resort could also be had to the concept of *force majeure;* arguably, full performance is excused when violence and disorder make normal academic work impossible, much as would be the case if the campus were destroyed by fire or closed down by an epidemic. Here too, the New York Small Claims Court was unpersuaded, apparently taking the view that neither faculty nor administrators could excuse their own dereliction by invoking the restlessness of students. In the NYU case the argument was also made that the contract had in fact been performed; although regular formal classes were not held at the precise times and places specified in the bulletin, members of the faculty were available for consultation, credit for all courses was given, etc. But again the judge insisted that only "business as usual" would meet the terms of the contract. In any case, it does seem that the measure of damages for a breach of contract would not exceed a refund of a pro rata share of tuition and fees, though given the NYU precedent others may seek incidental or consequential damages for the truncation of their academic expectation.

The possibility of recovery in tort is less certain but more alarming because of the higher monetary stakes. Before one can recover for the harm caused by another's default, he must show that some legal obligation has been breached. The nature of the duty involved here is uncertain at best. If a student suffers physical injury through the negligence of university officials—in a chemistry laboratory, on the athletic field, or even on a university-sponsored expedition—he may recover damages from the persons he proves to have been at fault, or from the institution itself, unless barred by sovereign or charitable immunities.

Perhaps some analogy could be drawn between physical injury suffered in this way and the far less tangible consequences of an interrupted spring quarter. But the measure of damages is far less certain, and the degree of culpability is manifestly lower. Is the chancellor legally liable for failure to call the police in the same way he is accountable for not repairing the broken seats in the stadium or for hiring a careless bus driver? The analogy seems implausible, but the student plaintiffs in the Washington University case and the state attorney general in the Terre Haute case appear to invoke precisely this theory of recovery. In addition, they seek substantial punitive damages for allegedly unsound administrative judgment about the timing and manner of quelling disorder.

There is a possibility of recovery based upon a statute or regulation like that of the New York City Board of Higher Education, requiring campus officials to keep the institution open and functioning. One New York court last summer ordered the administration of Queens College to give special instruction in several courses to plaintiffs who invoked this regulation in their injunctive suit. The court found that the board resolution left the campus officials "no discretion as to whether or not to continue the regular course of study" and that under it "the faculty had the responsibility to meet with and teach these students." But it seems most unlikely that such a regulation, even if inexcusably breached, would support a damage suit against administration or faculty. There is a well-settled rule of tort law that the intention of the lawmaking body governs resort to regulatory laws as a measure of civil liability. Here it seems quite clear that the purpose of the board's edict was to regulate the conduct of the campus presidents and not to leave them vulnerable to heavy damage suits.

Finally, there is the lurking possibility of a constitutional basis of recovery. It is true the courts have recognized in certain circumstances a student's constitutional right to attend college. But these cases protect only against the arbitrary or discriminatory denial of educational access or opportunity. They declare that a student may not be excluded or expelled because he happens to be a Black, a Catholic, a member of SDS, or of YAF for that matter. These precedents do not remotely ensure against interruption of one student's education because of the political activities of fellow students or the caution of administrators in calling the police.

How viable, then, are the theories of recovery in the Cambodia closing cases? It is too early to tell what kinds of proof may be offered in the many suits that now await trial. But to the extent the complaints reveal the strategy of their draftsmen, it seems unlikely that a proper recognition of student's claims could go much beyond that of the NYU tuition case. Meanwhile, a strong case will presumably be made for overturning the small claims court decision on appeal. The prospect of recovery for negligence, breach of a statutory duty, or infringement of constitutional rights now appears so remote as not to merit further attention.

Consequences and Implications of Litigation

However unlikely the prospect of civil liability, the mere filing of suits of this sort is enough to unnerve the most resilient university official. The mere threat of liability will undoubtedly constrict and may well distort administrative judgment at the very time when the need for flexibility in choosing among a range of options is greatest. The university president or dean who fears a lawsuit if he fails to call the police may make the wrong choice simply because he knows he will not be sued if he does summon outside aid.

The risks may be less obvious in other kinds of cases. Yet if the present resort to the courts does succeed in any substantial measure, the consequences for higher education are far reaching and extremely grave.

First, there is the risk that success in court will stimulate further attempts. Fred M. Hechinger of *The New York Times* recently observed that the NYU tuition refund decision "might not only tend to put extreme fiscal pressure on universities but also encourage parental efforts, through the courts, to demand or oppose specific courses, in return for their money."

Second, there is the ominous prospect of governance by injunction. An initially narrow range of questions committed to a court may steadily expand, because of the quest and counter-quest of various campus constituencies for protection against each other, until vital decisions about the way the university functions are being made by judges who have no particular expertise or sensitivity in these matters.

Third, long-range institutional planning obviously becomes increasingly difficult under these conditions. While one may be able to insure against heavy civil liability for mistaken judgment in calling the police or closing the campus, just as one insures against a variety of other potential hazards, there is no way to insure against an injunction.

Fourth, there is the danger that independently framed sanctions of different agencies may merge or interact in sinister ways. Henceforth if any Ohio court closes a state-supported or state-aided campus (as the Portage County Common Pleas judge closed Kent State in May), all public funds will cease flowing to the campus under a recent revision of Ohio regents regulations. Yet the judge who issues the closing order may be quite unaware of these harsh collateral consequences.

Fifth, the traditional and delegated authority of governing boards may also be impaired by mounting judicial surveillance of university governance. When a court accepts the complaint of even a single student against his university, it seemingly preempts the authority of other bodies to deal with subject matter during the pendency of the suit.

Finally, there is a real concern that increasing resort to the courts for settlement of campus disputes will cause the internal organs of conflict resolution to atrophy. If alternative external forms appear readily available to the campus constituencies, then the strongest pressure upon the university to put its own house in order may be removed at the very time that pressure is most necessary.

This recital of possible horrors is doubtless incomplete. The cases already pending in the courts carry grave threats to university autonomy and judgment. Additional types of suits against universities may have as yet unforeseen consequences. It is not too early to be vitally concerned about these hazards and to seek ways of averting them.

Alternatives and Antidotes to Litigation

The complaints already filed are not likely to be dismissed, and many others may be filed in coming months. What may the academic community do to protect itself? Several possible approaches may help.

First, a strong voice from the academic community may counsel courts to proceed with caution and even to abstain altogether in complex and sensitive academic disputes. Last summer, a number of higher education groups filed amicus curiae briefs in the Court of Appeals for the District of Columbia urging judicial deference to the accreditation process, which was challenged under the antitrust laws. Perhaps the court would have declined in any event to substitute its judgment for that of the regional association. But the active participation of so many concerned groups may have reinforced the judgment in favor of academic autonomy.

Second, it may be possible when cases are pending to do a far better job than we typically do of "educating" the courts about the issues and the way academic institutions operate. Several of the recent trial court decisions in New York reveal a serious misunderstanding of the nature of an academic community. If and when these decisions are appealed, academic groups may be able to play a vital role in informing the higher courts of the special needs and characteristics of institutions of higher learning.

Third, there may be some value in considering the possibility of special courts for university cases if the current volume of litigation is sustained. We have specialized courts for other sorts of highly complex and intricate subject matters on which judges of general jurisdiction are not expert. There are special military courts, courts of claims, tax courts, patent and customs courts, and others. Perhaps the time has come to consider the advisability of special education or university courts, at least in states where a large volume of litigation can be expected.

Finally, the best remedy of all is the simplest one to state and the hardest to implement. The best way to persuade the courts to abstain is to demonstrate the capacity of the university to solve its own problems. Of course, judicial abstinence will not bring peace to the campus any more than will judicial intervention. Yet one last effort must be made to develop tribunals on the campus that can adjudicate the issues now increasingly relegated to external forums. Rather than asking a civil court to issue an injunction, should we not still hope for an internal tribunal with comparable jurisdiction and vastly greater expertise? It is possible that the order of a campus court may not be obeyed; but there is also no guarantee that there will be compliance with the mandate of a civil court, as the number of recent contempt proceedings shows. The inherent advantages of seeking to utilize every available internal mechanism are substantial, and the hazards of surrendering control to external bodies are great enough without adding self-inflicted wounds.

CHAPTER EIGHTEEN

A Trial Lawyer's View of Lawsuits against Schools

*Richard M. Goodman**

Effect of Lawsuits on University Policy

The phenomenon of the closing of a university, followed by lawsuits, including suits for damages, arising out of the shut-down, is a new situation. When I attended The University of Michigan in the fifties and the University of Chicago in the late fifties, the confrontations of the sixties were neither contemplated nor predicted. We lived in an entirely different age, in a contemplative situation—many called it a lethargic condition—throughout our college years. The courts at that time had not turned their attention to such problems, because the student revolt had not surfaced; but in the past decade, courts have been called on repeatedly and have had to develop rules almost under emergency conditions. The flexibility of the common law and the courts to respond to the challenge of the swiftly paced social developments of this decade will be a measure of their basic soundness and ability to meet changing conditions. Historically, the common law has responded surprisingly well to this kind of challenge in other areas. I believe it will again.

The damage suit has been with us almost since the inception of the common law. It is, in my judgment, a somewhat misun-

* Goodman, Eden, Robb, Millender, Goodman & Bedrosian, Detroit, Michigan.

derstood animal, if I may use that word. Although a lawsuit claiming damages has many functions, most people today regard it as a method for securing compensation for individuals for the loss of property or for personal injury. This is the function of the damage suit in many contexts. It is the major, if not the exclusive, function in the ordinary automobile accident case. However, the damage suit fills another role in our society when it brings about changes in the policy of the institution being sued.

Litigation involving the design of products challenges corporate decisions regarding how such products are made or fabricated. These lawsuits inevitably affect the response of the corporation in the future; they force responsible officials to look more sharply at safety as a central factor in design. Similarly, the present-day environmental lawsuits have as their objectives not simply the recovery of money, but a change in the attitude and policy of an otherwise insensitive corporate or municipal establishment and the application of citizen pressure on groups responsible for decisions affecting the level of pollution. It is apparent that the recent suits filed against universities, suits which frequently ask substantial sums in damages, will also accelerate changes in university policy and governmental attitudes. The plaintiffs are aware that the lawsuit in which they are involved is in fact a vehicle to exert swift and expeditious pressure on these agencies. They seek answers defining the obligation of the university to maintain classes, secure the safety of the academic community, and preserve an open and free academic environment.

Some Recent Cases

Following the student strike in May 1970, and after the Cambodian situation arose, there were lawsuits filed against a number of universities. Many of these suits requested the court to grant injunctive relief in a particular situation. Some cases sought to compel the university officials to open the university; others requested the court to order the university closed; and some sought to supervise the way in which the university was responding to student protest. Most of these lawsuits appear to have been brought against the universities by students who were not participating in the protest activities, or by such students and their parents, or by the parents alone. The requests for relief were usually grounded on the claim that students were deprived of classroom time and the normal activities of the university because of the student protest activities and the police action which often followed in the wake of the protest.

The *College Law Bulletin*, a monthly newsletter published by the United States National Student Association in connection with the Association's Legal Rights Program, is an indispensable reference for those who wish to keep abreast of the latest suits arising out of student-university relationships. The cases I intend to talk about are reported in the monthly issues of that publication, in the section devoted to litigation growing out of the student strike in May 1970.

Cohen v. Stanford

An unreported case[1] filed in the circuit court in Dade County, Florida was a class action brought by a group of parents and students after the University of Miami was closed on May 7, following student turmoil on the campus. The students contended that the university had been shut down and classes cancelled without proper cause and without adequate justification. The action was brought under § 1983[2] of the federal civil rights legislation, one of the post-Civil War statutes passed by the Congress in 1871 to protect citizens who are deprived

1. Cohen v. Stanford, No. 70–8285 (11th Jud. Cir. Dade Co., Fla.), *writ of mandamus granted*, May 9, 1970, *writ amended*, May 11, 1970 (Balaban, Cir. J.); *see* COLL. LAW BULL. Vol. 11, No. 9, p. 69 (May, 1970).
2. 42 U.S.C. § 1983; Civil action for deprivation of rights. Every person who, under color of any statute, ordinance, regulation, custom or usage, of any State or Territory, subjects, or causes to be subjected, any citizen of the United States or other person within the jurisdiction thereof to the deprivation of any rights, privileges, or immunities secured by the Constitution and laws, shall be liable to the party injured in an action at law, suit in equity, or other proper proceeding for redress. R.S. § 1979. Act April 20, 1871, c.22, § 1,17 stat. 13.

of rights secured by the Constitution and federal law. Prior to a full hearing on the matter, the Florida circuit court granted a writ of mandamus ordering the university to be reopened on May 8. Three days later, the court issued an amended writ in clarification of this original order. The court stated that the writ should not be interpreted as a restriction on the university president's authority to set policy and make decisions regarding voluntary class attendance and academic grading.[3] I find the court's swift response to the student request to reopen the university by means of an order without hearing a rather startling act, especially since it was done under the civil rights legislation.

Bailey v. University of Minnesota

Another suit filed in a Minnesota trial court against the University of Minnesota and administrative officials at the time of the May student strike was clearly an attempt to bring direct pressure on the university to formulate policy acceptable to the plaintiffs.[4] The complaint alleged that the university and its officials had wrongfully allowed the perversion of university property and facilities by permitting or taking no measures to prevent commission of the crimes of sodomy, fornication, disorderly conduct, unlawful assembly, riot, malicious injury, and distribution of obscene literature. The complaint also alleged that the university permitted the use of university facilities by subversive organizations, permitted members of these organizations to speak on campus and teach students, and denied federal intelligence agencies full access to student records. A further charge against the university alleged that it interfered with national defense and the draft. Here is a lawsuit, certainly, which cuts a wide swath. These plaintiffs show a firm intent to use the court proceeding to coerce the university to formulate policy acceptable to the more conservative element

---

3. *See* COLL. LAW BULL., Vol. 11, No. 9, p. 69 (May, 1970).
4. Bailey v. University of Minnesota, No. 666859 (Dist. Ct. 4th Jud. Dist. Hennepin Co., Minn., *filed* May 5, 1970).

on the campus. No action has been taken by the court to this time.[5]

AAUP v. Nunn

Another interesting case is *Association of American University Professors v. Nunn*,[6] an unreported decision of the federal district court in Kentucky. Protest activities began on the University of Kentucky campus after Cambodia, and on May 5 an ROTC building was completely destroyed by fire. The next day Governor Nunn of Kentucky placed the campus under immediate curfew, to begin at seven-thirty in the evening and extend to six-thirty in the morning. The governor also called up National Guard units to enforce the curfew, authorizing them to carry bayonets and live ammunition and "to use such force as is necessary to perform their mission of protection." The plaintiffs were arrested by guardsmen and by security police for violation of the curfew. The complaint challenged the constitutional validity of the governor's order in setting up the curfew and calling out the National Guard and alleged bad faith and political motives. The suit was brought under the Civil Rights Act of 1871,[7] alleging that their rights to free speech, free expression, and free assembly had been denied by the Governor of Kentucky under color of state law, the operative language of the federal statute. They asked for an injunction dissolving the curfew and other relief which would effect reversal of the curfew and reversal of their arrests. The federal district court declined to grant the relief sought and dismissed the action, concluding that the governor and the university officials had authority to act as they did and that their actions were reasonable in the light of emergency conditions on campus. The court suggested that in the event the National Guard or the local police transgressed the orders of the governor, plaintiffs could sue for whatever relief was available under Kentucky law.

---

5. August 1970.
6. No. 2139 (E.D. Ky. May 14, 1970).
7. 42 U.S.C. § 1983.

Coppeler v. Cohen

The case of *Coppeler v. Cohen*[8] was filed in an Ohio court after disruptive incidents at Ohio State University resulted in the closing of the school for about two weeks in May. This action, probably the first of its kind, was brought by students and parents of students against the administration, a professor, teaching assistants, and several student organizations. The complaint alleged that the defendants, knowing that violence would probably occur as a result of their activities, incited students to engage in disruptive incidents. The complaint asked for, and the court granted, a permanent injunction against students and faculty who were engaged in protest activity. The court found that the activities of all of the defendants except one professor did, indeed, cause, contribute to, or aggravate civil disorder. However, the court refused to enjoin three of the organizations because of impracticalities, and refused to bar one defendant from the campus because the plaintiffs had not shown that the ordinary administrative and legal processes were inadequate to deal with his presence on campus. The permanent injunction was extremely broad, prohibiting speeches and pamphlets that would incite to riot, disrupt, or in any way hinder the operations of the university; blockading of streets, passageways, or halls in campus buildings; threatening or intimidation of any persons lawfully on the campus; and loud noises, stench, or commotion which would in any way interfere with persons lawfully using the campus.

State v. White

Another example of a very broad injunctive relief is found in *State v. White, President, Kent State University,*[9] another unreported decision. Following the Kent State affair, the county prosecutor of Portage County asked the local judge to enter an order closing down the campus immediately, restricting access

---

8. No. 240,650 (Common Pleas Ct., Franklin Co., Ohio, *filed* June 8, 1970).
9. No. 39346 (Common Pleas Ct., Portage Co., Ohio, *filed* May 4, 1970).

to the campus of all persons, including administrators of the
school, except by express permission of the National Guard.
Students living in dormitories were to be given time to arrange
their departures. The petition for injunction was granted without hearing—a far-reaching order, summarily granted, shut-
ting down the entire campus and preventing access by all
unauthorized personnel.

Ziglar v. George Washington University

A complaint against George Washington University, now
pending in the District of Columbia Court of General Sessions,[10] is a class action by sixteen students on behalf of the
rest of the student body, alleging breach of contract by the
university in causing or permitting the cancelling of classes in
May 1970. The plaintiffs claim more than a million dollars in
damages and request the appointment of a master to determine the amount due each member of the class.

University Defenses against Liability

Where are we going with this type of litigation? There is
good reason to believe that it will be used with increasing
frequency, if student disruption again becomes substantial and
affects numerous schools and universities. The matter of released time for students to engage in political activity in the fall
of 1970 raised the question as to whether this, too, would
expose universities and administrative officials to lawsuits by
disgruntled students claiming that such a practice would interfere with their right to an education and to attend classes on
an uninterrupted schedule.

The Doctrine of Governmental Immunity

I wish to suggest some possibilities concerning the defense
in such lawsuits, speaking as a trial lawyer generally, not as one
who has been active in representing university administrations.

---

10. August 1970.

We do, however, represent students from time to time. First, there are many states in which a lawsuit seeking damages cannot be brought directly against a university because the university shares the sovereign immunity of the state. Michigan is one such state. Consequently, no such action could be brought in a circuit court in Michigan. Plaintiffs in a suit claiming damages from any of the state universities of Michigan would have to resort to the court of claims, a special statutory court with exclusive jurisdiction over claims of more than one hundred dollars against the state or any of its arms or agencies, except those claims enforceable in federal courts. The creation of the court of claims did not change the sovereign immunity of the State of Michigan.

The rule of immunity, applicable in many jurisdictions throughout the United States, offers some protection to state universities in suits of this kind. However, plaintiffs in such suits will name particular officials as defendants, seeking to avoid the rule of sovereign immunity.[11]

Plaintiff's Difficulty in Proving Damages

The question of proving damages in a suit based upon a temporary closing of classes and other activities may be difficult. Where a university is shut down for a week, two weeks, or a month, but provides for a longer session to make up the lost time, in what way is the student damaged? And on what basis can his parents claim damages? I seriously question the possibility of proving damages in such circumstances. Moreover, how does one measure the damages suffered by students unable to attend classes, if the university does not allow additional time for the classes lost? This would appear to be a difficult burden of proof to sustain. Can the defendant officials or the academic community show that the student plaintiff voluntarily passed up the opportunity to attend classes

---

11. Asher v. Harrington, No. 70–C–309 (E.D.Wis. *filed* Oct. 12, 1970) was such an action, filed against the president, chancellors, and regents of the University of Wisconsin.

on any number of occasions when there was no disruption on campus?

Defenses in Actions for Breach of Contract

Many of the suits that have been brought and will be brought by students claiming damages for the closing of campus operations are brought on the theory of breach of contract. The student, or someone for him, pays money at the beginning of the school year so that the student may attend school. The university, for that consideration, promises to afford him continuous, systematic education for the entire period of the school year. When the school arbitrarily closes down because of protest activities or upon the demand of other students, the argument is that there has been a breach of contract by the school. In my judgment, however, the university or school clearly has the right to close its operations in emergencies, to protect the safety or the lives of the members of the academic community — students, faculty, and staff.

In other contractual actions of this type we have a principle of law called *force majeure:* The law recognizes that when insurrection or other wholly unforeseeable or extraordinary circumstance makes the performance of any contract impossible, from a practical point of view, performance is excused for the duration of the emergency. It is reasonable to suppose that this traditional principle of the law of contracts has application to student suits claiming damages for breach of contract.

University and school administrators might employ a technique which has been adopted in other circumstances involving the law of contracts and of torts. If schools and universities promise to provide continuing and systematic education for the entire school year, it would seem that the institution may properly ask the students, as they enroll, to agree to a modification of that contract under emergency conditions requiring a temporary closing of university facilities. Such an agreement could be in the nature of a waiver or other document similar to those used in hospitals in connection with possible medical-legal litigation. The wording of such waivers would, of course, need to be construed in the light of legal principles, but the idea is perhaps worth exploring.

The tragic and damaging events of May 1970, at Kent State and elsewhere, were the result of protests against our national policies in Southeast Asia. If universities are going to be challenged in the courts and possibly held liable for damages for the closedowns of the universities in the May 1970 student strike, I suggest that the universities have a right to ask the government of the United States to participate in their defense. They might request financial help for their defense, or, in an extreme situation implead the federal government under the Federal Tort Claims Act. Many people believe that much of the responsibility for the tragedies of May 1970 lies in Washington.

University Liability for Injury or Death of Student

The other side of the coin involves the responsibility of universities for the injury or the death of a student in the wake of student protest activity. Just running through *The New York Times* and the *Detroit Free Press* for a two-year period, covering approximately a dozen universities in the United States, I have counted 9 deaths and 885 student injuries of a moderate to severe nature. It is apparent that universities should give serious consideration to their liability to these students and to their families.

In my judgment, most students are not interested in bringing court actions against universities for the recovery of money. But consider that Arthur Krause filed an action in federal district court in June 1970, against former Governor Rhodes of Ohio and officials of the Ohio National Guard.[12] As administrator of the estate of his daughter, Allison, one of the four students killed at Kent State University, Mr. Krause is asking $1 million in compensatory damages and punitive damages of $5 million, under the Civil Rights Act of 1871.[13]

---

12. Krause v. Rhodes, No. C–70–544 (E.D. Ohio, *filed* June 10, 1970).
13. 42 U.S.C. § 1983.

Universities can very definitely be liable in civil actions for damages, both compensatory and punitive, in similar situations. University officials certainly have a duty to use due care — a common law duty, if nothing else — in carrying out their functions. Certainly this embraces the concept of using due care in requesting the assistance of National Guard forces in an academic community; due care in arranging for such forces; due care in the supervision of these forces along with university security personnel; and due care in determining whether or not the National Guard personnel invited or sent to the campus do in fact have specific orders in reference to their firearms. These are ordinary principles of negligence law.

The *Krause* suit in Cleveland was filed pursuant to the federal Civil Rights Act.[14] The complaint alleges that former Governor Rhodes of Ohio committed acts designed by him to deny to the students on the campus of Kent State their rights under the first amendment, and to interfere with their expression of views and their constitutionally protected activity on that campus. It is not only the state officials and the university officials who may be subject to liability in this setting. Under the Federal Tort Claims Act the federal government frequently can be brought in as a party defendant, where federalized National Guard is used, and even, perhaps, where it is not used. Moreover, in situations where the guard had not been federalized, as in the Kent State affair, I suggest that it could be successfully argued that the United States did not use due care in the training of the guard to control student protest activities, and in the proper use and handling of firearms in such situations.

Conclusion

I am firmly convinced that litigation, although it may provide a very temporary relief of the symptoms of campus problems, is not the vehicle for solving such problems. They are

14. 42 U.S.C. § 1983.

substantial, long-term, and very real. Students have valid complaints which must be dealt with not only by the academic community, but by the whole community and the nation. I have long been impressed by the fact that the student seems to stand in a very special relationship to the university, as compared to other kinds of relationships in the society. His lack of power in the university structure is marked, in contrast to other kinds of relationships in society—the employee-employer relationship, for example. Since the 1930s, unionized employees have had tremendous bargaining rights and effective economic power, controlling, to a substantial extent, the terms and conditions of their working lives. Voters, including taxpayers, can vote to remove elected officials—local, state, and federal. Shareholders in corporations have the right to review records, to vote for directors, and to affect policy decisions at all levels of the corporation. Students have no comparable rights. Although changes are beginning to emerge, institutional forms granting permanent, ongoing rights to students in the universities have not been created. This is the challenge that confronts us today.

CHAPTER NINETEEN

The Administrator's Dilemma

*Carroll L. Wagner, Jr.**

Tax Exemption

Ordinarily one would not think that tax law and student protest bear any relationship to one another. Recently, however, the Internal Revenue Service (IRS) has turned its attention to certain campus political activities. The Service has challenged plans for coordinating student campaigners through campus centers, plans such as the Princeton-based Movement for a New Congress. Concern has been expressed over the granting of preelection recesses to allow students and faculty to work in political campaigns.[1] A number of institutions had formally announced that they would recess for one or two weeks prior to the November[2] election and reduce other vacations accordingly. Not only has the institution itself been challenged but some of the smaller groups which are a part of the institution. The federal government announced that it would probe the tax-exempt status of the *Columbia Daily Spectator*, a college newspaper that has taken stands on political issues and candidates.[3] *Spectator* sources said that among the issues under examination by the tax officials is one which endorsed Black Panther leader Eldridge Cleaver for President of the United

---

* Hansell, Post, Brandon & Dorsey, Atlanta, Georgia.
1. Bur. Nat'l Affairs Daily Tax Report, p. G-1 (June 26, 1970) (letter from Rep. O'Neill, Mass., to Commissioner of Internal Revenue).
2. The election of November 1970.
3. The New York Times, June 27, 1970, p. 1, col. 7.

States. Another issue backed Nelson Rockefeller for Governor of New York. Surely there was a change of management in the interim between those two issues of the paper. Columbia University recently ordered certain politically active student groups to remove their operations from the Columbia campus.[4]

Two tax factors must be considered in discussing this problem. As most of you know, an educational institution which is nonproprietary is exempt from federal income taxation. In addition, donations made to that educational institution are deductible by the donor, a great incentive to give money to a tax-exempt organization as opposed to one which is not tax-exempt. For our purposes, the relevant section of the Internal Revenue Code is § 501(c)(3), applicable to private, nonproprietary educational institutions. It provides that in order for an institution to be exempt from federal income taxation, it must be organized and operated exclusively for educational purposes, among others. Further, § 501(c)(3) states that no substantial part of the activities of the institution can be devoted to carrying on propaganda or otherwise attempting to influence legislation; and finally, the school cannot "participate in or intervene in (including the publishing or distributing of statements), any political campaign on behalf of any candidate for public office." If an educational institution meets these requirements it is exempt from federal income taxation. Section 170 of the code provides that persons who make "charitable contributions" to "an educational organization which normally maintains a regular faculty and curriculum and normally has a regularly enrolled body of pupils or students in attendance at the place where its educational activities are carried on" are allowed a deduction from taxable income. The organization to which gifts are made must also meet the specific requirements of § 501(c)(3) which I mentioned earlier.

A few examples of the application of these principles to

---

4. Bur. Nat'l Affairs Daily Tax Report, p. G–1 (August 5, 1970) (letter from Rep. Rosenthal, N.Y., to Commissioner of Internal Revenue).

various organizations which have sought tax exemptions will convey some idea of how the IRS applies them. With respect to nonpartisan political activity, the IRS has ruled that a nonprofit organization created for the purpose of elevating the standards of ethics and morality in the conduct of campaigns for election to political office by publicizing its code of fair campaign practices through newspapers and other news media and by furnishing aids to political science teachers may qualify for exemption from federal income tax.[5] The IRS emphasized that the organization under review performed political activities on a nonpartisan basis.

In another instance, the IRS has ruled[6] that a nonprofit organization created to conduct public forums at which lectures and debates on social or political matters are presented qualifies for a tax exemption, even though some of its programs include controversial speakers or subjects. The IRS emphasized that the primary purpose of the organization being considered was to bring about a fair and open-minded consideration of social, political, and international questions.

Partisan political activity, no matter how beneficial it may be to the community or to society, will cause an institution to lose its tax exemption. The IRS has ruled[7] that a nonprofit organization created to improve a public educational system is not exempt from federal income tax where it campaigns on behalf of candidates for election to the school board. Finally, the IRS has ruled[8] that an organization which, as its primary objective, advocates the adoption of a theory or a doctrine which can become effective only by the enactment of legislation is not entitled to a tax exemption, since it is not operated exclusively for education purposes within the meaning of § 501(c)(3). It is important to note that this organization had as its primary objective the influencing of legislation. Thus, an organization can influence legislation if it makes sure that this is not a substantial part of its total activity.

5. Rev. Rul. 66–258, 1966–2 C.B. 213.
6. Rev. Rul. 66–256, 1966–2 C.B. 210.
7. Rev. Rul. 67–71, 1967–1 C.B. 125.
8. Rev. Rul. 62–71, 1962–1 C.B. 85.

More recently, in Revenue Ruling 70–449, 1970–35 I.R.B., page 9, the IRS recognized that a university is not engaged in restricted legislative activities where, at the request of a committee of the United States Congress for a person to testify on a proposed bill, the university sends the head of its biology department to testify. The IRS stated in this ruling as follows:

> In the instant case the university did not initiate any action with respect to pending legislation, but merely responded to an official request from a Congressional committee to testify. It cannot, therefore, be described as attempting to influence legislation by contacting members of a legislative body to propose, support, or oppose legislation or by advocating the adoption or rejection of legislation. The attempts to influence legislation as described in the regulations imply an affirmative act and require something more than a mere passive response to a Committee invitation.

In an analagous area of tax law, a business corporation was allowed to deduct, under § 162 of the code, expenses in connection with advertisements to encourage the public to register to vote and contribute to the political party or campaign fund of a candidate of their choice, the sponsoring of a political debate among candidates for a particular office, the granting to employees of time off with pay for registration and voting, and the maintenance of a payroll deduction plan for employees wishing to make political contributions.[9] Section 162(e) of the code provides that "ordinary and necessary" business expenses are deductible by business corporations unless they are expenses of "participation in, or intervention in, any political campaign on behalf of any candidate for public office." However, employees were not given paid vacations to campaign for the candidates of their choice.

The Tax Reform Act of 1969 contains some very stringent rules to be applied to charitable organizations which are "private foundations" within the meaning of § 509 of the code.

---

9. Rev. Rul. 62–156, 1962–2 C.B. 47.

While these regulations are not relevant to student protest problems, they are relevant to the tax-exempt organization and should be mentioned here. Private, nonproprietary educational institutions will not be deemed "private foundations" if they make the proper notification to the Internal Revenue Service.[10] Unless the Secretary of the Treasury exempts, by regulations, educational organizations from the notification requirements of § 508(a) of the code, private educational institutions will be presumed to be "private foundations" unless they notify the Internal Revenue Service to the contrary, pursuant to § 508(a). On July 13, 1970, the IRS announced temporary regulations setting out the procedure for § 501(c)(3) organizations to follow in notification. A new form, "Form 4653, Notification Concerning Foundation Status," was mailed to all § 501(c)(3) organizations. It should be filled out and returned to the IRS promptly.

Recently, the American Council on Education published a statement[11] which applies the principles which I have discussed to the matter of campus unrest and political activity on campuses. John Holt Myers[12] prepared this excellent statement. He was able to persuade Commissioner Thrower of the Internal Revenue Service to read the document and state that he believed it provided fair and reasonable guidelines with respect to the applicability of the relevant provisions of the Internal Revenue Code. This superb accomplishment deserves our congratulations.

Accreditation

As many of you may know, there are seven regional accreditation associations in the country. They are all members of a federation and their practices are somewhat similar. They accredit all of the nonproprietary educational institutions with-

---

10. I.R.C. §§ 509(a)(1), 170(b)(1)(A)(ii).
11. Guidelines on Questions Relating to Tax Exemption and Political Activities, *reproduced as* Appendix IX.
12. *See* chapter 15 *supra*.

in their respective regions. At the time I prepared my remarks for this seminar there had been no official position on campus unrest taken by any of the accreditation associations. I spoke informally with the Southern Association of Colleges and Schools to get their unofficial reaction. Their feeling was one of great sympathy for the institutions which are having problems with student unrest. Their general reaction was to attempt to aid the institution in correcting the situation. To this end, they discussed, with the institution, procedures to handle problems, and supported and assisted the institution in any way they could. In many cases they send observers to a campus in trouble, to try to get an accurate and objective viewpoint about the situation. Moreover, the Southern Association felt that revoking accreditation of a school served only to help the student protesters to achieve their goal of closing the school.

The Board of Directors of the Western Association of Schools and Colleges adopted formally an official statement on July 1, 1970, expressing sentiments similar to those expressed to me earlier by the Southern Association. The concluding paragraph in the policy statement of the Western Association states:

> Disruption of the work of a Western Association member institution by forces beyond its control, although not condoned, will not necessarily result in summary loss of accreditation. Prolonged inability, for whatever reasons, to conduct its academic programs will require a review of the institution.

If a regional association takes measures to revoke accreditation of a member school because of continuous campus disruption, some form of judicial review may be available to the institution to challenge the decision. Two recent cases have considered the matter. The first was *Parsons College v. North Central Association*.[13] The association withdrew Parsons' accreditation and Parsons sought to enjoin the association to prevent withdrawal of accreditation. The court rejected Parsons' con-

---

13. 271 F. Supp. 65 (N.D. Ill. 1967).

stitutional claims, noted that Parsons had made no attempt to invoke antitrust laws, and discussed the application of common law principles to the facts of the case. The court declared that no judge-made principles or statutes ought to be applied to control the actions of private associations. The court held that the standards of accreditation are not guides for laymen, but for professionals in the field of education. In answering a claim by Parsons that the standards under which it was judged were void because they were too vague, the court stated that the association was entitled to make a conscious choice in favor of flexible standards to accomodate variation in purpose and character among its constituent institutions and to avoid forcing all into a rigid and uniform mold. Regarding the procedure by which Parsons was reviewed by the association, the court held that the nature of the hearing, if indeed one was required, could be adjusted to the nature of the issue to be decided. In this case the issue was not one of innocence but excellence and the procedures appropriate to decide whether a specific act of plain misconduct was committed are not suited to an expert evaluation of educational quality. The court held that a trial-type hearing, with confrontation, cross-examination, and assistance of counsel, would not have been suited to resolving the issues.

More recently, the United States Court of Appeals for the District of Columbia demonstrated a similar reluctance to intervene in association affairs.[14] Marjorie Webster Junior College, a proprietary school, was refused accreditation by the Middle States Association. The college then brought an action on common law grounds, on constitutional grounds, and under the Sherman Antitrust Act, alleging that the Middle States Association was unreasonably boycotting the school. The court found that there was no violation of the Sherman Act and that there was "no necessity" for the court to intervene under the common law principles governing exclusions from member-

14. Marjorie Webster Junior College v. Middle States Association of Colleges and Secondary Schools, 432 F.2d 650 (D.C. Cir. 1970), *appeal pending.*

ship in private associations. The court added that "even assuming that Middle States' activities do constitute 'state action' which subjects Middle States to constitutional restraints, Marjorie Webster did not show that the exclusionary policy was unreasonable."

I believe that accreditation associations are going to be sympathetic and do everything in their power to aid member institutions in solving their problems. Reevaluation of the accreditation of any school which had been disrupted by student protest would be an action of last resort.

Interest Rates

Most of the financing of educational institutions depends upon gifts from private sources or grants from government agencies, legislative appropriations, borrowing, or a combination of these sources. Schools do not ordinarily borrow money to meet their operational expenses. Loans are obtained primarily for the construction of facilities, often by the issuance of bonds. A bond is an interest-paying IOU. In return for cash, the borrower provides an engraved certificate, therein promising to pay the bondholder a fixed rate of interest (usually twice a year) and to repay the principal amount at the maturity date of the bond. Public schools can issue bonds which entitle the individual who holds the bond to exclude from his taxable income the amount of interest paid on the bond.[15] These so-called municipal bonds are much more salable at lower interest rates than bonds issued by private schools, as interest on the latter is not tax-exempt.

The payment of principal and interest on bonds is usually secured by granting the bondholder a security interest in some form of collateral or the security of a guarantee of payment by the state. Such bonds may be general obligation bonds of the state, regarded by investors as most secure, and therefore salable at relatively low interest rates. Some states have building authorities which issue bonds; or states may enable single

---

15. I.R.C. § 103.

institutions or governing boards of several institutions to issue revenue bonds. Institutions may pledge the entire resources of the institution as collateral for the payment of revenue bonds; or they may pledge the income to be derived from the facility to be financed through the bonds, in which case the facility is termed self-liquidating.

I would imagine that the effect of student unrest on interest rates is minimal. There might be difficulty in finding a lender, but I doubt that the interest rate would be appreciably higher. It should be noted, however, that the public usually buys such bonds, and the public is concerned about possible damage to the buildings which serve as security or collateral for the payment of the bond. Full insurance or higher interest rates may be required to make the bonds salable. A lessening of public confidence in the ability of the institution to operate peacefully and safely, with little risk of property damage, could require the pledging of more security and higher interest to attract purchasers.

Property Insurance

In general, campus unrest has had little effect upon the published property insurance rates; but it has become increasingly difficult for certain universities which have been subjected to property damage during student protest to find an insurer willing to underwrite the property loss. Where insurance rates are controlled by state regulation, insurers are faced with either insuring at the prevailing rate or not insuring at all. If there has been unrest on the campus, they may well refuse to insure property, or they may impose a very high deductible—as much as fifty thousand to a hundred thousand dollars. The institution must, of course, act as self-insurer to the extent of the deductible amount. Institutions having problems with property insurance will need to consult their own state statutes and insurance companies operating in the state for answers, as the regulations vary from state to state.

CHAPTER TWENTY

Questions and Answers

Moderator:
John W. Reed

Participants:
Karl J. Bemesderfer
Richard M. Goodman
John P. Holloway
John Holt Myers
Carroll L. Wagner, Jr.
Robert G. Zumwinkle

Waiver of University Contract Obligation

Reed: I have a question for Mr. Goodman. You spoke of the possibility of having students execute a waiver relieving the school of contractual obligation in the event of a shutdown of the school. Would you explain the nature of such a waiver, so that we can be sure we know what we are talking about?

Goodman: The legal theory advanced for such suits was based on the breach of contract between the student and the university.

Reed: But you have some kind of document—the agreement which the student would have signed.

Goodman: Yes. If in fact this is a contract, it is simply an addendum to the main contract or a provision of that document.

Reed: Mr. Zumwinkle, do you think this idea is feasible?

Zumwinkle: The idea is certainly new to me. Would the waiver have to be signed before a student could register?

Goodman: Frankly, I don't know. I imagine many students would be perfectly willing to sign such a document.

Zumwinkle: If it were not mandatory for all students, it would be ineffective with respect to those students the administrators might want to get at.

Goodman: Not at all. If a student signs it he is bound by it, regardless of other signers or nonsigners.

Zumwinkle: Most students, of course, are not particularly rights conscious, but those who are might refuse to sign.

Goodman: At this point in time, I would say that students who would be willing to sign such a waiver would be members of the silent majority, not those already engaged in protest activity.

Zumwinkle: It seems that this waiver would potentially affect students at both extremes—either those who would be involved in protest activity or those who are against the protest.

Goodman: In the cases we have found to this time, protesters have not sued universities because of shutdowns. It has been . . .

Zumwinkle: Perhaps I am belaboring the point, but I think student dissenters could bring such suits, if, let us say, the president or other official of the university had taken certain disciplinary action that the student considered unconstitutional.

Goodman: I suppose that might be possible. Moreover, if asked to sign such a waiver, protesters might insist on an exculpatory provision, saving them from possible liability if the university should sue for damages arising out of protest activity.

Zumwinkle: I have the feeling that in order for such a waiver to be effective, it would have to be mandatory for all students.

Reed: I have one more question: Have there been any lawsuits by students who felt that the university should have been closed during disruption—suits against universities for damages suffered because the administrations failed to close down?

These would be suits for damages other than physical injury. Is that really the substance of the *Krause* suit, for example?
Goodman: Right.

Impact of Lawsuits on Future School Obligations

Reed: Those who are lawyers in the audience will note that much of the development of the law, in terms of the care that people need to take with regard to the doing of various tasks in their lives, has been in response to lawsuits that have been brought. Indeed, plaintiffs' lawyers frequently say that they have made doctors more careful by their malpractice actions, hospitals more careful by negligence suits against the hospitals, automobile manufacturers more careful by suits against the automobile manufacturers. Mr. Goodman, would you be willing to say something about your assessment of the impact of lawsuits on future obligations of administrators? The feeling of the people gathered here is that the strictures of the law rest rather uncomfortably on many sectors of the educational establishment; that academic life is somehow different; that to worry about all the details of the law is really too late and after the fact; and that much needs to be done in other ways. Do you, nevertheless, see the lawsuit against the school, the administrator, and the faculty, or the dissident people as effecting any change?
Goodman: There are two kinds of actions involved. One is the negligence action, a conventional kind of lawsuit. The university carries on all kinds of activities, including hospitals and medical care. Doctors commit malpractice; nurses commit malpractice; campus police fail to use due care in connection with security on campus and people are beaten up; injuries occur because of inadequate recreational equipment or poor supervision. These examples represent typical negligence litigation. It has a therapeutic effect, because in many instances it results in an upgrading of the quality of service.

The second category is the political litigation: suits arising from the closing down of universities and civil rights suits against administrators of universities for failure to accord constitutional rights to students. In my judgment, the second kind of litigation is more significant. It is designed to affect the policymaking of universities at the highest level, and it does so. We are going to see more of it, both from the right and from the left. Unlike typical tort litigation, this kind of suit is designed to affect policy rather than to get money compensation for injuries. And it makes no difference whether it is denominated tort, contract, or what-have-you. It would not surprise me to see lawsuits brought by students against universities, perhaps under a contract theory, basing complaints on poor curricula or incompetent faculty. These actions will say to the university, "You promised us a good education and we're getting a lousy education. You have breached your contract. Now pay up." Why shouldn't a lawsuit for damages be brought under such circumstances?

Perhaps the idea is novel to some of us, but consider the employer-employee situation. Forty years ago the idea that workers should have the right to bargain collectively and to affect the terms and conditions under which they worked was a novel idea. Today it is accepted practice. Consumers exercise their right to challenge a bad product. Although these are not totally analogous situations, I think students are beginning to assert such rights.

Holloway: You will find it difficult to believe this, but in Colorado we were sued by a coed seeking a grade of *B* in English Literature 110. The suit, in the nature of mandamus, was initiated in the state district court. She claimed that she and another student had been given grades of *F* in the course for disciplinary reasons—namely, cheating. She sought a grade of *B* because she understood that was the worth of the course. I had more trouble with the deans and professors than I did with the plaintiff and her lawyer, because to the school people it was a shocking thing. Many academicians feel that they can give whatever grades they want for whatever reasons.

We went through all the machinations and were all set for trial. We had a pretrial conference with some twenty-three exhibits attached to the pretrial order. Then, one night the judge called counsel in the case to his chambers. He looked at us very seriously and said, "Gentlemen, I've read all the exhibits attached to this order. If you think this court is going to sit here and grade papers in English Literature 110, you're crazy. Now one of you move to take it back to the university. If you don't move to remand the case to the university, the court is going to move it back, because this is purely a matter of discretion. The court is not going to enter into it."

Bemesderfer: I think Dick Goodman may be a prophet, though. Some of you may have noticed a suit in Wisconsin which was decided recently. The suit involved a faculty member at the University of Wisconsin in Milwaukee. His contract had expired. At the end of six years he did not receive tenure. Some of you may know that the AAUP rules require an up or out decision at the end of six years, to maintain status with the AAUP. The faculty member brought a suit requesting a show cause order to compel the university to show cause why he should not be given tenure, and he won. They are now in litigation preparing a documented case on his nonrenewal. The case is also on appeal. The interesting thing about this case is that Judge Doyle said, in effect, that any faculty member, whether for a standard renewal or for a tenure decision, could get a show cause order from his court to compel the university to state its case for not renewing or for refusing tenure.

Goodman: All of this seems quite bizarre, but look again at the industrial analogy. Before the National Labor Relations Act of 1935, employees tried to adjust their grievances with employers by lawsuits. It was the only way they had, but a ridiculous way to attempt to change working conditions. In the same way, a lawsuit is a poor substitute for adequate machinery inside the academic community itself. I think the machinery will come; and as the machinery is devised and student power is institutionalized we will see fewer lawsuits.

The Legislative Reaction

Faults and Fallacies

Reed: I have a question for Karl Bemesderfer. The questioner states, "You believe that there is not wisdom in some of these legislative enactments. In your wisdom, what is a good approach?"

Bemesderfer: There are two ways to answer that question: One is simply to say that special legislation directed at colleges and universities, enacted under stress in order to appease angry constituents, is usually bad. It will almost certainly be poorly drafted. It will put pressure on institutions which are already under tremendous pressure internally—the attrition rate of college presidents is probably higher than the attrition rate of field commanders in Vietnam. They do not really need an additional kick in the pants from the legislature.

I have another concern which is somewhat more philosophical. I do not see why it is considered good practice to single out college students, teachers, and employees of colleges as people who are particularly in need of restrictive legislation. Take that Ohio statute, for example. The statute says that somebody who shoots somebody else or commits arson ought to be automatically terminated. He would surely be in jail for twenty years and unavailable to teach or to attend school anyway. It is excess baggage, I suggest, to tack that kind of penalty onto the existing penalty for bad behavior.

If the state is concerned about people who commit crimes of various kinds, then let us pass laws which prohibit them from doing that and let us punish them if they do. Why particularize crime on a college campus, and why single out college teachers and students as people who have to be specially surveyed for fear that they might commit such crimes? It works both ways. Some statutes tack a trivial penalty onto a much more serious offense; some tack a severe penalty onto a trivial offense. For example, what is meant by "committing a nuisance in a building"? Painting a sign on a wall? Scattering files? For the offense, the individual loses his job and his right to employment in the state educational system for a year. There is a failure to fit punishment and crime.

The most serious objection I have to such statutes is a little more difficult to explain. I am distressed when legislators take the attitude that colleges and universities can be reduced to—or should be made to resemble—other institutions in society. The truth is that colleges and universities have a limited and special function. There is a very narrow range of things which they do in a way that other agencies do not—they research and they teach.

Finally, it seems to me that this legislation, in a sense, tries to take college and university officials off the hook. And they ought to be on the hook. That is, if a college president or his faculty have any belief that what they are doing is good to do and the kind of place they are running is good to run, then they will defend it. They will do so by holding hearings and they will expel people who are disruptive. That is what they ought to do and they should not be taken off that hook. I believe that the responsibility for maintaining order should rest with the officials of the institutions and that they ought to discharge that responsibility. I do not believe that their authority should be supervened by the state. I do not believe in being pressured by the state any more than I believe in being pressured by students.

Trespass Statutes

Reed: Mr. Myers, you spoke kindly of the trespass statutes to fill a hole that you saw in that area. Is there anything else in the recent legislation that you applaud, or do you agree with Mr. Bemesderfer?

Myers: I am essentially in agreement. There are several problems. Many statutes are badly constructed and drafted. They can't accomplish what they are meant to accomplish. Second, they will not serve the purpose of the legislature—they will not solve the problems. The students will react by continuing to disregard laws, especially these laws, which they consider even more unfair than the ones already in force. Where the penalty is expulsion, the institutions will try to avoid imposing it, just as they have avoided expulsion in recent years because of the draft situation. I wish that legislatures would listen to what is going on at the institution and accept the institution's advice about the kind of legislation which would be useful. I believe some of the trespass legislation will be useful. But the inflexible imposition of expulsion or firing is not going to work. There must be flexibility in making a decision as vital and important as a man's job or his chance to go to school.

Bemesderfer: I completely agree with Jack Myers that some of the recent legislation, especially that which has reworked ancient trespass statutes, criminal contempt statutes, and the like, is to the good. My point is simply that most such legislation is passed under circumstances which almost guarantee that it will be bad, and it is bad.

Tax Exemption Problems

Reed: Mr. Wagner, you mentioned the problems of the *Columbia Spectator,* suggesting that the tax-exempt status of the paper might be lost because they took positions in favor of particular candidates. Could this have any practical impact other than with respect to gifts to them? I have the impression that most school papers simply eke out an existence.

Wagner: The greatest damage to an institution or to an organization such as a college newspaper would be the inability of the institution to offer its contributors a tax deduction for their contributions. Generally, these organizations operate, as I am sure the *Columbia Spectator* does, without making any profit.

Reed: Then the problem is that of the status of gifts, not taxable income.

Summary

Reed: In the sessions here we have had numerous questions which have suggested that the law seems to be late in the picture and that the real answers lie elsewhere. Almost every speaker has made this point. It has been said here that if only a minority of students are involved in a campus disruption, then these legal procedures seem to work fairly well; but if the issue has attracted the interest and the sympathy and the participation of a majority of students, it is not a matter for the law, it is the people who need to sit down and try to work the thing out. This is a counsel of hope and expectation which cannot always be met, but at least it suggests that the law is not the full answer.

APPENDIXES

RIGHTS, RESPONSIBILITIES, AND RULES

A Statement of the
Rights and Responsibilities
of College and University Students*

Preamble

Our universities bear a special obligation to serve as exemplars of respect for individuals. Such respect underlies the relations of trust which are the foundation of our free institutions. In the past, too many educational institutions have insufficiently heeded this obligation. As a consequence, few were prepared to meet the great challenge of youthful unrest now disturbing our society. Today, most institutions appreciate the necessity to give careful attention to relations with individual students. This statement is intended to help that effort by members of a profession which has long been concerned with the development of individual rights and responsibilities.

The "rights and responsibilities" expressed herein are not intended as a proclamation of existing law, but of desirable administrative practice. The accompanying comment, which is a part of the statement, does attempt to describe briefly the

---

* The views expressed in this Committee Report are those of the American Bar Association Section of Individual Rights and Responsibilities and its Committee on Civil Rights and Responsibilities. This Statement has not been considered by the House of Delegates of the American Bar Association and pending approval by it cannot be considered an official Statement of the Association.

existing state of the law. As the comment indicates, some of the rights and responsibilities expressed are not legally enforceable and may never become so. Courts have long exhibited a reluctance to expand student rights. To some extent, this reluctance may reflect a restraint on the part of judges who have not wished to divert students from the educational process by encouraging them to test their rights against the legal powers of their educators. On the other hand, many courts have come to recognize the old concept of the university as parent to its student-offspring as an anachronism which has been invoked to justify the nonrecognition of student claims. Most of our institutions have become far too large and impersonal to resemble a family in any important respects. The exercise of unbridled power over mature offspring is, in any event, not a characteristic of American family life. Also, the need for order and fairness in the exercise of institutional power has been much increased by the growing reliance of our society on academic credentials. Finally, there is a general trend in our society to control power by subjecting it to legal norms. Officials of all kinds are increasingly required to exercise their powers in orderly and even-handed ways which will bear public inspection. For all these reasons, there is ferment in the law which takes the form of the developing recognition of the rights of students. This statement is intended also to help in pointing the way for that development.

In the general attitude which it seeks to evoke, this statement resembles the *Interim Statement on Campus Disorder* of the National Commission on The Causes and Prevention of Violence, of June 9, 1969. In important respects, this statement has been influenced by the *Model Code for Student Rights, Responsibilities & Conduct,* prepared by a committee of the Law Student Division of the American Bar Association, and published on May 31, 1969. Especially, this statement has been influenced by the *Joint Statement on Rights and Freedoms of Students* which was promulgated in 1967 by the National Student Association, The American Association of University Professors, the Association of American Colleges, and other groups involved in educational administration. Much of our language is drawn directly from that statement. The differences in the several statements which are significant are described in our accompanying comments. We have added provisions for the purpose of expressing our conviction that the existence of students' rights is dependent on the fulfillment of student responsibilities.

We also invite attention to the excellent *Report of the American Bar Association Commission on Campus Government and Student Dissent* which was issued in February, 1970. That report, while it generally does not set forth detailed recommendations, elaborates on the principles and procedures designed to insure freedom for dissent while preserving the order required for those endeavors that constitute the reasons for the existence of universities.

This statement is made subject to the following general qualifications. We have directed our attention at institutions of higher learning which purport to exist for the discovery, collection and transmission of knowledge and which promote the development of relatively mature students by engaging them in a quest for undiscovered truth. We have not attempted to define the rights and responsibilities of students in secondary schools. Moreover, we recognize that institutions which promote military discipline, or moral dogma, or a variety of other goals, surely have a right to exist and to maintain their character as special institutions. To the extent that this may require departure from the ordinary norms for the treatment of students and that this is understood by those who freely choose to attend such institutions, our statement may also be inapplicable. We also note that universities are not integers; our statement may, in some particulars, be applicable to one part of an institution, and inapplicable to another.

I. The Right to Study

Admission standards should be stated as clearly as possible and should, in general, be based on the capacity of individual students to contribute to or profit from the particular educational program. Under no circumstances should a student be barred from admission on the basis of race or ethnic background. The facilities and services of an institution should be open to all of its students and the institution's influence should be used to secure equal access for all students to public facilities in the local community. It is also the responsibility of all students to refrain from any conduct which would obstruct fellow students in their enjoyment of the benefits of institutional programs.

Comment To Article I

(a) Similar provisions are contained in the Joint Statement and in the Model Code, except for the last sentence.

(b) As applied to public institutions, discrimination on the basis of race is, of course, proscribed by *Brown v. Board of Education,* 347 U.S. 483 (1954). It seems probable that a private institution would be similarly barred from racial discrimination, at least if it administers public funds. *Guillory v. Tulane Univ.,* 203 F.Supp. 855 (E.D.La., 1962). See *Evans v. Newton,* 382 U.S. 296, 321–322 (1966) (Harlan, J., dissenting); but cf. id. at 300. Dorsen, *Racial Discrimination in "Private" Schools,* 9 Wm. & Mary L. Rev. 39 (1969). Discrimination on the basis of intellectual qualification is well-supported. E.g., *Lesser v. Board of Education,* 18 App. Div. 2d 388, 239 N.Y.S.2d 776 (1963); but cf. *Hobson v. Hansen,* 269 F.Supp. 401 (D.D.C., 1967), aff'd sub nom. *Smuck v. Hobson,* 408 F.2d 175 (D.C.Cir., 1969). The obligation not to discriminate on the basis of ethnic background does imply a duty to use inculturated intellectual qualifications with care. The statement does not deal with the problem of "reverse discrimination."

(c) The law of discriminatory tuition fees will have to be re-evaluated in the light of *Shapiro v. Thompson,* 394 U.S. 618 (1969). Meanwhile, public institutions should not unduly burden non-residents so as to restrict free movement to affluent students.

(d) The next to last sentence expresses the policy of the public accommodations provisions of the Civil Rights Act of 1964, 42 U.S.C. § 2000a.

II. Rights with Respect to Standards of Conduct

For the purposes of advancing its educational program and protecting its facilities and internal relationships, a university has the responsibility for promoting student conduct which is consistent with the educational program. Counseling and guidance should be the preferred means for expressing this concern, but institutions have the duty and power to impose discipline for these limited purposes. Depending on the severity of an offense, disciplinary sanctions may include admonition, censure, probation, restitution, fines, suspension, or expulsion. Generally, such sanctions should not be imposed for violations of standards of conduct unless the standards are publicized in advance through such means as a student handbook or otherwise generally understood. The discipline system of the institution should not be used merely to duplicate the function of general laws. Only where the institution's interests as an academic community are clearly involved should the special authority of the institution be asserted. The student who incidentally violates institutional regulations in the course of his off-campus activity, such as those relating to class attendance, should be subject to no greater penalty than would normally be imposed. Institutional action should be independent of community pressure.

Comment to Article II

(a) Similar provisions are contained in the Joint Statement, except for the list of sanctions, which is taken from the Model Code. Fines are added to the list. Some courts might still hold that such fines would be "penal" and not subject to administrative adjudication. Inasmuch as the ultimate means of enforcement would have to be suspension or enforcement, most would accept the characterization of such fines as "civil." See Davis, *Administrative Law* § 2.13. Fines are instruments for precise measurement of culpability and do not disrupt the violator's education; hence, they are a very useful sanction. They contrast most favorably with the arbitrary sanction of scholarship revocation which has been fostered by some recent "anti-riot" legislation.

(b) "Void for vagueness" is a contention unsuccessfully invoked against university rules in such recent cases as *Jones v. Board of Education,* 407 F.2d 834 (6th Cir., 1969); *Carr v. St. John's University,* 17 App. Div. 2d 632, 231 N.Y.S.2d 410 (1962), aff'd 12 N.Y.2d 802, 187 N.E.2d 18 (1962); *Buttny v. Smiley,* 281 F.Supp. 280 (D.Colo., 1968). A well-reasoned opinion expressing a requirement of reasonable specificity is *Soglin v. Kauffman,* 295 F.Supp. 978 (W.D.Wis., 1968). A requirement of a writing is expressed in *Zanders v. La. State Bd. of Educ.,* 279 F.Supp. 747 (W.D.La., 1968); *General Order,* 45 F.R.D. 133 (W.D.Mo., 1968).

(c) The purpose of the publication requirement is notice. It is not intended to disapprove the use of a "common law" standard of behavior to support application of sanctions to blatant offenders against institutions which had not published carefully drawn standards.

(d) The law does not forbid the overlapping of criminal and academic penalties; the defense of "double jeopardy" does not apply. *Goldberg v. Regents of the University of California,* 248 Cal. App. 2d 867, 57 Cal. Rptr. 463 (1967). The purposes served by the two systems of regulation of conduct are sufficiently distinct that there may be a few instances in which overlapping penalties are justified, but these should be the exception. It should not be an occasion for institutional punishment that a student has impaired his own standing in the community by being convicted of an offense. Educational institutions should provide an opportunity for rehabilitation of offenders, unless there is a special reason for not doing so. See generally, Van Alstyne, *The Student as University Resident,* 45 Denver L.J. 582, 598-603 (1968).

III. The Right to Share in Policy-Making

Students have a collective right to an appropriate voice in the making of institutional policy generally affecting their social or academic affairs, but this right is subject to the supervening responsibility of governing boards to assure adequate protection for essential interests and policies of each institution. The form by which this collective right is recognized is left to each institution to shape with regard to particular administrative and academic functions. To the extent that students are foreclosed from sharing in the making of particular decisions, or kinds of decisions, the institutional policy or interest deemed to require the foreclosure should be explicitly stated, where possible with approval of the governing boards. Students should always share in the formulation of standards of student conduct.

Comment to Article III

(a) There is no legal right to participate in institutional decision-making. *Grossner v. Trustees of Columbia Univ.*, 287 F.Supp. 535 (S.D.N.Y., 1968). But a wise governing board will consult its constituent groups. Many university students are already participating as voters in public elections; all others are expected to do so within a few months or years. An institution which fails to provide any opportunity for such individuals to make themselves heard with respect to its policies is not performing adequately as a training ground for citizens. This statement is more affirmative in making this assertion than the Joint Statement. For a criticism of the Joint Statement provisions, see Bloustein, *The New Student and His Role in American Colleges,* in *Dimensions of Academic Freedom* 92, 118–121 (1969).

(b) The sharing of power may take many appropriate forms. Such matters as dormitory administration may be left almost entirely to governance by representatives of the occupants. Other matters may best be handled by joint committees of faculty and students. Others may be best suited to disposition by non-voting participation of the kind provided with respect to other governmental rule-making activity by administrative procedure legislation. E.g., 5 U.S.C. § 553. With respect to some matters, a combination of these methods might be employed. Regular reconsideration of methods is appropriate; no person or group should be deemed to have a fixed right in any particular mode of decision-making. Representation through students selected by administrative officials is not ordinarily an appropriate means of sharing.

(c) To the extent that students are dissatisfied with the means of participation provided, they should be provided with a statement of the reasons dictating against a more satisfying mode of operation. If possible, this statement should be made on behalf of the governing board, and not merely by the officials who are being asked to share their own delegated power. It may be a sufficient reason to curtail the students' share of power over curriculum that minimum standards of academic performance must be maintained. It may be a sufficient reason to curtail student participation in the selection and retention of faculty that the independence of judgment and integrity of the faculty requires freedom from student governance. The research enterprise of a faculty could be aborted by the intrusion of majoritarian control. It may be a sufficient reason for other strictures on student participation that excessive energy should not be invested in trivial decisions. Some repose for decisions once made is also permissible. Moreover, it may be a sufficient reason to restrict student participation that too meagre a minority of the students have exercised their franchise to sustain the recognition of any representatives. A balanced consideration of some of the problems of student participation is found in Frankel, *Education at the Barricades* 40–59 (1968). The strictures on student participation should not be greater than required by these competing policies or interests.

IV. The Right to Speak

Every aspect of the educational process should promote the free expression of ideas. The right of expression extends to matters of institutional administration and policy. Students have the right to publish written material, and to distribute it without prior approval. Distribution should not disrupt or unreasonably burden the operations of the institution. Should the institution support a written publication at least part of it should be available for student journalism free of prior censorship or institutional control of editorial policy, except that student journalists editing an institutionally supported publication (or broadcasting on an institutional installation if available) may be subject to removal from office, as well as other punishment, for breach of reasonable standards of journalism, such as reasonable proscriptions against libel, obscenity, intentional distortion, or reckless disregard for the facts. The institution and its teachers should assure that academic evaluations are not prejudiced or capricious such as may deter students from expressing views contrary to those of the person making the evaluation. Students should be protected from public disclosure of views or beliefs which may have been tentatively expressed in academic discourse. Students are responsible for respecting the equal rights of all other members of the academic community. For student journalists editing an institutionally supported publication, this responsibility extends to an obligation to provide reasonable opportunity for the expression of views by fellow students differing from editorial policy. Students are also responsible for respecting the personal rights of other students and of teachers and administrators by avoiding the utterance of willful or malicious defamatory statements or other incivilities so grave as to impair the ability of students or educators to perform their duties effectively.

Comment to Article IV

(a) In *Tinker v. Des Moines School District,* 343 U.S. 503 (1969), the Supreme Court of the United States laid down the following principle significant to the rights expressed in this Article.

(b) Similar provisions are contained in the Joint Statement and the Model Code. Unlike the Joint Statement, but as in the

Model Code, specific provision is made for the "underground" press. A provision not common to either of the other statements is that of establishing a right of access to the institutional press. See generally, Barron, *Access to the Press—A New First Amendment Right,* 80 Harv.L.Rev. (1967) and *An Emerging First Amendment Right of Access to the Media?,* 37 Geo.Wash.L.Rev. 487 (1969). While a right of access may not be manageable in the setting of mass media, the need is greater and the administrative difficulty of accomodation less with respect to the institutionally supported press. E.g., *Zucker v. Panitz,* 299 F.Supp 102 (S.D.N.Y., 1969).

(c) The Joint Statement urges "orderly procedures" for protecting against prejudiced or capricious evaluation. This statement recoils from any suggestion of judicial review of academic grading, but there should be some internal check for extraordinary cases. An unusual case expressing willingness to entertain a suit to prove malice on the part of a grader is *Connelly v. University of Vermont and State Agricultural College,* 244 F.Supp. 156 (D.Vt., 1965).

(d) It seems probable that the disclosure of the views and beliefs of students by educators cannot be required by subpoena. Cf. *Sweezy v. New Hampshire,* 354 U.S. 234 (1957). Neither should such disclosures be volunteered by teachers or fellow students. Improper disclosures which are harmful to the student whose tentative thoughts are publicized are proper occasions for institutional discipline. Note that the privilege is limited to the expression of ideas in academic discourse; voluntary confession, even in academic discourse, of criminal *behavior* is not privileged.

(e) Provisions of the Joint Statement seeking to inhibit confidential evaluations of intellectual capacity are omitted; no position is taken with respect to the propriety of such evaluations.

(f) The right of the students to criticize their institution is expressed in *Dickey v. Alabama State Bd. of Educ.,* 273 F.Supp. 613 (M.D. Ala., 1967). It would seem to be a necessary corollary to *Pickering v. Will Cty. Board of Education,* 391 U.S. 563

(1968). On the other hand, teachers and administrators may be fully protected by the civil law of defamation. *Curtis Publishing Co. v. Butts*, 388 U.S. 130 (1967). But cf. *Klahr v. Winterble*, 4 Ariz. App. 158, 418 P.2d 404 (1966). As an institutional matter, it is proper to use discipline to protect them from willful or malicious defamation or gross incivility of the kind which belittles their office and impairs their ability to perform their duties. Doubtless, the dignity required to teach is less than that required to judge. But gross incivility is an offense comparable to contempt of court in that it violates a constraint necessary to protect institutional relationships and processes. Cf. *Robson v. Malone*, (7th Cir., 1969). Compare, also, the right of a witness to be treated with civility. E.g., *Hamilton v. Alabama*, 376 U.S. 650 (1964), rev'd 275 Ala. 574, 156 So. 2d 926 (1963).

V. The Right of Association

Students should be free to organize and join associations to promote their common interests and to make reasonable use of institutional facilities for such purposes. This right should be limited by a requirement of institutional recognition only insofar as necessary to preserve the openness of the institution and its receptivity to free inquiry. Thus, it may be appropriate for an institution to withhold the use of its facilities from associations which impinge on the rights of others by obstructing their study or self-expression or otherwise subjecting them to harassment. It may also be appropriate to require that student organizations be open to all students without respect to race or ethnic background. Sectarian groups may have religious qualifications. It may also be appropriate to take reasonable precautions to prevent the misuse of student funds. Extramural affiliation should not be proscribed, but reasonable provisions for local autonomy may be required. The policy of a student organization should not be subject to the control of an "adviser." At the same time, student organizations should avoid representing that their action reflects the views of the university. An organization may properly be required to identify officers handling student funds or to designate a person to receive institutional communications, but no organization should be required to submit its membership list, except for the limited purpose of assisting in an investigation of alleged improper discrimination. A membership list used for the purpose stated should be destroyed upon completion of the investigation.

Comment to Article V

(a) Similar provisions are contained in the Joint Statement. The provisions of the Model Code are more detailed and contain a number of minor divergent provisions. Neither of the other statements contains the last clause of this Article, but it is probably needed to give meaning to the provision for anti-discriminatory regulation. This Article permits, but does not require, anti-discriminatory regulation; the Model Code and Joint Statement provisions are mandatory. This statement is permissive because, in some communities, it may well be possible to permit arbitrary ostracism by some social organizations without adverse effect on the general openness of the institution. This statement is not addressed to the problem of controlling the use of the institution's name; more stringent conditions may be imposed on organizations engaged in such use.

(b) Traditionally, institutional power over student organizations has been unqualified. A recent case has upheld the power of the university to exclude an organization on grounds of racial discrimination. *Sigma Chi Fraternity v. Regents of the University of Colorado*, 258 F.Supp. 515 (D.Colo., 1966). The court in *Beta Sigma Rho v. Moore*, 41 Misc. 2d 1030, 261 N.Y.S.2d 658 (1965), upheld the power to exclude social groups with national affiliations; that decision is disapproved by the statement. To the extent that the extramural relations are political or religious, rather than social, the right to such relations may be protected by the First Amendment, at least with respect to public institutions.

(c) The last sentence goes beyond the holdings with respect

to membership lists of political organizations in *NAACP v. Alabama ex rel. Patterson,* 357 U.S. 449 (1957) and *Bates v. City of Little Rock,* 361 U.S. 516 (1959). Those opinions imply that a public institution could require disclosure upon a showing of significant need.

VI. The Right to Listen

Students should be allowed to invite and to hear any person of their own choosing for the purpose of hearing his ideas and opinions. Those routine procedures required by an institution before a guest speaker is invited to appear on campus should be designed only to insure that there is orderly scheduling of facilities and adequate preparation for the event. Charges may be imposed for any unusual costs. The institutional control of campus facilities should not be used as a device of censorship. Correspondingly, students should be constrained from disrupting a meeting of their fellows or others lawfully using the university's premises. It is not a sufficient reason for suppressing the peaceful expression of ideas that they are so outrageous to others that there is a risk of misconduct by those offended. The students' right of self-expression does not extend to protect noise intended to prevent self-expression by others. Students should be held to account for the defamatory statements of their invited speakers only if they might reasonably have anticipated and prevented the defamation.

Comment to Article VI

(a) This is similar to provisions of the Joint Statement, but the last two sentences are entirely new. It is intended that this statement go beyond the dictum of *Tinker v. Des Moines Independent Community School District,* 393 U.S. 503 (1969), which suggests that suppression of ideas might be tolerable if necessary to achieve the educational purpose of the institution. It should be noted that the Court was there contemplating the problem in the setting of a public secondary school dealing with immature students who may, in fact, be uncontrollable when confronted with inflammatory ideas. A university and its students have an unqualified obligation to suffer the presence of an unwelcome idea as long as any student feels impelled to entertain it.

(b) The proscription of censorship of outside speakers is probably required of public institutions by the First Amendment. *Snyder v. Board of Trustees of University of Illinois,* 286 F.Supp. 927 (N.D.Ill., 1968); *Brooks v. Auburn University,* 296 F.Supp. 188 (M.D.Ala., 1969). Cf. *Dickson v. Sitterson,* 280 F.Supp. 486 (M.D.N.Car., 1968). Perhaps a private institution might lawfully engage in censorship of speakers, but this would be difficult to justify if the institution is, indeed, committed to inquiry. Note that the statement does not inhibit the control of illicit *behavior* which might accompany tolerated speech.

VII. The Right to Private Quarters

An institution has an obligation to respect the right of all students living or working on its premises to privacy in their living and working quarters. This obligation must be observed by establishing appropriate procedural safeguards on such institutional activity as may be necessary to the fulfillment of the institution's cognate obligation to protect the health and safety of all persons resident and working on its premises. Intrusions by police or other officials exercising responsibility for the enforcement of civil law (penal or otherwise) should be governed by standards and procedures no less stringent than those applicable to intrusions on private quarters outside the institution.

Comment to Article VII

(a) This provision is, in an important respect, more restrictive of searches by university officials than the Joint Statement or the Model Code. This statement takes the position of the minority of the committee which drafted the Model Code in holding that it is not a proper function of a university to "keep the police off campus" in situations in which searches are lawfully justified to enforce the criminal law.

(b) The law with respect to students living in dormitories has yet to progress beyond the concept of the dormitory as university property. In *Moore v. Student Affairs Committee,* 284 F.Supp. 725 (M.D.Ala., 1968), it was held that a dormitory resident waived any objection to a search conducted in aid of discipline. The concept of waiver should not be applied on the basis of a student's acceptance of university quarters. For rejection of such an idea in a different setting, see *Dixon v. Alabama St. Bd. of Educ.,* 294 F.2d 150 (5th Cir., 1961). And see *Camara v. Municipal Court,* 387 U.S. 523 (1967). Cf. *Griswold v. Connecticut,* 381 U.S. 479 (1965).

(c) An appropriate procedure for institutional searches might employ the authority of a responsible official designated by institutional rule as the one to whom application must be made before student quarters are searched. For fuller development of this idea, see Note, *The Fourth Amendment and Housing Inspections,* 77 Yale L.J. 521 (1968).

VIII. The Right to Private Records

To minimize the risk of improper disclosures, academic records should be kept separate from disciplinary records. The conditions of access to each should be set forth in an explicit policy statement. Transcripts of academic records should contain only information about academic status. Information from disciplinary or counseling files should not be available to unauthorized persons within the institution or to any person outside the institution without the express consent of the student involved except under legal compulsion or in cases where the safety of persons or property is involved. No records should be kept which reflect the political activities or beliefs of students. Special provision should be made to prevent misuse of old disciplinary records of former students. A student should have access to his records under reasonable circumstances. Administrative staff and faculty members should respect confidential information about students which they acquire in the course of their work. Students are likewise bound to respect the confidentiality of the files and records of faculty and administrators.

Comment to Article VIII

(a) This Article is almost identical to the Joint Statement. The distinction between academic and disciplinary records is helpful in making effective confidentiality rules because the two kinds of records are used by different persons for different purposes. Two sentences have been added: one assuring a student access to his records and another proclaiming the confidentiality of institutional files against invasion by students. The Model Code provisions are more detailed and are somewhat more restrictive as to the kind of information that may be kept, and the circumstances under which information may be used or released. This statement is not intended to express disapproval of tighter restrictions which institutions may choose to impose. In general, the standards expressed here seem to be descriptive of emerging general practice. Whittaker, *The Rights of the Student as Related to the Protection of His Transcript,* 42 College and University 78 (1966).

(b) Licensing bodies or employers seeking access to student discipline files should be required to present evidence of the consent of the applicant whose file is sought. Such consent can be routinely obtained by such users of records. The same requirement may be imposed on access to academic records, although this is not required by the statement.

(c) An institution might presently be enjoined from giving "unreasonable publicity" to the private lives of its students, or otherwise held to account for an invasion of privacy. But cf. *Time, Inc. v. Hill,* 385 U.S. 374 (1967). This Article goes beyond the existing tort law in imposing an obligation on institutions to protect their constituents from improper snooping. It does not impose an obligation on the institution to risk contempt by challenging a subpoena of records, but students affected should be given sufficient notice of prospective compliance to permit them to invoke judicial assistance against an improper subpoena. The institution need not require a subpoena before disclosing information to investigators seeking to identify perpetrators of crimes against persons or property. The statement may raise doubt about the propriety of the action of some institutions in disclosing to the Department of Health, Education and Welfare, the names of students engaged in "disruptive activity."

(d) Misuse of old disciplinary records can be avoided by the sealing of such records, although some institutions may appropriately prefer to destroy them.

(e) As the Model Code suggests, an administrative tribunal which imposes discipline might also be authorized to provide a remedy against improper or inaccurate maintenance of records.

IX. The Right to Procedural Fairness

The administration of discipline should guarantee procedural fairness to an accused student. Procedure may vary in formality with the gravity of the offense and the sanctions which may be applied; it may also be varied to take account of an honor code which imposes responsibility on students to enforce standards of conduct against one another. The jurisdiction of judicial bodies, the disciplinary responsibilities of institutional officials, and the disciplinary procedures should be clearly formulated and published. Minor penalties may be assessed informally under such procedures, but in all situations, the student should be informed of the nature of the charges against him, given a fair opportunity to refute them, and provided with some avenue for appeal from arbitrary official action. In the course of investigations, a student may be questioned about alleged acts of misconduct committed by him or by others, except that a student should be told that he need not discuss his own alleged misconduct while criminal proceedings arising from the same event are pending. Information obtained from a student in the course of an institutional investigation or hearing should not be made available for use in criminal proceedings against him. Before a serious penalty such as a substantial fine, extended suspension, or expulsion is imposed, the student should be advised of his right to a fair hearing to determine his guilt. The right to such a hearing is satisfied if the following procedural requirements are met:

1. Pending action on the charges, the status of a student should not be altered, or his right to be present on the campus and to attend classes suspended, except for reasons relating to his physical or emotional safety and well-being, or for reasons relating to the safety and well-being of students, faculty, or university property, or to the maintenance of order or to the effective continuation of the educational process. Provisional suspension by the Administration should be subject to review by the hearing committee.

2. At the option of the student, and subject to the provisions of paragraph 1, adjudication on the merits should be deferred until final disposition of any criminal proceedings arising out of the same conduct, provided that the student effectively insists upon a speedy criminal trial.

3. The hearing committee should include students not selected by the Administration. On objection by any party, a member who is otherwise personally interested in the particular case should not sit in judgment during the proceeding.

4. The student should be informed, in writing, of the reasons for the proposed disciplinary action with sufficient particularity, and in sufficient time, to insure opportunity to prepare for the hearing.

5. The student appearing before the hearing committee should have the right to have his defense conducted by an adviser of his choice. At the request of the student, hearings should be conducted in private. In any event, the hearing committee may impose a reasonable limit on the number of persons to be present, and should exclude from the hearing any person whose behavior detracts from the seriousness of the proceeding. In blatant cases, such behavior by students may be the basis for summary discipline by the committee.

6. The burden of proof should rest upon the officials bring-

ing the charge. It is the responsibility of all students, as well as other members of the community, to serve as witnesses if called. If supporting evidence is presented, an inference of guilt can be drawn from a student's refusal to cooperate in a proper institutional investigation.

7. The student should be given an opportunity to testify and to present evidence and witnesses. He should, except under exceptional circumstances, have an opportunity to hear and question adverse witnesses. On a showing of good cause, the institution should be required to produce relevant records or documents to the student for use as proof.

8. A decision may be based upon disputable information only if it is introduced into evidence at the proceeding before the hearing committee. Improperly acquired evidence should not be admitted.

9. At the request of the student, there should be a transcript, or both a digest and a verbatim record, such as a tape recording, of the hearing.

10. The decision of the hearing committee should be final, subject only to the student's right of appeal.

Comment to Article IX

(a) These provisions are generally in accord with the Joint Statement. The Joint Statement makes no provision for the production of records or documents by the institution and limits the student's appeal to the president or governing board. In departing from these features, this statement follows the Model Code. The Model Code provides for a formal hearing in all disciplinary cases, and provides for severance of cases involving more than one student. These features were deemed unduly burdensome to the administrative process. The provision of a contempt power in paragraph 5 is novel to this statement.

(b) These provisions are consistent with the generally accepted concept of procedural due process as a plastic standard requiring only such procedural scruples as fit the event. For public institutions, procedural due process seems to follow from *In re Gault*, 387 U.S. 1 (1967). It was clearly recognized as early as *Dixon v. Alabama State Bd. of Educ.*, 294 F.2d 150 (5th Cir., 1961); see also, *Knight v. State Bd. of Educ.*, 200 F.Supp. 174 (M.D.Tenn., 1961). With respect to private institutions, the issue of the applicability of due process requirements remains open. In *Powe v. Miles*, 407 F.2d 73 (2d Cir., 1968), it was held that students in the state-supported ceramics department of Alfred University were entitled to constitutional protection, while their associates in other departments of the institution were not. However, the concept of "state action has so far expanded and the presence of government so far penetrated in educational finances that few colleges are likely to be found immune from the reach of the Fourteenth Amendment." See Van Alstyne, *The Judicial Trend Toward Academic Freedom*, 20 Univ. of Fla. L. Rev. 290, 291 (1968). There seems to be no practical reason for distinguishing private institutions for this purpose; procedural due process is not likely to conflict with proper private goals. Alternatively, due process might be imported into the private contract as a non-negotiable term of an "adhesion" contract. See Note, *Private Government on the Campus — Judicial Review of University Expulsions*, 72 Yale L.J. 1362, 1378 (1963).

(c) There is no legal right to remain silent on the basis of threatened non-criminal sanctions. E.g., *Buttny v. Smiley*, 281 F.Supp. 280 (D.Colo., 1968). But this statement does recognize that a student also facing criminal prosecution may be reticent to discuss his conduct and should not be prejudiced in his right to remain silent in the criminal proceeding by a preliminary institutional investigation. This may be a constitutional right. Cf. *Spevack v. Klein*, 385 U.S. 511 (1967). The restraint on the use in criminal proceedings of information obtained by institutional investigation is declaratory of the principle of *Garrity v. New Jersey*, 385 U.S. 493 (1967). It is, in essence, an evidentiary privilege for communications between students and deans. The requirement that a student be advised of his right to refrain from discussion of events pending criminal proceedings is a variation on the concept of *Miranda v. State of Arizona,* 384 U.S. 436 (1966). If institutional investigations were to be used as the basis for criminal proceedings, it is arguable that the full panoply of *Miranda* warnings should be given. Cf. *Mathis v. United States,* 391 U.S. 1 (1968); but cf. *United States v. Mackiewicz,* 401 F.2d 219 (2d Cir., 1968). If, however, the *Garrity*-type restraint on the use of the information is observed, there is no occasion for such warning.

(d) The body of paragraph 1 was explicitly approved as constitutional doctrine in *Stricklin v. Regents of Univ. of Wisconsin,* 297 F.Supp. 416 (W.D.Wis., 1969). Note that the student's status may be frozen; in the event of inordinate delay, as might occur under paragraph 2, graduation or the accrual of credits may be deferred. The last sentence of paragraph 1 is original to this statement. The issue of the need for quick suspension can be decided by a hearing committee without full consideration of the merits.

(e) Paragraph 2 recognizes that the *Garrity*-type restraint on the use of information revealed by a public hearing in the institutional setting is not a full protection for a student's right to remain silent in subsequent criminal proceedings arising from the same misconduct. Although perhaps not legally required to do so, *Furutani v. Ewigleben,* 297 F.Supp. 1163 (N.D.Cal., 1969), the institution should defer its proceedings. Note that duplicate proceedings are seldom appropriate; see Article II, *supra.* It should also be noted that provisional suspension may be imposed under paragraph 1 of this Article in dangerous situations. And, finally, it should be emphasized that the right to defer discipline imposes an obligation to demand a speedy criminal trial.

(f) The requirement of student participation in paragraph 3 goes well beyond existing law. In *Powe v. Miles, supra,* the hearing committee was a single dean. *Wasson v. Trowbridge,* 382 F.2d 807 (2d Cir., 1967), did affirm the necessity of impartiality. The Joint Statement suggests, but does not require, student participation. But the adequacy of the procedure rests on the capacity of the tribunal to command acceptance; student participation seems vital to that objective. There is no reason, however, to require that the selection of the students be entrusted to student leaders who may themselves be the objects of disciplinary proceedings or whose bias may otherwise be questionable. All university students are fully qualified to understand the nature of the issues of fact and are no less likely to take an appropriate view of their responsibility than those who have been self-propelled into the seat of judgment through a student political process. For this reason, this seems to be a very suitable place in which to invoke the tradition of jury selection. If this is done, random selection should be available at the request of either party, and each party should be permitted to remove a reasonable number of members from the panel without stated reasons. The Model Code would require a hearing committee composed entirely of students.

(g) Paragraph 4 is declaratory of existing law. *Jones v. Board of Educ.*, 407 F.2d 834 (6th Cir., 1969); *Dixon v. Alabama State Bd. of Educ., supra; Esteban v. Central Mo. State College*, 277 F.Supp. 649 (W.D.Mo., 1967); *Schiff v. Hannah*, 282 F.Supp. 381 (W.D.Mich., 1966); *Scoggin v. Lincoln Univ.*, 291 F.Supp. 161 (W.D.Mo., 1968); but cf. *Due v. Florida A. & M. Univ.*, 233 F.Supp. 396 (N.D.Fla., 1963). Presumably, a reasonable effort to give notice will suffice. E.g., *Wright v. Texas So. Univ.*, 392 F.2d 728 (5th Cir., 1967).

(h) In connection with the first sentence of paragraph 5, it should be emphasized that the statement applies only in cases involving potential application of "serious penalties," or situations "requiring a high degree of formality." With this caveat, the statement may be declaratory of existing law. *Esteban v. Central Mo. State College, supra; Moore v. Student Affairs Comm. of Troy State Univ.*, 284 F.Supp. 725 (M.D.Ala., 1968); *Goldwyn v. Allen*, 281 N.Y.S. 2d 899 (1967); *Madera v. Board of Educ.*, 267 F.Supp. 356 (S.D.N.Y. 1967), rev'd, 386 F.2d 778 (2d Cir., 1967) (on grounds that the hearing was not disciplinary, but in the nature of counseling); cf. *Buttny v. Smiley, supra; Jones v. Board of Educ., supra; Goldberg v. Regents of Univ. of Calif.*, 248 Cal. App. 2d 867, 57 Cal. Rptr. 463 (1967); but cf. *Barker v. Hardway*, 399 F.2d 638 (4th Cir., 1968), cert. denied, 395 U.S.

905 (suspension only; plenary hearing with counsel granted in District Court); *Wasson v. Trowbridge, supra* (Merchant Marine Academy); *Dunmars v. Ailes,* 348 F.2d 51 (D.C.Cir., 1965) (military academy). There is no requirement that the institution supply counsel to indigent students. *Buttny v. Smiley, supra.* It is the duty of the institution to restrain members of its community who would disrupt or prevent a presentation of evidence by others.

(i) Paragraph 6 would overrule one holding of *Jones v. Board of Educ., supra;* but cf. *Knight v. State Bd. of Educ., supra.*

(j) The first sentence of paragraph 7 expresses fairly well-settled principles of administrative procedure. Hearsay should be very sparingly employed in a punitive proceeding, but the rule should not be formulated in such detail as to make it unworkable by laymen. *Dixon v. Alabama State Bd. of Educ., supra,* suggests that there may be no right to cross-examination and the court in *Esteban v. Central Mo. State College, supra,* was satisfied by a procedure which permitted the student, not counsel, to cross-examine. The general practice is certainly to permit it. The Model Code states the right in more absolute terms. The university should provide some appropriate penalty for refusals of students and others to serve as witnesses.

(k) *Jones v. Board of Educ., supra,* upheld the practice of permitting an investigating official to sit on the hearing committee and disclose all he knew of the case outside the record. This would not be permitted by paragraph 8. The last sentence of this paragraph imposes an exclusionary rule. Exclusionary rules have not generally been applied to evidence obtained by private litigants. *Sackler v. Sackler,* 15 N.Y.2d 40, 203 N.E.2d 481 (1964); *Del Presto v. Del Presto,* 97 N.J.Super. 446, 235 A.2d 240 (1967). The exclusionary rule may be inapplicable to civil proceedings. There seems to be sparse precedent for applying it to administrative proceedings. E.g., *Finn's Liquor Shop v. State Liquor Authority,* 24 N.Y.2d 647, 249 N.E.2d 440 (1969). As stated, the rule would forbid the use of evidence obtained as a result of fraud or harassment, or in violation of principles of the sort stated in Articles VII or VIII.

It would not forbid the use of evidence obtained by advising an accused student or witness that he may be subject to appropriately modest sanctions for failing to cooperate with an administrative investigation or proceeding.

(l) There is no legally enforceable right to appellate review within the institution. The principal consequence of paragraph 10 is to cut off prosecutorial appeals. The president or governing board may retain power to give relief from punishment. Moreover, an additional level of appeal may be provided. Such an appeal may be limited in its scope to review of interpretations of standards of conduct and review of the fundamental fairness of the proceeding. The procedure, jurisdiction, and scope of appeal should be explicitly detailed in the institutional rules.

X. Student Responsibility

In addition to the specific responsibilities arising in connection with these rights, students bear a general responsibility to support the institution's effort to maintain a spirit of free inquiry and respect for the rights of others. This responsibility arises from the fact that students are the present beneficiaries of that traditional spirit, and are best positioned to preserve, improve, and transmit it to future generations. This responsibility imposes a duty on students not only to refrain from conduct which obstructs such effort of the institution, but also to support the enforcement of institutional discipline designed to deter or prevent such conduct and the enforcement of civil laws where such enforcement is reasonably deemed by responsible officials to be necessary to the continued operation of the institution.

Note

This project was initiated by our Section's Committee on Civil Rights and Responsibilities. The Chairman of that Committee is McNeill Smith, Esq., Jefferson Standard Building, Greensboro, N.C. 27402, and the Vice-Chairman is Professor Paul D. Carrington, University of Michigan Law School, Ann Arbor, Mich. 48104.

The Committee on Civil Rights and Responsibilities formed a sub-committee on Rights and Responsibilities of Students under the chairmanship of Professor Paul D. Carrington. It was this sub-committee which was responsible for drafting the foregoing statement. The draft was then reviewed and revised by the Committee on Civil Rights and Responsibilities and by the Council of the Section of Individual Rights and Responsibilities. The members of the sub-committee who prepared the draft under Professor Carrington are listed below.

Berl Bernhard Washington, D.C.	Hon. George N. Leighton Chicago, Illinois
Robert L. Ackerly Washington, D.C.	Stuart M. Glass New York, New York
Melvin Zarr New York, New York	Martha Wood Fayette, Mississippi
Charles deY Elkus, Jr. San Francisco, California	Herbert B. Richmond LaJolla, California
Aubrey V. McCutcheon Detroit, Michigan	Harry J. Roper Chicago, Illinois
Dean Charles O. Galvin Dallas, Texas	John H. Titley Nagatuck, Connecticut
Peter W. Salsich, Jr. St. Louis, Missouri	Jeremy E. Butler Phoenix, Arizona
Dean E. Clayton Bamberger Washington, D.C.	Prof. Edward A. Mearns, Jr. Chicago, Illinois

Melvin C. Hartman
New York, New York

Section of Individual Rights and Responsibilities

Officers

Chairman........................Jerome J. Shestack
Philadelphia, Pennsylvania

Chairman-Elect.................Louis H. Pollak
New Haven, Connecticut

Vice-Chairman.................Cecil F. Poole
San Francisco, California

Secretary........................Robert R. Richardson
Atlanta, Georgia

Recording Secretary...........Carole Kamin Bellows
Chicago, Illinois

Council

Joseph Harrison
Newark, New Jersey

William T. Coleman, Jr.
Philadelphia, Pennsylvania

Ben R. Miller
Baton Rouge, Louisiana

Albert E. Jenner, Jr.
Chicago, Illinois

Whitney North Seymour
New York, New York

Rufus King
Washington, D.C.

Charles W. Joiner
Detroit, Michigan

McNeill Smith
Greensboro, North Carolina

Orrin G. Judd
Brooklyn, New York

Samuel R. Pierce, Jr.
New York, New York

Paul Freund
Cambridge, Massachusetts

Warren M. Christopher
Los Angeles, California

Basic Rights and
Responsibilities for
College and University Presidents*

The history of American higher education strongly supports the contention that no college or university has made important progress except under the leadership of an outstanding president. At the present time, unfortunately, colleges and universities are experiencing increasing difficulty in attracting and holding able persons as chief administrative officers. And individuals remaining in such positions stand virtually unanimous in the opinion that their role has become much more difficult and demanding.

It is the purpose of this document, therefore, to identify certain basic principles that must be accepted if colleges and universities are to function in an orderly, purposeful way and to lay down those conditions necessary to insure the presence of effective leadership on the campus.

Basic Principles

(1) Before anything else, a college or university (particularly a public one) exists to serve the general society which created it and which supports it; such an institution does not belong to a particular group of persons within that society or within that institution.

---

* A Statement Adopted by the Board of Directors of the American Association of State Colleges and Universities, May 6, 1970.

(2) A college or university serves many constituencies — faculty, staff, students, alumni, and parents of students being the closest ones. All of these constituencies have a stake in the institution and its development, and all should be provided with an opportunity to be informed and heard.

(3) Legally defined, a college or university does not consist of any one or combination of these constituencies. In the eyes of the law, a college or university is its governing board, most commonly known as the board of trustees.

(4) The major functions of a public college or university are teaching/learning, scholarship/research, and appropriate public service, as determined ultimately by the board of trustees. These functions cannot be illegally interfered with or eliminated except at the risk of destroying the institution.

The Role of the College President

I Executive Officer: The president serves as chief executive officer of the college or university. In this capacity, he reports and recommends directly to the board of trustees. Although the president listens to the voices of all constituent groups, it must be recognized that he functions primarily as the administrative arm of the board and that all legal governing authority resides with the board.

II Authority: The selection of the president is the board of trustees' most important decision. Having once made that selection, the board must insure that the president is vested with all the authority necessary to carry out the duties and responsibilities for which he is held accountable. The board (and, if the institution is part of a multi-college system, its central staff) must operate in a manner which does not erode the authority of the president but which enhances the autonomy of the institution.

III Responsibilities: As chief executive officer, the president is responsible for recommending broad policies for consideration by the board and implementing these policies once they have been approved by the board. Major areas of presidential responsibility include:

(1) The direction of current and long-range planning related to institutional goals, academic programs and teaching approaches, research, public service, enrollment projections, and physical plant development.

(2) The development and maintenance of appropriate administrative organization and policymaking structure for the most efficient and effective utilization of institutional resources.

(3) The development and maintenance of a personnel system concerned with the recruitment, selection, assignment, supervision, evaluation, and promotion and tenure of all personnel employed by the institution.

(4) The preparation and presentation of the financial budget and the allocation and supervision of all appropriated and other funds that finance any activities under the jurisdiction of the college.

(5) The development and maintenance of the facilities and equipment necessary for the support of the college's functions.

IV Relationship with Governing Board: As chief executive officer of the institution, the president deserves to have a clear understanding with his governing board concerning the following working relationships:

(1) The board of trustees should invite the president to attend all meetings of the board (the only exception being when the board meets in executive session to act on the president's salary and other personal matters). The board should not meet with any representatives of the college's various constituencies without the presence of the president.

(2) The board of trustees should ask the president for his recommendations on all matters before the board that may affect the college. No changes affecting an institution in any regard should be made by the board (or a coordinating board, commission for higher education, central staff, or other state agencies) without appropriate prior consultation with and recommendations from the president of that institution.

(3) The board of trustees should hold the president free of any personal liability in the execution of his duties and responsibilities so long as he is acting as the board's chief executive

officer. This should include protection against claims from damage suits and physical and psychological harassment.

(4) The board of trustees should recognize that it, and not the president, holds final responsibility for the health, safety, and welfare of the institution and its personnel, particularly students. The president's main responsibility is that of providing students with reasonable opportunities to obtain an education, in accordance with the laws of the surrounding community, the policies of the board, and the resources of the institution.

* * *

The American Association of State Colleges and Universities is an organization of 270 regional state colleges and universities located in 45 states, the District of Columbia, Guam and the Virgin Islands. Many evolved from former teacher-training and technical schools; some are new institutions. All are now four-year institutions of arts and sciences; two-thirds have graduate programs. Together AASCU institutions enroll 1.7 million students, or over 20 per cent of the total national student population. They represent the fastest growing group of degree-granting colleges and universities in the country.

Examples of Campus Rules, Disciplinary Structures and Procedures, Arranged by Subject

This appendix consists of portions of the disciplinary rules of a selected group of colleges and universities, arranged under the following subject heads:

(1) Composition, Selection, and Jurisdiction of Tribunals;

(2) Hearing and Review Procedures;

(3) Sanctions;

(4) Proscribed Conduct.

These materials are included to illustrate the broad range of disciplinary systems on campuses. Because it is believed that the exact language of the rules and regulations will be of great interest, we have chosen to reproduce the applicable portions of the rules rather than to summarize them. The school administrator, attorney, or academic legislative body may well find helpful guidelines in the partial codes of discipline included here.

Composition, Selection, and Jurisdiction of Tribunals

Bennington College

The Judicial Committee

6. There shall be a Judicial Committee composed of five students and one non-voting faculty adviser serving one-year terms. (*As amended, spring 1961*) Two students shall be elected at the end of the Fall Term and three students and the faculty

adviser shall be elected at the end of the Spring Term by the student electorate in a preferential secret ballot conducted by the Legislative Council. They shall elect a chairman from the student members who have experience on the Committee.

No student shall be eligible for election until she has served at least one semester on a House Committee or on a divisional Educational Policies Committee; but no student shall be a member of the Judicial Committee while she is serving as a House Chairman. No faculty member shall be eligible for election until he has been a member of the faculty for two years. Candidates shall be nominated by the Legislative Council, by house meetings, or by petition of fifteen eligible members of the community, and a preliminary election shall be held one week before the final balloting to reduce the number of candidates to three times the number of vacancies. The authority of the Judicial Committee shall extend to all infractions of rules and regulations voted upon by the student electorate. It shall have power to rescind campus motor vehicle permits issued by the College, to limit individual students' sign-out privileges and to campus individual students, to suspend the social privileges of a student house, to suspend or expel students from the College, or to employ such other penalties as it deems appropriate. The Committee shall operate at all times as a full committee, except in instances in which it has specifically and publicly delegated authority to an individual member. *(As amended, spring 1966)*

7. Every student shall have the right to appeal to a Judicial Review Committee to reduce a penalty imposed by the Judicial Committee. Sentences of suspension or expulsion must be appealed to the Judicial Review Committee, and shall require the approval of the president of the College before they may be carried into effect. The Judicial Review Committee shall be composed of the Director of Student Personnel and two faculty members serving two-year terms and elected in alternate years by the student electorate in a preferential secret ballot conducted by the Legislative Council. No one shall be eligible until he has been a member of the faculty for two years.

Candidates shall be nominated by the Legislative Council, by a Faculty Meeting, by a House Meeting, or by petition of fifteen members of the community; and a preliminary election shall be held one week before the final balloting to reduce the number of candidates to three times the number of vacancies.

University of Delaware

C. *Membership*

The membership of the JUDICIAL POLICY BOARD shall be:

1. The Vice President for Student Affairs.

2. Three other faculty members elected or appointed for staggered two-year terms, in accordance with the Faculty By-laws.

3. The President of the Student Government Association or his designee, a member of the Student Government Association.

4. Three other students selected in accordance with the Constitution and Bylaws of the Student Government Association.

5. A quorum shall consist of five members.

6. Should a vacancy occur in the faculty or student membership during the school year, such vacancies shall be filled as provided for in the Bylaws of the Faculty or in the Constitution and Bylaws of the Student Government Association, respectively.

7. The Chairman of the Judicial Policy Board shall be elected by the Board at its first meeting each year from among the elected or appointed members of the Board.

III. *Faculty-Student Appellate Court*

A. *Authority*

The authority of the FACULTY-STUDENT APPELLATE COURT is derived from the JUDICIAL POLICY BOARD to which it is responsible.

B. *Jurisdiction*

This Court normally shall serve as the highest student appellate Court. In the most extraordinary circumstances, further appeals may be heard by the faculty at their option, upon petition of the student found guilty by any court.

C. Membership

The membership of the FACULTY-STUDENT APPELLATE COURT shall be:

1. Four faculty members, one of whom is elected by the court to serve as Chairman, appointed or elected with provision for continuity of membership as provided for in the Faculty Bylaws.

2. Four student members, appointed or elected with provision for continuity of membership as provided for in the Student Government Association Constitution and Bylaws, which shall set forth the qualifications for such appointment or election.

3. Members shall begin their terms on the court immediately following their appointment/election in May of each year.

4. A quorum shall consist of five members.

5. Should a vacancy occur in the faculty or student membership during the school year, such vacancies shall be filled as provided for in the Bylaws of the Faculty or in the Constitution/Bylaws of the Student Government Association respectively.

IV. Student Court

A. Authority

The authority of the STUDENT COURT is derived from the JUDICIAL POLICY BOARD to which it is responsible.

B. Jurisdiction

The STUDENT COURT is the highest student judicial body. It shall have two primary functions:

1. To serve as a judicial body to hear and decide cases of student misconduct referred to it by members of the Student Services staff designated by the Vice President for Student Affairs, or by other judiciaries.

2. To serve as an appellate court to hear appeals of dis-

ciplinary actions by any immediately subordinate student judicial body, or by administrative action.

C. *Membership*

The STUDENT COURT shall be composed of:

1. A student chairman and six other student members, appointed in the manner provided for in the Student Government Association Constitution/Bylaws.

2. Two non-voting advisers. One of these advisers shall be a faculty member appointed by the JUDICIAL POLICY BOARD. The other adviser shall be a member of the Student Services staff, appointed by the Vice President for Student Affairs.

3. The term to be served by members of this court shall be for one year beginning in May. Members may be reappointed to serve for successive terms.

4. A quorum shall consist of five student members and one adviser.

5. A vacancy in the student membership of this court shall be filled as provided for in the Student Government Association Constitution/Bylaws. A vacancy which may occur in the adviser positions shall be filled promptly by an appointment made by the respective board or officer responsible for such appointments.

V. *Judicial Bodies below the Student Court*

Residence Hall Judicial Bodies and/or Men's or Women's Courts and/or such other judiciaries subordinate to the STUDENT COURT as may be required, may be established and assigned responsibilities for reviewing and imposing penalties for infractions of residence hall rules and other rules of social conduct appropriate to the level of the judiciary. The authority and responsibility for establishing lower judiciaries shall rest with the JUDICIAL POLICY BOARD.

VII. *Administrative Disciplinary Hearings*

A. Administrative disciplinary hearings shall be conducted

by the Vice President for Student Affairs, or other Student Services Officer(s) designated by him in the following circumstances:

1. In those types of cases designated by the JUDICIAL POLICY BOARD.

2. In any case referred to him by the judicial body having primary jurisdiction over the offense.

3. In any case when the student chooses not to appear before a judicial body and requests an administrative disciplinary hearing.

4. In any case when the Vice President for Student Affairs or his designee determines that timely action (normally within ten class days) is not possible by the judiciary which normally would hear the case.

B. Appeals of administrative disciplinary action are heard by the body normally having appellate jurisdiction of the code violation. For example, if jurisdiction for a particular code violation is assigned to the STUDENT COURT an appeal of an administrative action for a similar violation would be to the FACULTY-STUDENT APPELLATE COURT.

University of Kentucky

Article I — The University Judicial System

1.1 Authority of the President of the University

Pursuant to the provisions of K.R.S. 164.200, 164.210 and 164.220, the Board of Trustees hereby delegates the responsibility for student discipline to the President of the University.

1.41 *The Role of the Office of the Dean of Students*

1.411 When the Dean, after investigation into an alleged violation of the disciplinary rules, believes a student has committed a disciplinary offense defined in Section 1.2 or 6.1, he shall notify the student that he is charged with said offense. Thereafter, he may counsel with the student and may outline proposed disciplinary punishment and/or counseling.

1.412 In the counseling process, the accused shall enjoy the right to have the assistance of an advisor of his choice and shall be informed of this right.

1.413 If the Dean and the student are unable to resolve the matter to their mutual satisfaction in the counseling process, the Dean shall forward the reports and evidence concerning the case to the office of the University Counsel for evaluation and prosecution before the appropriate University judicial agency. The Dean is thereafter concerned with furnishing testimony as requested by University Counsel, keeping the records of the University Judicial Board and Appeals Board and in aiding the student to comply with any punishment decreed by either Board.

1.414 Within the rights of the student at the University of Kentucky, the Dean of Students may contact the parents, or other persons he deems appropriate, in matters of discipline.

1.415 All student grievances involving rights stated herein shall be reported to the Dean of Students within 30 days of their occurrence. Grievances reported after this period or which otherwise come to the attention of the Dean of Students may be acted upon according to his determination of the circumstances.

1.416 The Dean of Students shall investigate each student grievance to determine whether it contains merit.

a. If he decides that it does, he shall use moral suasion, negotiation, personal appeal, and the prestige of his office to settle the case to his satisfaction and that of the student.

b. When he is unable to satisfy the grievance to the satisfaction of the student or when he has notified the student that the grievance does not contain merit, the student has the right to appeal within 30 days to the University Appeals Board.

1.417 The Dean of Students shall have broad investigatory powers in non-academic cases and he shall receive prompt and full cooperation from students, student organizations, faculty and administrators. He may recommend policies or practices that should be terminated, modified or initiated to Student Government, the Senate Council, deans, department heads, or other appropriate persons.

1.42 *The University Judicial Board*

There shall be a University Judicial Board, hereinafter referred to as the U. J-Board, with appellate jurisdiction over the

decisions of any Residence Judicial Board and original jurisdiction over cases involving alleged violations by students of
the University disciplinary offenses defined in Section 1.2.

1.421 Authority

a. The U. J-Board shall receive appeals by accused students
from decisions of any Residence J-Board pursuant to Section
2.4 of this document, and shall have the authority to reverse
the decision of the Residence J-Board regarding the student's
guilt or to mitigate, but not to increase, the punishment imposed by the Residence J-Board.

b. The U. J-Board shall have the sole authority to determine the issue of guilt in those cases referred to it pursuant to
Section 1.413. It shall have the sole authority to impose punishment short of actual suspension, dismissal, or expulsion
upon any student found guilty of a violation of University
disciplinary rules defined in Section 1.2. If the U. J-Board
believes that actual suspension, dismissal, or expulsion is the
appropriate remedy, it shall recommend such action to the
Vice President for Student Affairs.

1.422 Composition

The U. J-Board shall consist of eighteen persons; seven
graduate or professional students, five male undergraduate
students, five female undergraduate students, and a Hearing
Officer.

a. The Hearing Officer shall be the Chairman of the Board
and of each division thereof. He shall convene meetings of the
Board at such times and places as he deems necessary to carry
out its duties. The Hearing Officer shall be a non-voting member of the Board as to the issue of guilt or innocence and as to
the quantum of punishment, but shall decide and rule upon all
questions of law, whether they be substantive or procedural,
and upon all procedural questions arising under this Code.

b. When the accused is a graduate or professional student,
the Board shall be composed of its graduate or professional
members.

c. When the accused is an undergraduate student, the
Board shall be composed of all the undergraduate members

with at least two members of each sex present, except that the accused student may request, prior to his or her hearing, a Board composed only of the members of his or her sex. (The requirement as to sex shall not apply to the Hearing Officer.)

d. In any proceeding of the graduate board or the full undergraduate board, at least five members of the appropriate board, in addition to the Hearing Officer, must be present to hear the case. Any decision of the U. J-Board must be by majority of the voting members of the board sitting on the case.

1.423 Eligibility Requirements

a. A graduate or professional member of the U. J-Board shall be a full-time student enrolled in the Colleges of Dentistry, Law, Medicine or in the Graduate School, who has been in residence at least one semester and is in good standing within his or her appropriate school or college.

b. An undergraduate member of the U. J-Board shall be a full-time undergraduate student, other than a freshman, who has had at least one year of residence on the Lexington campus and has at least a 2.5 cumulative average.

c. The Hearing Officer shall be a person with training in the law, possessing at least the degree of Bachelor of Laws or its equivalent.

1.424 The Appointment Process

The Student Government shall screen all applications for membership and forward those approved to the President of the Student Body who, with the advice and approval of the Vice President for Student Affairs, shall make the final appointment of the members of the U. J-Board.

State University of New York

(g) There shall be constituted at each state-operated institution a Hearing Committee to hear charges against students of violation of the rules for maintenance of public order prescribed by or referred to in this Part. Such committee shall consist of three members of the administrative staff and three members of the faculty, designated by the chief administrative officer, and three students who shall be designated by the members named by the chief administrative officer. Each such member shall serve until his successor or replacement has been designated. No member of the committee shall serve in any case where he is a witness or is or has been directly involved in the events upon which the charges are based. In order to provide for cases where there may be such a disqualification and for cases of absence or disability, the chief administrative officer shall designate an alternate member of the administrative staff and an alternate member of the faculty, and his principal designees shall designate an alternate student member, to serve in such cases. Any five members of the committee may conduct hearings and make findings and recommendations as hereinafter provided.

At any institution where the chief administrative officer determines that the number of hearings which will be required to be held is, or may be, so great that they cannot otherwise be disposed of with reasonable speed, he may determine that the Hearing Committee shall consist of six members of the administrative staff and six members of the faculty to be designated by him and of six students who shall be designated by the members so designated by him. In such event the chief administrative officer shall designate one of such members as chairman who may divide the membership of the committee into three divisions each to consist of two members of the administrative staff, two faculty members and two students and may assign charges among such divisions for hearing. Any four members of each such division may conduct hearings and make recommendations as hereinafter provided.
[Off. Comp. of Codes, Rules and Regulations of SUNY, Tit. 8, Ch. V, Pt. 535, §535.9(g), amended April 29, 1970.]

University of Oregon

II. The Administration of the Code

A. The Student Court

1. The Student Court shall be composed of five students and two faculty members, each appointed by the President of

the University. The student members shall be recommended by the President of the Associated Students and shall serve for a term of two years with two members retiring in alternate years. Whenever possible, one member shall be a second or third-year law student. The Court will elect a chairman from its student membership.

E. The Student Conduct Committee

1. The Student Conduct Committee, by faculty legislation and by delegation of the President of the University, is designated as the agency within the University which has primary responsibility for the student-conduct program. The Committee shall be responsible to the faculty and the President of the University for recommending policies relating to student conduct, for formulating or approving rules and enforcement procedures within the framework of existing policies, for disposing of such individual cases as may properly come before it, and for recommending to the President of the University changes in the administration of any aspect of the student-conduct program.

2. The Committee shall consist of four faculty members and three student members, each appointed by the President of the University. Each student member shall serve for a period of one year with one member retiring at the end of each academic term (Fall, Winter, Spring). Members of the Committee may be reappointed. The President may appoint temporary members of the Committee to serve during a summer session or such other times as are necessary to assure full membership of the Committee.

5. The Committee may delegate jurisdiction to handle infractions of University rules to the Student Court and such other tribunals as may be established. With the consent of the President of the University, the Committee also may delegate such jurisdiction to appropriate University officials. In all instances such jurisdiction shall be defined by the Committee, ordinarily in terms of specified offenses, maximum sanctions, or designated living units. The Committee may, at its discretion, withdraw delegation of jurisdiction in any case and dispose of such case itself.

F. Student Tribunals

1. The Student Court shall be composed of five students and two faculty members, each appointed by the President of the University. The student members shall be recommended by the President of the Associated Students. The jurisdiction of the Student Court and its procedural rules shall be established or approved by the Student Conduct Committee.

2. The Student Conduct Committee, with the assistance of the Associate Dean of Students, may establish minor tribunals composed of students. When appropriate, University officials or faculty members may serve as advisers. No minor tribunal shall have jurisdiction to impose the sanction of expulsion or suspension.

3. No tribunal shall have any function except the enforcement of University rules or the performance of other duties which may be delegated to it by the Student Conduct-Committee.

University of Texas at Austin

Subchapter 11–200. Administration of Discipline

Sec. 11–201. Administration by Dean of Students

(a) Under direction of the president, the dean is primarily responsible for administration of student discipline.

(b) In carrying out his responsibility, the dean shall consult regularly with the Discipline Policies Committee.

Sec. 11–202. Discipline Policies Committee

(a) The Discipline Policies Committee has 9 members. The members are:

> (1) 5 representatives from the general faculty, appointed by the president for staggered 2-year terms;
>
> (2) the Chief Justice of the Student Court who serves for a 1-year term; and
>
> (3) 3 student assemblymen, designated by the Student Assembly for 1-year terms.

(b) The dean serves the committee as an administrative adviser without vote.

(c) The president shall appoint the committee chairman, who presides over committee meetings and serves as the committee's chief executive officer. The chairman may appoint as many subcommittees as are necessary to carry out the committee's business.

(d) The committee shall
(1) consult regularly with the dean on student disciplinary policies, rules and practices;
(2) recommend to the dean and to the Faculty Council changes in student disciplinary policies, rules, and practices; and
(3) hear appeals from faculty-student discipline committees.

Sec. 11-203. Faculty-Student Discipline Committees

(a) The dean shall appoint discipline committees to hear complaints under Subchapter 11-400. Each committee shall have 3 faculty representatives and 2 students appointed by the dean in alphabetical rotation from available members of the discipline panel.

(b) The discipline panel has 80 members. The members are:
(1) 50 representatives from the general faculty, appointed by the president for staggered terms not exceeding 5 years; and
(2) 30 students, nominated by the Student Assembly and appointed by the dean for 1-year terms.

(c) The Student Assembly may nominate only junior, senior or graduate students for appointment to the discipline panel. The dean may reject any nomination, in which case the Student Assembly shall nominate another, but the dean may not appoint a student not nominated by the Student Assembly.

(d) The Chairman of the Discipline Policies Committee shall instruct the discipline panel members on student disciplinary policies, rules, and hearing procedures as soon as practicable after the members are appointed.

Hearing and Review Procedures

University of California at Los Angeles

5.6 *Scheduling and Notice of Hearing*

5.6.1 Upon receipt of the notice of charges against the student from the Campus Advocate, it is the responsibility of the Chairman promptly to schedule a hearing of the case before either the Student Conduct Committee or a Hearing Officer, and to give written notice of the time and place of the hearing to the student and to the Campus Advocate.

5.6.2 The hearing shall be scheduled so as to permit the student reasonable time to prepare his case.

5.6.3 Hearings which may begin or extend into the student's off-quarter shall be so scheduled unless to do so would create substantial hardship for the student.

5.7 *Discovery*

5.7.1 The student shall be entitled to request and receive from the Campus Advocate:

5.7.1.1 Information in the possession of the University, whenever acquired, which will be adduced by the Campus Advocate at the hearing; and

5.7.1.2 Other non-confidential information in the possession of the University which the Chairman finds to be relevant and necessary for a fair and just hearing.

5.7.2 The notice of charges sent by the Campus Advocate to the student shall inform the student that:

5.7.2.1 He is entitled to request and receive the foregoing information; and

5.7.2.2 If he wishes to obtain such information, he must make the necessary arrangements with the Campus Advocate in advance of the hearing.

5.8 *Hearing Procedures*

Committee hearings shall be conducted in accordance with the following principles:

5.8.1 Any member shall disqualify himself if he believes such disqualification would serve the interests of a just and fair hearing. In the event that such disqualification prevents the convening of a quorum, members of the Committee who have disqualified themselves, shall be replaced, in accordance with 5.2 of this Code, by persons who shall serve during the period of disqualification.

5.8.2 The hearing shall be in private unless the student specifically requests an open hearing.

5.8.3 The student is entitled to be present throughout the hearing. He may, however, elect not to appear. His failure to appear shall not be construed as proof of culpability.

5.8.4 The student is entitled to be represented or assisted by an attorney or adviser of his choice throughout the hearing.

5.8.5 The Committee's findings and recommendations shall be based only upon the evidence received at the hearing.

5.8.5.1 The Committee shall receive and consider oral and documentary evidence of the kind on which responsible persons are accustomed to rely in serious matters, and the Committee may exclude irrelevant or unduly repetitious evidence.

5.8.5.2 Evidence shall not be considered if obtained by means which under the circumstances were either unfair or unjustified.

5.8.6 The student shall have the right to confront witnesses and, as the Campus Advocate, cross-examine them.

5.8.7 The student, the Campus Advocate, and the Committee may produce witnesses at the hearing.

5.8.7.1 No witness shall be permitted to testify unless prior to his testimony he agrees to submit to cross-examination.

5.8.7.2 If it is certified that a University employee or student who has declined voluntarily to testify is a material witness, the Chairman, if he finds with substantial certainty that such is the case, shall so inform the Chancellor who shall require said employee or student to testify, subject, however, to 5.8.9 of this Code.

5.8.8 The student shall not be compelled to incriminate or bear witness against himself by word or action, and his silence shall not be taken as an inference of culpability.

5.8.9 No witness shall be compelled to incriminate or bear witness against himself.

5.8.10 Where a witness is or may become unavailable to testify at a hearing, the Chairman shall arrange for his deposition under circumstances complying with 5.8.6 of this Code.

5.8.11 Hearings shall be concluded as speedily as possible without creating substantial hardship for the student or for witnesses.

5.8.12 The hearing shall be recorded. Such recording may be by tape.

5.8.13 Findings of violations of University policies and/or campus regulations shall be based upon clear and convincing proof.

5.8.14 Findings of violations of University policies and/or campus regulations require an affirmative vote of a majority of the Committee members deciding the case.

5.9 *Findings and Recommendations*

5.9.1 Promptly after the conclusion of the hearing, the Committee, through the Chairman, shall submit to the Chancellor the Committee's report setting forth:

(a) Findings as to each of the charges including:

(1) the facts surrounding the alleged misconduct; and

(2) whether such facts do or do not amount to a violation of the University policies and/or campus regulations alleged to have been violated.

(b) Recommendations as to:

(1) the disposition of the case, proposing any sanction to be imposed and/or reimbursement to be required; and, if so inclined,

(2) the revision or elimination of a University policy and/or campus regulation deemed by the reporting body to be inappropriate.

5.9.1.1 Where the decision is not unanimous, a minority report may be submitted to the Chancellor.

5.9.1.2 These reports shall be treated as confidential if the hearing was private; if the hearing was open, they may be made public by the Chancellor.

5.9.2 A copy of the Committee's reports shall be mailed to the student at the same time they are furnished to the Chancellor.

Hearing Officers

6.1 *Number and Appointment*

A minimum of three qualified members of the campus community who are not members of the Student Conduct Committee shall be nominated by the Chairman, approved by the Committee, and appointed by the Chancellor to serve under the coordination of the Chairman as Hearing Officers.

6.2 *Term of Service*

Hearing Officers shall serve for a period of three to five consecutive quarters, and may be reappointed at any time to successive terms of service.

6.3 *Assignment of Cases*

6.3.1 The Chairman of the Student Conduct Committee may assign individual cases for hearing by a Hearing Officer.

6.3.1.1 Normally, cases involving minor breaches of conduct which do not raise issues of extraordinary importance should be assigned to a Hearing Officer.

6.3.1.2 The Committee shall be notified by the Chairman of his decision to assign a case to a Hearing Officer.

6.3.2 When a case is so assigned, the selection of the Hearing Officer shall be made in rotating, alphabetical order, subject to the principle set forth at 5.8.1 of this Code, except in cases in which the Chairman anticipates that the hearing may have to be held following, or extend beyond, that Hearing Officer's term of service.

6.4 *Procedures*

Cases assigned to a Hearing Officer shall be dealt with in accordance with all of the discovery and hearing procedures set forth in 5.7 and 5.8 of this Code, provided, however, that:

(a) the Hearing Officer (rather than the Chairman or the Committee) shall rule on all issues arising prior to and during the hearing conducted by him; and

(b) such further modifications of them shall be made as are necessary by reason of having a single-member, rather than a multi-member, hearing body.

6.5 *Findings and Recommendations*

Promptly after the conclusion of the hearing, the Hearing Officer shall:

6.5.1 Submit to the Student Conduct Committee, which will review his findings and recommendations, the record of the hearing; and

6.5.2 Submit to the Chancellor, through the Committee, his report setting forth:

(a) Findings as to each of the charges including:

(1) the facts surrounding the alleged misconduct; and

(2) whether such facts do or do not amount to a violation of the University policies and/or campus regulations alleged to have been violated.

(b) Recommendations as to:

(1) the disposition of the case, proposing any sanction to be imposed and/or reimbursement to be required; and, if so inclined,

(2) the revision or elimination of a University policy and/or campus regulation deemed by the Hearing Officer to be inappropriate.

6.6 *Review by the Student Conduct Committee*

The Student Conduct Committee shall, as to every case assigned to a Hearing Officer, automatically review his findings and recommendations.

6.6.1 Ordinarily, such review shall consist of no more than an examination of the record for the purpose of determining whether:

(a) the Hearing Officer's findings are supported by substantial evidence, and his recommendations are warranted by the findings, and

(b) the proceedings conformed to the requirements of 6.4 of this Code.

6.6.2 Where the review consists of no more than the foregoing:

6.6.2.1 Persons other than Committee members may not be present during the deliberations unless their presence is requested by the Committee. The Campus Advocate shall not be invited to be present unless an invitation is also extended to the student or his attorney or adviser.

6.6.2.2 The Committee may adopt the findings and endorse

the recommendations of the Hearing Officer, or, by a majority vote of the members reviewing the case, either:

(a) modify his recommendations, other than by increasing any sanction he has proposed, or

(b) refer the case back to him for further proceedings.

6.6.3 By majority vote of the Committee members reviewing the case, the Committee may, as to limited issues specified by the Committee, hold its own hearing. Such hearing shall be held in accordance with all of the discovery and hearing procedures set forth in 5.7 and 5.8 of this Code.

University of Kentucky

3.3 *Rights of the Accused*

3.31 The student shall be guaranteed the following rights in all proceedings of the University Judicial System.

3.311 All students shall be guaranteed a fair hearing in all proceedings of all judicial agencies.

3.312 No student shall be compelled to give testimony which might tend to incriminate him, and his refusal to do so shall not be considered evidence of his guilt.

3.313 The accused student shall be informed in writing of the reasons for his appearance before any judicial agency with sufficient particularity and in sufficient time to insure an opportunity to prepare for the hearing.

3.314 The accused shall be entitled to receive upon request a copy of all rules and procedures governing the judicial agency at least 24 hours prior to his appearance before the agency.

3.315 The accused student shall enjoy the right to hear and question the witnesses against him and to present witnesses in his own favor.

3.316 The accused shall enjoy the right to have the assistance of an advisor of his choice and shall be informed of this right in all processes of the University Judicial System.

3.317 Only impartial members of the judicial agency shall sit in judgment of any case.

3.318 The accused shall have access to a permanent verbal or written transcript of every hearing of every judicial agency.

3.319 The accused student shall have the right to either an open or closed hearing. All hearings before any judicial agency shall be closed unless the accused student requests that said hearing be open. If a student desires an open hearing, he must file a written request with the Hearing Officer at least 24 hours prior to the time set for the hearing. The Hearing Officer will then admit to the hearing, in addition to those admitted to closed hearings, one properly identified member of the working press from the student newspaper, and from each established newspaper, magazine, television or radio station requesting admission, four persons invited by the accused student, and four persons invited by the University Counsel. The Hearing Officer may order the removal of any disruptive person from the hearing.

University of New Mexico

B. Rules Governing Proceedings before the Student Standards Committee

Section 1. Statement of Charges — Answer — Hearing Date

(a) Proceedings before the Committee shall be commenced either by (i) a written communication from the complaining party to the student charged and to the Chairman of the Committee, or (ii) the filing of a notice of appeal by the student followed by a written communication from the original complaining party. The communication shall state with reasonable particularity the charges being made, and the copy sent to the student shall contain a statement of the functions, duties and composition of the Committee and a copy of these rules.

(b) Within one week of receipt of the statement of charges in cases of original complaint against the students (§ 1(a)(i)) above, the student shall submit a written answer which shall be sent to the complaining party and the Chairman of the Committee. The answer shall state whether the student desires a hearing before the Committee, and in the student's discretion, may detail the defense the student plans to present. In the discretion of the Chairman, the one-week period for answer may be extended.

(c) Upon receipt of the statement of charges and the answer in cases where one is called for, the Chairman of the Committee, after consulting the parties, shall set a time and place for the hearing. In setting such time, the Chairman shall take into account the parties' need for sufficient time to prepare their presentations.

Section 2. Student's Failure to Answer

If the student fails to answer the statement of charges or if he indicates that he desires no hearing, the Committee, at its option, may consider whether the complaining party's statement of charges constitutes adequate grounds for disciplinary action. If the Committee finds that the stated charges do constitute grounds for disciplinary action, it shall determine the extent of such action. In its discretion, the Committee may investigate the truth of the charges and request that the complaining party present proof thereof. The Committee shall forward its decision, with reasons stated, to the complaining party, to the student charged, and to the Dean of Students or Dean of Women, as the case may be.

Section 3. Failure to File Specific Statements of Charges

When a student appeals to the Committee concerning disciplinary action taken against him, the original complaining party must file the statement of charges contemplated by Section 1 within ten days of receipt of notice of the appeal or the disciplinary action appealed from shall be deemed reversed. The ten-day period can be extended for a reasonable period of time in the discretion of the Chairman.

Section 4. Proceedings Before Committee

If the student files an answer as contemplated in Section 1, the following procedures shall be followed:

(a) Unless both the complaining party and the student request a public hearing, the hearing before the Committee shall be private.

(b) If any facts are in dispute, testimony of witnesses and other evidence shall be received.

(c) The student and the complaining party shall have the option of being represented by counsel or an adviser, or both.

(d) The hearing normally shall proceed as follows: (i) presentation of evidence in support of the statement of charges; (ii) the student's evidence in answer; (iii) the rebuttal evidence; (iv) the student's rebuttal evidence; (v) closing arguments.

(e) The student and the complaining party, their representatives, and Committee members shall have the right, within reasonable limits, to question all witnesses who testify orally.

(f) The Committee, if it deems it desirable, may proceed independently to secure the presentation of evidence at the hearing.

(g) A verbatim record of the proceeding shall be kept, the cost of such record being borne by the University. In the usual case, the record shall consist of a tape recording of the proceeding. Such recording shall be retained by the Committee until the time for appeal to the President shall have passed. Unless both parties agree to its necessity, no typed record shall be made. The University shall bear the cost if a typed record is made.

(h) The student shall have the aid of the University administration and the Committee, when needed, in securing the attendance of witnesses and in obtaining information necessary to answer the charges made against him.

(i) Except as provided in this paragraph, the parties shall have the opportunity to be confronted at the hearing by all witnesses.

When it is impossible for either party to secure the attendance of a witness at the hearing, the statement which is to be introduced at the hearing shall be reduced to writing and signed by the witness, and shall be disclosed to the other party sufficiently in advance to permit such other party to interrogate the witness prior to the hearing. If the other party fails to interrogate the witness within a reasonable time or if he does interrogate the witness and the reply is reduced to writing and signed by the witness, the original statement together with the replies, if any, shall be admissible in the hearing.

(j) The Committee shall not be required to follow formal court procedures or judical rules of evidence.

Section 5. Consideration of Matter by Committee

(a) After hearing the evidence, the Committee may request or accept written arguments from the parties.

(b) The Committee shall reach its conclusions in executive session.

(c) If the Committee finds that the student's conduct has adversely affected the University's educational function, has disrupted community living on campus, or has demonstrated the probability that the student constitutes a physical danger to himself or others on campus, it shall, in determining what disciplinary action should be taken, consider whether police or other official off-campus action has been taken or is likely to be taken against the student, and whether such off-campus action is likely to be effective in deterring similar conduct by the student in the future. If final off-campus action has not been taken by the time the Committee considers the case, the Committee may, in its discretion, delay its decision until the off-campus action has been taken.

(d) The Committee shall notify the complaining party and the student of its decision. If either of them so requests or if an appeal is taken, the Committee shall prepare an opinion containing specific findings of fact supporting its conclusions on each of the stated charges. These findings shall be sent to both parties. The Committee's decision shall be communicated to the Dean of Men or the Dean of Women, as the case may be, so that appropriate administrative action can be taken to implement the Committee's decision.

Section 6. Review by President

If a request is made by either party within ten days of receipt of notification of the Committee's decision, the President shall review the matter. His review shall be based on (i) the record made before the Committee; (ii) the Committee's written opinion; and (iii) oral or written arguments made to him by the parties or their representatives. After consulting the parties, the President may arrange for a hearing with all parties present.

If the President concludes that additional evidence should be taken, he shall remand the matter to the Committee for further proceedings. If he concludes that the record is complete, he may affirm, reverse or modify the Committee's determination. The President's decision shall be communicated in writing to the Chairman of the Committee, to the complaining party and to the student within thirty days of the case being appealed to him. If for any reason the President is unable to participate in the appellate process, the appeal shall be heard and the decision made by the Academic Vice President.

Section 7. Records

The Chairman of the Committee, or his appointee, shall keep a record of Committee actions, such record to be filed at the end of each academic year in the office of the Dean of Men.

Section 8. Parking Violations

In the Committee's discretion, the procedures outlined herein need not be followed in cases involving parking violations on campus.

Oberlin College

Article IV. Hearing Procedures for All Boards

A. Hearings

1. A date for a hearing will be set no more than one week after the notification of the accused.

2. The Chairman will notify all board members, the liaison from Judicial Board, the accused, the accuser and other persons concerned with the case, of the time and place of the hearing.

3. The Board will receive its first official information and report of the alleged violation during that scheduled meeting, at which time the accused will be present to hear the written statement of the case. He will be given an opportunity to comment on the information presented and to add any further information he feels is relevant.

4. The accused may have an advisor present at the meeting and, with the permission of the Board, may invite others to present relevant information. Students are permitted to invite their Floor Counselor to the meeting. In the course of the proceedings, any Board member may request the other per-

sons who might have relevant information to appear before the Board. The student has the right to confront his accuser or anyone else presenting the information to the judicial body, and said person(s) will be required to appear before the Board during the proceedings. The accused may request an open hearing.

5. If the Board is in doubt about the facts and seeks additional information to dispel this doubt, or if new information is submitted at any time, the accused will be present when such information is presented. The source may be requested by any member of the Board or by the accused.

6. Discussion by the Board, including interpretation of the facts presented in the accused's presence, and disciplinary action (if any), will occur after the accused and other participants are excused from the meeting by the Chairman.

7. The accused will be notified as soon as possible by the Chairman and one of the Deans of the action taken in his case. He may read the minutes taken during his presence at the Board meeting and, if he does so, must certify the minutes as correct.

8. A student disciplined by a board may request a rehearing of his case by the board of original jurisdiction provided he has new information relevant to his case.

9. Any decision by a board requiring disciplinary action will be reported in writing to the Dean of the division concerned with the vote of the Board indicated.

10. Decisions and actions of the Board must be reported to the College Community, but the name of the student will not be released. Additional publicity will be withheld on recommendation of the Board. Board members will not discuss the proceedings of disciplinary meetings with other persons except those required to know.

11. Any information sent to the parents of the student involved in cases appearing before the Board will be determined by the Board after consulting with the student. Normally parents will be informed when actions of probation, suspension, or expulsion are taken.

12. In student disciplinary cases in which it appears to the

264 • RIGHTS, RESPONSIBILITIES, RULES

Provost or the Dean of Students that the discussion in such judicial boards or committees as the General Faculty may have established or approved is impracticable (or inadvisable), or in the event of failure of the concerned boards or committees to act, the Provost or the Dean of Students may act with power. (College Bylaws, Article XVIII, Section 4)

13. Notwithstanding any other provision of the Bylaws, the President is authorized to act finally with respect to any student disciplinary matter affecting, in his judgment, the best interests of the College.

University of Oregon

11. Rules of Procedure (November 4, 1963)

A. Notice

1. A student who is charged with an offense under the Student Conduct Code shall receive written notice at least three days before his case is to be considered by the Court. The notice shall be in the form approved by the Student Conduct Committee as shown in Form A (Appendix I.) *A student may, in writing, waive the three day notice of hearing. (January 9, 1968)*

B. Outline of Proceedings

1. *Student does not appear.* A student may elect not to appear for a hearing. If, in writing, he agrees not to contest the case and, also in writing, waives a hearing, the Court will dispose of the case as provided for in Part II.E.5.e of the Student Conduct Program. If he does not so agree in writing or does not waive a hearing in writing, but still does not appear personally or through his representative at the hearing, the Court will dispose of the case in the manner it believes is just.

2. *Student not reasonably able to appear.* If the case is disposed of under paragraph 10 b.1. of Section II.A., and it is subsequently determined by the Court that the student was not reasonably able to appear and not reasonably able to give notice of this prior to or at the time of the hearing, the Court

may set aside its disposition and set the case for rehearing. Notice of any re-scheduled hearing will be given the student in writing three days in advance of the hearing.

3. *Student appears personally or through representative.* If a student appears at a hearing, the charge against him shall be read in his or his representative's presence. The student then shall state whether the charge is accurate and, if so, whether he has an excuse. If the student admits the facts as charged and offers no adequate excuse the Court will proceed to determine the sanction. If the student does not admit the facts as charged or assert an adequate excuse, the hearing will proceed as follows: the Associate Dean of Students, or his representative, will present the evidence he has obtained; the student will present his evidence; the Associate Dean of Students (or his representative), the student (or his representative), or the Court may ask questions. After it has been determined whether the student committed the offense as charged, the Court will proceed to dismiss the case or to impose sanction, whichever is appropriate. Before imposing sanction, the Court will listen to any statement on behalf of the student. In addition, the Court may conduct any investigation it believes is necessary to a fair disposition of the case.

4. *Variations in order of procedure.* The order of procedure set forth in this rule is not rigid. The Court may vary it whenever it believes a variation would be wise.

C. *Evidence*

1. *Hearsay evidence.* All statements that are proposed to be used against the student shall be reduced to writing, and the student shall be given the opportunity to examine them. If he objects to their use within the time set in the Notice of Hearing that he receives, the statement will not be used. If he does not object within that time, he will be understood to have waived his objection. If any other hearsay evidence is used at his hearing, the student may enter an objection based on the lack of opportunity to cross-examine at any time within the period established for appeals from decisions of the Court.

2. *Other evidence.* Except as provided in the case of hearsay evidence any evidence that the Court believes is relevant is admissible.

D. Objections and Motions

1. The Court may rule on objections and motions at the time they are made. However, the Court may reserve decision on an objection or motion, require that it be reduced to writing, and order that the proceedings continue.

E. Contempt

1. *Contempt of Adjudicative Proceedings.* When any person, in the presence of any tribunal created under this Code, and while sitting as an adjudicative body, exhibits contemptuous, boisterous, disorderly, or violent conduct tending to impair or to interrupt the due course of a trial or other adjudicative proceedings, such person may be held in contempt and sanctioned therefor.

2. *Sanction Imposed.* Any sanction which may be imposed for the violation of a rule promulgated pursuant to I.B.3.f. may be imposed for the commission of a contempt.

3. *Adjudication of Contempt and Imposition of Sanction.* The adjudication of contempt shall be made by the then presiding officer, alone and summarily. Thereupon the proceedings shall be recessed and the entire tribunal shall decide whether the presiding officer's adjudication shall be upheld and, if so, what sanction shall be imposed. Such decision shall be made as in any other case. Upon the adjudication and sanction, if any, the presiding officer shall certify to the Associate Dean of Students the facts constituting the contempt and the sanction imposed therefor. Persons so adjudicated in contempt shall have the same right to appeal as is afforded in any other case adjudicated in that tribunal. *(May 27, 1969)*

F. Decisions of the Court

1. *Vote Required.* A decision that a student has committed an offense requires an affirmative vote of two-thirds of the members of the Court deciding the case. Sanctions of suspension or expulsion may likewise be imposed only by two-thirds of the

members voting on the question. Sanctions of lesser severity than suspension or expulsion may be imposed by a majority of the members who vote. The Chairman of the Court may rule on all other questions that come before the Court. If no member of the Court objects to a ruling of the Chairman before the case has been disposed of, it stands as the ruling of the Court. If any member of the Court does object to a ruling of the Chairman before the case has been disposed of, a majority of the members voting will determine its effect.

2. *Student's Copy.* A written copy of the decision shall be given to the student. If a sanction of expulsion, suspension, or probation is imposed, the decision shall advise the student of his right to appeal.

G. *Standard of Proof*

1. No member of the Court shall vote that the student has committed the offense as charged unless the evidence is clear and convincing to him.

H. *Appeal*

1. A student may appeal from any decision by delivering to the Associate Dean of Students within five days of receiving written notice of his right to appeal, a signed statement containing: (1) a statement that he appeals from a designated decision; and (2) a brief statement of the respects in which he considers the decision is wrong.

Stanford University

E. *Defendant Cooperation*

1. A student does not have the right to refuse to cooperate with either the Judicial Aide or the Stanford Judicial Council. Sanctions for refusal to cooperate will consist (1) of placing a hold on next-quarter registration or (2) of refusal of graduation in the case of students in their last quarter.

2. A student may refuse to incriminate himself.

F. *Defendant Rights before the Stanford Judicial Council*

1. To be informed of the charge and of the alleged act upon which the charge is based;

2. To request that the Dean of Students decide the case;

3. To be allowed a reasonable time in which to prepare a defense;

4. To hear all evidence upon which charges are based, and to answer this evidence through rebuttal;

5. To call witnesses before the Council subject to the provisions of Article II, section C.4 and to confront any other witnesses before the Council;

6. To be assured that, unless the defendant asks for an open hearing, any matters of facts which would tend to identify the person or persons involved in a case would be kept confidential;

7. To have an open hearing;

8. To request that any member of the Council be disqualified because of prejudice;

9. To be informed of the above rights by proper summons;

10. To be considered innocent until proved guilty beyond a reasonable doubt;

11. To be assured that no record of the case is placed on his transcript;

12. To have no person presenting evidence against him sit in judgment upon him.

13. In instances of conviction under State or Federal law, the SJC shall not assess penalties if the circumstances of the case indicate that such penalties would be inequitable to the defendant when imposed in addition to civil or criminal penalties. This limitation shall not apply when SJC proceedings are deemed necessary by the SJC to protect the University from risk of harm. Nothing in this paragraph, however, shall be interpreted as barring or delaying action by the SJC on a case because a similar charge is pending before a civil court.

14. A defendant shall be entitled to a prompt decision by the Council and shall receive a written copy of the decision which shall include findings of ultimate facts and law and a notification of any penalty recommended to the University President.

G. Procedures of the Stanford Judicial Council

1. The Chairman of the Stanford Judicial Council has absolute authority to control the conduct of persons in the Council chambers (i.e. to maintain order) and, subject to being overruled by a majority of the other members present, has the power to rule on the relevance of evidence presented.

2. The Dean of Students will not be in charge of the presentation of evidence and will not conduct cross-examination. He may be present at any hearing, closed or open, and has the right to present in writing his opinion of the case and its implications. If he wishes to present his views orally, he may request permission of the Chairman of the SJC, whose decision on this request may be overruled by a majority of the other members present.

I. Alternate Judicial Procedure

1. A student may ask the Dean of Students to hear his case. The Dean may refuse to do so.

2. A student has the right to appeal the Dean's decision to a three-man subcommittee of the Stanford Judicial Council. The subcommittee is to consist of two faculty members and one student chosen by the Chairman of the Council at the beginning of the academic year, with the student defendant having the right to ask that the student member be replaced by a faculty member.

3. The SJC shall be informed of the Dean's decision in all cases and the reasons therefor.

4. To the extent appropriate the rights of students enumerated in Article II, section F shall be applicable to cases heard by the Dean.

University of Tennessee

Prior notice concerning the alleged misconduct or offense and the specific University regulations which apply is given to the student or organization involved. Evidence is presented to the Committee by the representative of the Dean of Students' staff in the presence of the accused student or, in the case of student groups, in the presence of the officers representing the student organization. The student or student organization so charged has the right to challenge the evidence as is deemed necessary. The student or student organization is then excused from the meeting before action is taken. When the recommendation has been approved or amended, the Dean of Students' representative then informs the student's parents, if the student is under 21 years of age, the dean of the college in which the student is enrolled, and the Admissions Office when notation is to be made on the official University record. In cases of cheating and plagiarism, the dean of the college in which the offense occurred is notified, if it differs from college of enrollment.

The Student-Faculty Discipline Committee may call for counsel or advice from university specialists in law, medicine, psychology, and similar fields. The Office of the Dean of Students will arrange assistance of this kind.

Personal confidences and the identity of students appearing before discipline boards are protected. Any member of a discipline board who discusses a case outside a meeting is subject to suspension from the panel.

Appeals. Appeals to the Administrative Council from decisions made by the Dean of Students on recommendation of a Committee are acceptable only when there is new evidence or where the penalty involves suspension for more than two quarter periods. If suspension is for one or two quarters only, appeals should be made in writing to the Dean of Students stating the bases for appealing the decision. Such appeals should be made within five days of the Committee's decision.

University of Wisconsin

(3) Faculty

(a) The faculty on each campus has the power to impose discipline upon any student for misconduct upon such terms and conditions, and pursuant to such procedures, as it finds appropriate, not inconsistent with these By-Laws.

(b) The faculty on each campus may establish such committee or committees as it finds appropriate to hear student disciplinary matters. Faculty discipline structure may be in two stages, an initial hearing committee and an appeals committee, if this is desired. In such a case it is desirable that the hearing committee include student representation, unless a student in a specific case chooses to be heard by faculty members only. Plenary power of review, however, either de novo or on the record, shall be vested in an all-faculty committee, and either the administration or the student may initiate an appeal within five (5) days of the hearing committee decision. Within seven (7) days of receipt of notice of an appeal, the appeals committee shall begin action on the appeal. Any hearing committee sitting in any case must be composed in fact of a majority of faculty members.

1. The student's right of privacy in disciplinary matters will be respected by the University, but students shall have the opportunity to be heard either in public or privately as they wish, unless it becomes necessary to close the hearing as provided herein. Committee deliberations as distinguished from hearings shall not be public.

2. For the purpose of conducting hearings, one faculty member on each committee shall be designated as chairman, a member of the Law faculty or with legal background, if available. It shall be his duty to inquire fully into the facts as to whether the student has engaged in misconduct as set forth in the charge. He has authority to:

(i) Rule upon offers of proof and receive relevant evidence.

(ii) Regulate the course of the hearing, and, if appropriate or necessary, summarily adjudge disciplinary penalties against students who unreasonably obstruct or impair its proceedings in its presence, or order removal of such students from the hearing, or both.

(iii) Strike all evidence of a witness refusing to answer any proper question unless the answer would involve privileged matter.

(iv) Dispose of motions and procedural matters or requests.

(v) Schedule filing of briefs and proposed findings by the student and dean or charging officer.

(vi) Take any other actions necessary to conduct the hearing.

3. Committee members may question any ruling by the chairman but such matters unless otherwise convenient should be decided in closed session. Committee members may, through the chairman, question any of the witnesses.

4. The committee and chairman are not bound by the common law or statutory rules of evidence. Evidence having reasonable probative value shall be admitted; but irrelevant, immaterial and repetitious evidence shall be excluded. Effect shall be given to the laws of privilege and relevancy; materiality and probative force shall govern proof on all questions of fact.

5. Without limitation by enumeration, each committee established by the faculty is empowered to maintain order and decorum during proceedings before them, to summarily impose discipline upon any student in violation of its oral or written rules of conduct for the hearing, to order any person from the hearing room for misconduct that impairs the proceedings, and to close or otherwise regulate admission to the hearing as the committee in its discretion finds necessary.

6. Following are procedures to be followed in hearings:

(i) A charge of misconduct shall contain a clear and concise statement of the facts constituting the alleged misconduct. The chairman may permit the reasonable amendment of any charge.

(ii) Papers may be served by mail or by delivery to the person.

(iii) Action before a committee is commenced by the filing of a charge of misconduct with the committee, with a statement that a copy has been mailed or provided to the student against whom the charge is made. The chairman shall cause a copy of these rules to be provided to the student and shall notify the student that he has ten (10) days within which to respond to the charge in writing.

(iv) Answer. The student shall within ten (10) days from the service of the charge file an answer thereto. The student shall specifically admit, deny, or explain each of the facts alleged in the charge, unless the student is without knowledge in which case he shall so state, such statement being a denial. All allegations in the charge, if no answer is filed, or any allegation in the charge not specifically denied or explained in an answer filed, unless the student states in the answer that he is without knowledge, is deemed to be admitted to be true and shall be so found by the committee unless good cause to the contrary is shown.

(v) Where to file; service. The answer shall be filed with the chairman. The answer shall contain the address of the student, and if represented the name and address of his representative, and shall be signed by the student. The student's signature constitutes a representation by him that he has read the answer; that to the best of his knowledge, information and belief it is true and that it is not made to delay. If the answer is not signed, or if signed to delay or with intent to falsify or misrepresent the fact, it may be stricken and the action may proceed as if no answer were filed.

(vi) Extension of time for filing. The chairman may extend the time for filing the answer, for cause, upon written request.

(vii) Amendment. The student may amend his answer at any time prior to hearing, upon leave of the chairman, upon such terms as are deemed just, and as of right in any case in which the charge is amended, within the time fixed by the chairman.

(viii) The chairman shall, upon receipt of the charge and answer, prepare a statement of the issues he believes are to be decided and furnish a copy of this statement to both the charging officer and the student. In addition, he should immediately furnish the committee members with copies of the charges, answer and statement of issues and set the matter for hearing.

Sanctions

University of Connecticut

In discussing disciplinary action the Committee is free to devise a particular action for each case. However, the following disciplinary actions have been used at the University of Connecticut.

Residence Hall Probation

When a student demonstrates either an unwillingness or inability to adjust or conform to the demands of a community living situation through a series of infractions of residence hall requirements, he may be placed on "Residence Hall Probation." Normally, further misconduct would constitute grounds for loss of the privilege to reside in a University residence. In view of the requirement that students live in residence or commute from their home, Residence Hall Probation has serious implications.

Official Reprimand

A student may receive an official oral or written reprimand when his conduct is unsatisfactory to the extent that the University must take "official notice." Generally, the student is admonished and advised that the misconduct has become a matter of record in the Affairs Office for future reference.

Disiciplinary Warning

Issued when a specific behavior or a series of actions is unacceptable to the point that repetition would most likely result in one of the more serious disciplinary actions, such as a form of Disciplinary Probation or Suspension. The student is literally and officially *warned* that further unacceptable behavior will result in *more serious action*.

Disciplinary Probation

One of the major sanctions which may be imposed. This

status means that for reasons of conduct, the student is no longer in "good standing" in the University community. Certain restrictions may be placed upon his activities and privileges for a stated period.

Disciplinary Probation is of *two* types:

1. Office Probation—student is "on probation" with the appropriate Affairs office. The status is intended to serve as a constant reminder that the infraction has become a part of his permanent record in the Affairs Office and that repetition of similar or other unsatisfactory conduct will be cause for further action, at a minimum, Probation with Restrictions.

2. Disciplinary Probation with Restrictions—involves a review of the student's eligibility to receive or continue under scholarship or other financial aid, to participate in extracurricular activities (those which entail authority or involve public recognition), to hold Student Counselor, Resident Advisor, or Chapter Assistant positions, etc. Several or any number of restrictions may be placed upon the student's activities or privileges during the period of probation.

Students who are on disciplinary probation of either type may be required to schedule periodic interviews with a staff member of the appropriate Affairs Office for the purpose of necessary counseling.

Further improper behavior during a period of disciplinary probation of either type is likely to result in the student's immediate separation from the University.

Disciplinary Suspension

When a student's behavior resists correction through counseling or other measures or is unacceptable to the extent that it reflects most unfavorably upon his character, judgment, and maturity and/or is harmful to the well-being of the student body and the University, he may be suspended from the University. Suspensions are of *two* types:

1. "Suspended Suspension"—the period of suspension is not instituted; instead, the student is permitted to continue on the understanding that further misconduct during the period stated will result in immediate separation. The "suspension" is

noted on the permanent record in the Affairs Office and the restrictions of probation are instituted.

2. Actual Suspension — the student temporarily forfeits the privilege of attendance at the University. Such a suspension may be for less than a semester, a full semester, or indefinite. Students are subject to the normal procedure and regulations governing readmission to the University.

A student who has been suspended may not receive "a statement of honorable dismissal" during the period of suspension.

Disciplinary Dismissal

The ultimate disciplinary action which may be taken is dismissal. Dismissal involves permanent separation from the institution. No student who has been dismissed for disciplinary reasons may receive "a statement of honorable dismissal."

University of Illinois

Section 7

The panel shall hear cases brought before it in the manner outlined in Section 10 below. It shall discuss each case in executive session as soon as possible, but not later than twenty-four hours, after the conclusion of the hearing. It shall rule separately on each point of the charges in secret balloting, a majority of affirmative votes being necessary to declare a charge proven. The chairman shall announce the results of the voting. The panel shall then discuss the disciplinary action that might be taken, following which each member of the panel shall recommend by secret ballot the disciplinary action which he considers appropriate. If no majority is reached, all recommendations shall be tabulated and panel members shall then cast a secret "yes" or "no" ballot on each recommendation in descending order of severity until a majority of "yes" votes is obtained.

The penalties which the panel may impose include but are not restricted to:

a. *A warning* issued in the form of a letter to the student. Its purpose is to make him aware of the incompatibility of his behavior with the Student Code and with other University regulations. It shall be used for minor transgressions, particularly when there is good reason to believe that the student was not fully aware of the nature or implications of his actions.

b. *A reprimand* is a formal censure of the student's actions and is issued in the form of a letter.

c. *Disciplinary probation* imposes certain requirements on the student for a specified time. For example, the terms of the probation may require the student to report regularly to a member of the administration or faculty, restrict his participation in nonacademic student activities, or impose other appropriate conditions. The panel shall name the person charged with supervising the terms of the probation and shall specify how compliance shall be verified. Should the student violate the terms of his probation, the panel shall meet and specify further disciplinary action.

d. *Suspension* deprives the student of all of the rights and privileges of membership in the University community for a specified period of time, including those of attending classes, taking examinations, and participating in University sponsored activities. Normally, the student shall automatically be permitted to register for the next quarter.

e. *Dismissal* provides for the expulsion of the student from the University. The panel may specify a period after which the student will be entitled to apply for readmission.

The secretary shall inform the student by letter of the panel's decisions. He shall file copies with the Director of Admissions and Records, who will enter a notation of the disciplinary action on the student's ledger, and with the Dean of Student Affairs. However, only disciplinary probation, suspension, or dismissal shall appear on the student's official transcript and only then if the transcript is requested during the time when the disciplinary action is in effect.

University of Kentucky

1.45 *Temporary Sanctions*

In the event that the Vice President for Student Affairs has reasonable cause to believe that a student's presence may result in injury to himself, others or University property, or in the event that he has been charged with a crime so serious as to threaten the welfare of the University community, the Vice President may impose such temporary sanctions as he considers necessary to protect members of the University community or its property, including exclusion from University property. Upon taking such action, the Vice President shall notify the University Appeals Board. The student may appeal the Vice President's decision to the University Appeals Board in writing within 30 days. If requested in the written appeal, the Chairman will call a meeting of the Board to hear the case within 48 hours, or as soon as practicable thereafter. The Board shall consider the student's academic needs to attend class, use the library, and fulfill his other academic responsibilities in making its recommendation. This Board may recommend to the President of the University changes or extensions of the Vice President's action. The President then shall determine the sanctions to be imposed.

Such temporary sanctions shall be enforced only for such time as the conditions requiring them exist. Accordingly, the circumstances shall be reviewed by the Board whenever there are indications that they have changed and upon an appeal in writing from the student involved.

1.5 *Punishments*

1.51 *Warning*

The Dean of Students or his authorized representative may notify the student that continuation or repetition of specified conduct may be cause for other disciplinary action. (This action is not appealable.)

1.52 *Reprimand*

A written admonition which may include a reasonable requirement for additional labor in keeping with the offense committed.

1.53 *Probation*

Exclusion from participation in privileges or extracurricular University activities as set forth in the notice of probation for a specified period of time. If a student, while on probation, violates any of the terms set forth in the notice of probation or violates the Code of Student Conduct, as determined after the opportunity for a hearing, he shall be subject to further discipline in the form of undated suspension, suspension, dismissal or expulsion.

1.54 *Undated Suspension*

Exclusion from participation in any and all privileges or extracurricular University activities, except for attendance in classes in which officially enrolled, for a specified period of time. If a student, while on undated suspension, violates any of the terms set forth in the notice of undated suspension, or violates the Code of Student Conduct, as determined after the opportunity for a hearing, he shall be subject to further discipline in the form of suspension, dismissal or expulsion.

1.55 *Suspension*

Forced withdrawal from the University for a specified period of time, including exclusion from classes, termination of student status and all related privileges and activities, and exclusion from the campus if set forth in the notice of suspension. If a student, while on suspension, violates any of the terms set forth in the notice of suspension or violates the Code of Student Conduct while on a campus of the University, or in relation to a University sponsored activity, as determined after the opportunity for a hearing, he shall be subject to further discipline in the form of dismissal or expulsion.

1.56 *Dismissal*

Exclusion from the campus and termination of student status for an indefinite period. The student may be readmitted to the University only with the specified approval of the President of the University. If a dismissed student violates the Code of Student Conduct while on a campus of the University, or in relation to a University sponsored activity, or is present on a University campus without the written permission of the Dean of Students or Vice President for Student Affairs, as determined after the opportunity for a hearing, he shall be subject to further discipline in the form of expulsion.

1.57 *Expulsion*

Permanent termination of student status without possibility of readmission to any campus of the University.

1.58 *Monetary Reimbursement*

In cases where personal or public property has been stolen, defaced, disfigured, damaged or destroyed, the disciplinary action shall also include an appropriate monetary reimbursement for compensatory damages.

Occidental College

Sanctions

The Judicial Council shall be authorized to impose any of the following penalties:

1. *Disciplinary Probation:* Status for a specified period during which time any infraction of College regulations will automatically result in a more severe penalty.

2. *Suspension:* Termination of student status for a specified period of time.

3. *Dismissal:* Termination of student status for an indefinite period. The student may be readmitted to the College only with the specific approval of the President, given after recommendation of the Judicial Council, on the basis of a hearing held by it.

4. *Expulsion:* Permanent termination of student status without possibility of readmission to the College.

Other penalties, such as warnings, censures, fines, and restitution for damages may be imposed by the Judicial Council as deemed appropriate for a particular case.

Authority of the President

As set forth in the preceding sections, the Judicial Council shall be responsible for adjudicating cases of student misconduct. However, as the College officer directly responsible to the Board of Trustees for enforcement of all policies and regulations of the College, the President of the College in extraordinary circumstances is authorized to take whatever action he deems necessary with respect to any student disciplinary matter.

University of Texas

Subchapter 11–500. Penalties

Sec. 11–501. Authorized Disciplinary Penalties

The dean, under Subchapter 11–300, or a faculty-student discipline committee after a hearing under Subchapter 11–400, may impose one or more of the following penalties for violation of a regents' rule, university regulation, or administrative rule:

(1) admonition;
(2) warning probation;
(3) disciplinary probation;
(4) withholding of transcript or degree;
(5) bar against readmission;
(6) restitution;
(7) suspension of rights and privileges;
(8) suspension of eligibility for official athletic and nonathletic extracurricular activities;
(9) failing grade;
(10) denial of degree;
(11) suspension from the university;
(12) expulsion from the university.

Sec. 11–502. Nature of Disciplinary Penalties

(a) An admonition is a written reprimand from the dean to the student on whom it is imposed.

(b) Warning probation indicates that further violations of regulations will result in more severe disciplinary action. The dean shall impose warning probation for a period of not more than 1 calendar year, and the student shall be removed automatically from probation when the imposed period expires.

(c) Disciplinary probation indicates that further violations may result in suspension. Disciplinary probation may not be imposed for more than 1 calendar year.

(d) Withholding of transcript or degree is imposed upon a

student who fails to pay a debt owed the university, and the penalty terminates on payment of the debt.

(e) Bar against readmission is imposed on a student who has left the university and fails to pay a debt owed the university. The penalty terminates on payment of the debt.

(f) Restitution is reimbursement for damage to or mis-appropriation of property. Reimbursement may take the form of appropriate service to repair or otherwise compensate for damages.

(g) Suspension of rights and privileges is an elastic penalty. The dean or the discipline committee may impose limitations to fit the particular case.

(h) Suspension of eligibility for official athletic and nonathletic extracurricular activities prohibits, during the period of suspension, the student on whom it is imposed from joining a registered student organization; taking part in a registered student organization's activities, or attending its meetings or functions; and from participating in an official athletic or nonathletic extracurricular activity. A suspension may be imposed under this subsection for not more than 1 calendar year.

(i) A failing grade may be assigned to a student for a course in which he was found guilty of scholastic dishonesty.

(j) A student found guilty of scholastic dishonesty may be denied his degree.

(k) Suspension from the university prohibits, during the period of suspension, the student on whom it is imposed from entering the university campus, except in response to an official summons; from being initiated into an honorary or service organization; and from receiving credit at a component of the university system for scholastic work done in residence or by correspondence or extension. Except when suspension is imposed for scholastic dishonesty, the dean or faculty-student discipline committee may permit the receipt of credit for scholastic work done during the period of suspension.

(l) Expulsion from the university is permanent severance from the university.

Willamette University

Participation in an academic community is a privilege contingent upon the acceptance of responsibility. The student who violates his responsibility to abide by the Standards of Conduct of Willamette University jeopardizes his status as a member of the community and becomes subject to any one of the following actions, depending upon the nature of the violation. Such conduct sanctions, except in the case of Conduct Reprimand, are noted on the student's official transcript for the duration of the period of sanction and are made a part of his personal record until such time as he transfers or graduates.

Conduct Dismissal

The student's participation in university life is severed indefinitely with loss of all fees and all academic credit for the semester in which the dismissal takes place.

Conduct Suspension

The student's participation in university life is severed with a loss of all fees and all academic credit for the remainder of the semester in which the suspension takes place. The student's privilege of continuing within the University following the suspension period is contingent upon a demonstration of his willingness to accept his responsibility to abide by the Standards of Conduct. Any subsequent failure to accept his responsibility to abide by the Standards of Conduct following reinstatement may result in dismissal from the University.

Conduct Probation

The student's participation in university life is placed on a provisional status. The student must demonstrate a willingness to accept his responsibility to abide by the Standards of Conduct or forfeit the privilege of continuing in the University for at least the remainder of the current semester.

Conduct Reprimand

The student is given notice that his actions have brought into question his willingness to accept his responsibility to abide by the Standards of Conduct and that further failure to accept this responsibility may result in the application of additional sanctions.

Proscribed Conduct

University of Illinois

Student Conduct and Discipline

The University may at any time exclude or impose conduct probation on a student whose conduct is considered to be undesirable and/or not in the best interest of the University community. Generally, undesirable conduct may consist of one, or a combination of several, of the following:

1. Disruptions of normal and necessary academic, administrative, and extracurricular functions of the University.

2. Conduct which prevents, seriously limits, or creates hazards for regular University activities of students, faculty, and staff, *including, but not limited to, disruption of elevator service, access to classes and University facilities, and all other scheduled University or University-approved events.*

3. Violations of national, state, or city laws on campus or at University functions.

4. Withholding information or giving false information on an application for admission, readmission, or registration. Such action may result in ineligibility for admission to the University or be cause for dismissal.

5. Failure of the student to respond to requests from University officials for conference on matters pertaining to his status in the University, *including, but not limited to, failure to respond to mail and telephone messages.*

6. Violations of University rules on the use of intoxicants (See *Student Code, Part V, Section A, Item 1*).

7. Violations of regulations on demonstrations, picketing, distribution of mimeographed and printed materials (See *Student Code, Part V, Section D*).

8. Alteration or mutilation of an official University docu-

ment or permission for the use thereof by an unauthorized person; I.D. cards, course-program cards, change slips, receipts, transcripts of credit, and like documents are official documents.

9. Violations of regulations established for student organizations (including financial regulations and student election regulations).

10. Academic irregularities.

University of Maine

Within the sphere of university interest mentioned above—conduct on or involving university property and conduct indicating substantial potential physical danger to members of the university community—not all conduct is appropriate for university regulation. Further distinctions must be drawn, which admittedly cannot be absolutely precise, with as great a degree of exactitude as possible. This conclusion does not demand that every conceivable act of misconduct must be anticipated with a correlative rule: it does require, however, that categories of forbidden conduct, appropriate for university regulation, ought to be delineated in such a way as to give reasonable warning to students that the conduct is forbidden. If the categories of forbidden conduct prove to be inadequate, as occasionally they may, to comprehend certain acts deemed appropriate for university regulation, then additional formulation will be necessary from time to time. The university must be prepared to refrain from punishing a student for an act that does not fall within any category of acts prohibited at the time it was committed. Elementary considerations of justice forbid punishment without warning.

Disciplinary Code

I. Purpose

The University of Maine Disciplinary Code is designed primarily to ensure peaceful pursuit of intellectual and subsidiary activities at the University of Maine or under its auspices and to ensure the safety of persons engaging in those pursuits while they are at the University or under its auspices.

II. *Jurisdiction*

The Disciplinary Code is limited to the regulation of individuals'

A. conduct

1. occurring on any campus of the University of Maine, on other real property held by the University, or on University-related real property, or

2. involving University-held or University-related personal property, or

3. occurring at activities pursued under the auspices of the University, or

4. occurring on another college or university campus, except where such conduct is permissible under the rules and regulations governing that campus.

B. conduct, regardless of where it occurs, indicating that the presence of the student at the University results in a substantial danger of physical harm to persons in the University community.

As used in this section, the following definitions apply:

"Real property held by the University" and "University-held personal property" are to include property held in any manner, whether owned, rented, chartered, or otherwise engaged. Regulation of conduct occurring on or involving such property shall not be made to depend upon the manner in which that property is held.

"University-related real property" and "University-related personal property" shall include only such property as is held by members of the faculty or administration, by other University officers or employees, or by University-approved organizations. "University-related personal property" shall include also any document or record issued or purporting to be issued by the University.

"Activities pursued under the auspices of the University" shall include any activities specifically sponsored or participated in by the University or by any University organization. Such activities do not include informal off-campus gatherings of students.

The conduct referred to in subsection B. shall include only acts physically harming another individual or threatening him with physical harm, and acts, although not resulting in physical harm, that are committed in reckless disregard of possible physical harm.

IV. Regulations

A. Dismissal is the maximum sanction that may be imposed for the following forms of conduct:

1. Theft, occurring under the conditions of section II. A.

2. Destruction, damage, misuse, or defacement of property by acts committed deliberately or in reckless disregard of possible harm to property, occurring under the conditions of section II. A.

3. Lewd or indecent conduct, occurring under the conditions of section II. A.

4. Cheating, including plagiarism, on University work.

5. Knowingly falsifying University records or documents, or knowingly causing University records or documents to be falsified.

6. Knowingly furnishing false information to members of the University faculty or to other officers or employees of the University in pursuit of their official duties.

7. Possession or use of narcotics, marijuana, hallucinogens, amphetamines, or similar drugs, occurring under the conditions of section II. This provision is not applicable to any drug prescribed for the student by a licensed physician.

8. Intentional infliction of physical harm to another individual or acts committed for the purpose of inflicting such harm or in reckless disregard that such harm might result, occurring under the conditions of section II.

9. Knowingly assisting in the infraction of any of the provisions of subsections 1. to 8. of section IV. A.

10. Any infraction of the provisions of this Code while under disciplinary sanction or the conditions of a disciplinary sanction.

11. Two or more acts in violation of a single subsection of section IV. B.

B. Suspension is the maximum sanction that may be imposed for the following forms of conduct:

1. Violation of rules establishing house closing or visiting hours.

2. Trespass on any University-held or University-related property access to which is by rule or convention denied to students in general or to the individual student at a time when such access is prohibited. This conduct shall include trespassory violation of dormitory or housing rules. "Property" indicates such property as is included in section II.

3. Possession or use of alcholic beverages under the conditions of section II. A. 1., excluding such possession or use by persons over twenty-one years of age in homes of members of the faculty or other officers or employees of the University or of married students. "Possession or use" shall not include internal presence of alcoholic beverages.

4. Intentionally placing a person in reasonable fear of imminent physical harm.

5. Two or more acts in violation of a single subsection of section IV. C. within a twelve-month period.

6. Assisting in the infraction of any of the provisions of subsections 1. to 4. of section IV. B.

C. Disciplinary probation is the maximum sanction that may be imposed for the following forms of conduct:

1. Disorderly behavior, occurring under the conditions of section II. A.

2. Violation, after written warning, of parking or traffic regulations of the University.

3. Violation, after written warning, of University library regulations.

4. Unauthorized use of a motor vehicle, occurring under the conditions of section II.

North Dakota

The status of the University of North Dakota as a residential academic community and the student's position as a citizen in that community make necessary certain regulations designed to protect and promote positive learning activity, maintain order, and control behavior that infringes on the rights and freedom of others. The University's primary objective is to provide human and physical resources—and an environment—for the complete education of its students. A college education is primarily academic/intellectual in nature, but it also includes the development of attitudes and values which facilitate mature, responsible behavior. Student conduct, then, is not considered in isolation within the University community, but as an integral part of the educational process.

In general, the behavioral norms on the campus, in University buildings, and in classrooms are those of common decency and decorum, recognition of the rights and property of others, honesty in classwork and elsewhere, and obedience to the laws of the land.

Academic Honesty

Each student is expected to be honest in his academic work. Dishonesty in examinations, papers, or other work is considered an extremely serious offense by the faculty and students.

Respect for Property

It is expected that students show respect for public and private property. Theft of any kind is unacceptable. The destruction or mutilation of books, magazines, or other library material will not be condoned. Equally repugnant is the unauthorized use of, damage to, or destruction of University buildings, equipment, and property.

Financial Obligation of the Student

It is the responsibility of the student to make satisfactory arrangements for the settling of accounts with the University.

Failure to settle a University account will result either in cancellation of the student's enrollment or the placing of a "hold" on the student's official records and future registration.

The intentional passing of worthless checks to the University or the failure to redeem promptly a worthless check passed unintentionally to the University is considered sufficient cause for stringent disciplinary action.

Distributing Printed Materials

Students may distribute leaflets or other free printed material outdoors on-campus if the individual or group responsible for the materials is clearly identified and if the distributors do not obstruct traffic, block entrances to buildings or driveways, harass or interfere with passers-by, disturb others by excessive noise, or litter the premises. Those who wish to distribute at a sponsored outdoor event must have the approval of the sponsoring group.

Distribution inside University buildings is *not* permitted except at properly authorized meetings, with consent of the sponsor, or in areas of the University Center designated by the Director. Housing units may or may not permit distribution, according to their own rules.

Solicitation

All solicitation on University property must have the approval of the responsible University administrator or student group.* If approved, the solicitation in residence halls, fraternity houses, or sorority houses must be confined to the public areas of the hall or house; solicitors are not to enter the living quarters of an individual student. Door-to-door solicitation in University family housing projects is not permitted.

University I.D.

Misuse, alteration or forging of University identification to obtain privileges to which you or others are not entitled is an offense against the University.

Examples of misuse are using an I.D. card issued to another person or using an altered or forged card.

* The Director of the University Center and the Director of Housing are the responsible University administrators who must authorize solicitation within the University Center and in University on-campus housing, respectively. Solicitation within fraternity and sorority houses is determined by the residents of the houses. Other campus solicitation must be authorized by the President or his representative.

Falsification of Documents

The falsification, defacing, altering, or mutilating of any official University document — I.D. card, receipt, transcript, etc. — or the withholding or falsification of information on an admissions application, subjects the student to cancellation of registration.

Fireworks & Firearms

The detonating of fireworks or other explosives, or the discharging of firearms on campus without the express knowledge and consent of appropriate University officials is prohibited.

Keys

The possession of keys to University buildings by students who have not been authorized to use such keys is strictly forbidden. The duplication of a key issued to a student by the University is prohibited.

Hazing

Hazing is prohibited on- or off-campus. Hazing is defined to include any actions, activities, or situation intentionally created to produce unnecessary or undue mental or physical discomfort, embarrassment, harrassment, ridicule, excessive fatigue, interference with scholarship or personal lives, or exposure to situations wherein one's physical or mental well-being may be endangered.

Drugs

The University unequivocally disapproves of, and will not condone, the illegal possession or professionally unsupervised use of hallucinogenic or narcotic drugs by any member of the University community. It is considered an especially serious offense to sell, provide, share, or distribute such drugs illegally.

Disorderly Behavior

Behavior which is disturbing or disorderly, e.g., physical or verbal abuse of another person, obscene language or actions, disrespect for the rights or privileges of others, or drunkenness, detracts from the academic environment and is therefore contrary to the best interests of the University community.

Disorderly behavior by students or non-students at public events on-campus, e.g., athletic contests, or University Center programs, subjects the violator(s) to arrest and referral to civil authorities.

Alcoholic Beverages

The consumption or possession of beer or other alcoholic beverages on the campus or in University housing, including sorority houses and fraternity houses, is forbidden. State and local laws govern family housing.

Persons observed at public events in violation of the City ordinance regarding possession or consumption of alcoholic beverages are subject to arrest and referral to civil authorities.

Telephone Abuse

Students who defraud the University and the telephone company by failing to give correct information on long distance calls or on charge numbers are subject to disciplinary action, as are individuals who use unauthorized attachments or extensions to telephones.

Gambling

University students are expressly forbidden to gamble for money or other things of value.

Cheating or Plagiarism

These words refer to the use of unauthorized books or notes or otherwise securing help in a test; copying tests, assignments, reports or term papers; or being in unauthorized places like offices, buildings after hours, or a professor's office without his permission. These forms of dishonesty are very serious matters in a University.

In cases of cheating or plagiarism, the instructor shall refer the case to his academic dean. After meeting with the instructor and student involved, the academic dean shall have the authority to act.

A student has the right to appeal the academic dean's action to the Student Relations Committee. The student's appeal is initiated with his academic dean.

Purdue University

Student Conduct

2.01. *General*

Students are expected and required to abide by the laws of the State of Indiana and of the United States and the rules and regulations of Purdue University, to conduct themselves in accordance with accepted standards of social behavior, to respect the rights of others and to refrain from any conduct which tends to obstruct the work of the University or to be injurious to the welfare of the University.

2.02. *Misconduct Subject to Disciplinary Penalties*

The following actions constitute misconduct for which students are subject to the disciplinary penalties of expulsion or suspension from the University or disciplinary probation, as such terms are defined in Part 3, Section 3.01.

(a) Dishonesty, such as cheating, plagiarism, or knowingly furnishing false information to the University.

(b) Forgery, alteration, or misuse of University documents, records, or identification.

(c) Obstruction or disruption of teaching, research, administration, disciplinary procedures, or other University activities (as defined below). Such obstruction or disruption, whether involving individual or group conduct, and whether taking the form of force, trespass, seizure, occupation or obstruction of buildings, facilities or property, or of other conduct having such obstructive or disruptive effects, or the inciting of others to any conduct having such effects, is directly opposed to the maintenance of academic freedom and to the accomplishment of the mission of the University. Consequently, any student found guilty, under hearing procedures now or hereafter prescribed or approved by the Board of Trustees, of violation of this subsection, will automatically be subject to a minimum disciplinary penalty of suspension for the remainder of the semester (or summer session) during which the offense occurred, and for the next full academic semester (and any intervening summer session) thereafter, and to any additional disciplinary penalty which may be imposed in a particular case by the appropriate tribunal under the hearing procedure.

(d) Physical abuse of any person on University property (as defined below) or in the course of a University activity, or conduct which threatens or endangers the health or safety of any such person.

(e) Theft of or damage to property of the University or of a member of the University community or campus visitor.

(f) Unauthorized entry to, or use, or occupancy of University facilities.

(g) Violation of University policies, rules or regulations concerning student organizations, the use of University facilities, or the time, place and manner of meetings or demonstrations on University property.

(h) Use, possession, or distribution of narcotics or dangerous drugs except as expressly permitted by law.

(i) Violation of University regulations governing students who live in University-owned or controlled property, or in fraternities, sororities, and cooperative houses.

(j) Disorderly conduct or lewd, indecent, or obscene conduct or expression on University property, or on the property of fraternities, sororities, and cooperative houses, or at University-sponsored or supervised functions.

(k) Failure to comply with directions of University officials acting in the performance of their duties.

(l) Conduct which materially and adversely affects the student's suitability as a member of the Purdue University community.

University of Tennessee

Standards of Conduct

Misconduct for which students are subject to discipline falls into the following categories:

1. Plagiarism, cheating, or knowingly furnishing false in-

formation to the University or other similar forms of dishonesty in University-related affairs.

2. Forgery, alteration, destruction or misuse of University documents, records, or identification.

3. Obstruction or disruption of teaching, research, administration, disciplinary procedures, or other University activities, including its public service functions, or of other authorized activities on University premises.

4. Physical abuse of any person on University-owned or controlled property or at University-sponsored or supervised functions, or conduct which threatens or endangers the health or safety of any such person.

5. Theft of or damage to property of the University or of a member of the University community or campus visitor.

6. Unauthorized use of or entry to University facilities.

7. Use, possession, distribution, or being under the influence of narcotics or drugs, except as permitted by law, while on University-owned or controlled property or at University-sponsored or supervised activities.

8. Disorderly conduct or lewd, indecent, or obscene conduct or expression on University-owned or controlled property or at University-sponsored or supervised functions.

9. Possession, while on University-owned or controlled property or at University-sponsored or supervised activities, of any weapons such as, but not limited to, rifles, shotguns, ammunition, handguns and air guns, including explosives such as firecrackers, etc., unless authorized in writing by the Superintendent of Safety and Security.

10. Failure to pay promptly all University bills, accounts, and other University financial obligations when due.

11. Gambling on University-owned or controlled property.

12. Groups of students gathering on or adjacent to the campus in a manner which causes damage to public or private property, causes injuries to persons, or interferes with the orderly functioning of the University or the normal flow of traffic.

13. Arrest for violation of local, state, or federal law when it appears that the student has acted in a way which adversely affects or seriously interferes with the University's normal educational function, or which injures or endangers the welfare of any member of the University community.

14. Possession or use of alcoholic beverages on University-owned or controlled property, except as allowed by law.

15. Violation of properly constituted rules and regulations governing the use of motor vehicles on University-owned or controlled property.

16. Refusal to respond to a request to report to a University administrative office.

17. Failure to comply with directions of University officials acting in the performance of their duties.

18. Violation of written University policies and regulations as stipulated herein or as promulgated and announced by authorized personnel.

19. Inciting other students to violate written University policies and regulations as promulgated and announced by authorized personnel.

Willamette University

Standards of expectation include, but are not limited to the following:

Section 1

Conduct in general should be in accord with common decency, public order and a respect for others.

Section 2

Dress should be appropriate and in good taste. Specific dress regulations within each living organization may be decided by the residents of that living organization.

Section 3

Organization and group functions should be conducted in a manner consistent with Standards of Conduct and the responsibility for the same shall rest with the officers of the organization or leaders of the group. Failure to accept this responsibility shall result in action being taken by the personnel deans.

Section 4

In order to promote the well-being of the university as a whole, the following specific activities are deemed improper:

(a) The possession or use of intoxicants, illegal drugs or narcotics on the campus and on or in any university facility.

(b) The possession and use of firearms on the campus and on or in any university facility, except that rifles and shotguns for recreational purposes may be stored on campus in accordance with established procedures.

(c) Smoking in areas designated by the university in areas within living organizations so designated by the governing bodies of such living organizations.

University of Wisconsin

Section 4

To permit it to carry on its functions, the University may discipline students in non-academic matters in these situations:

(1) For intentional conduct that seriously damages or destroys University property or attempts to seriously damage or destroy University property.

(2) For intentional conduct that indicates a serious danger to the personal safety of other members of the University community.

(3) For intentional conduct that obstructs or seriously impairs University-run or University-authorized activities on any campus, including activities either outdoors or inside a classroom, office, lecture hall, library, laboratory, theater, union, residence hall, or other place where a University-run or University-authorized activity is carried on. The kind of intentional conduct referred to is conduct which by itself or in conjunction with the conduct of others prevents the effective carrying on of the activity—a result which the student knew or reasonably should have known would occur.

In order to illustrate types of conduct which paragraph (3) is designed to cover the following examples are set out. These examples are not meant to illustrate the only situations or types of conduct intended to be covered.

(a) A student would be in violation if he participated in conduct which he knew or should have known would prevent or block physical entry to, or exit from, a University building, corridor, or room to anyone apparently entitled to enter or leave in connection with a University-run or University-authorized activity.

(b) A student would be in violation if, in attending a speech or program on campus sponsored by or with permission of the University, he engaged in shouted interruptions, whistling, derisive laughter, or other means which by itself or in conjunction with the conduct of others, prevented or seriously interfered with, a fair hearing of the speech or program.

(c) A student would be in violation if in a classroom he used techniques similar to those specified in the preceding paragraph, or filibuster-type tactics, or other tactics, which by themselves or in conjunction with the conduct of others, prevented or seriously interfered with the carrying on of the teaching and learning process.

(4) The principles stated in the present section are not intended to preclude discipline for intentional conduct violating any University rule or order which may not fall within one of the above specified categories but is issued pursuant to authorized University functions.

NEW ANSWERS–
ACTUAL AND PROPOSED

Office of Students' Attorney –
The University of Texas:
Student Assembly Bills
and Regents' Rules

The University of Texas Student Assembly in 1969 created the full-time position of students' attorney, to provide group legal services for the members of the Students' Association of the University at Austin. The attorney was selected by a student-faculty committee and his salary comes from a student activities fee. James Boyle, the author of chapter 5 of this volume, is the first attorney to serve in the new position.

Certain difficulties regarding the position of students' attorney surfaced rather quickly after Mr. Boyle's employment in June 1970. The board of regents adopted rules relating to the office of students' attorney, restricting his activities substantially. In January 1971 the board amended those rules to impose even more severe restrictions on the activities of the attorney.

We have reproduced in this appendix the students' assembly act creating the office; the Regents' Rules and Regulations, Chapter X, Sec. 11, as amended; and four measures adopted by the student assembly, presumably to clarify its stand in this matter and to attempt to counter the regents' restrictions. One of the more contentious matters concerns Mr. Boyle's status—whether he is or is not a university employee. The Negotiation of Lease Bill, here reproduced, delineates one attempt of the student assembly to reinforce its claim that the office of students' attorney is an independent position.

Office of the Students' Attorney Act

[*University of Texas Student Assembly Acts 1969, B-75-68-69*]

Section 1. Statement of Purpose

There is found to exist a need for competent, continual legal advice and representation by the Students' Association of the University of Texas at Austin. The concern of this Assembly is that the Students' Association, through its President, would better advance the programs and activities of this association, and the interests of the students which it represents, by having an attorney available at all times. It is further found that the individual students of this association would greatly benefit by having an attorney available to advise them or refer them to an attorney on civil and criminal legal matters. In order to fulfill this need, there shall be a Students' Attorney, and this office is hereby created.

Section 2. Qualifications

The Students' Attorney shall be an attorney admitted to the Bar of the Supreme Court of Texas.

Section 3. Selection

1. The Students' Attorney shall be nominated by a selection committee composed as follows:

    a. the President of the Students' Association as chairman

    b. two members of the faculty; one must be from the School of Law and appointed by the Dean of the School of Law, the other appointed by the President of the Students' Association

    c. two students; one must be from the School of Law and appointed by the President of the Student Bar Association, the other appointed by the President of the Students' Association.

2. The selection committee shall extend efforts in soliciting qualified men for the position of Students' Attorney, and choose one man for the nomination.

3. The nomination of the selection committee shall be submitted to the Student Assembly for approval by a majority vote.

4. The selection committee shall draft a contract, consistent with this act, in order to maintain the office of Students'

Attorney. The attorney shall be given a three year contract, subject to an initial six month probation clause, and subject to removal in accordance with section 7 of this act.

Section 4. Duties of Office

1. The Students' Attorney shall act as counsel to the Students' Association. He shall be available to aid in matters of contracts, suits, complaints, negotiations, and any other activity within the scope of the legal practice as may be required by the Students' Association. His duties shall include, but shall not be limited to the following:

    a. He shall be familiar with state and federal legislation and proposed legislation as it pertains to students, and advise this association thereon. He shall act as agent for this association when requested to do so by the Student Assembly.

    b. He shall consider all matters referred to him by the Student Assembly and the House of Delegates.

    c. He may aid in drafting legislation for the Student Assembly and the House of Delegates and advise the Attorney General.

2. The Students' Attorney may establish a legal referral service program for the benefit of the individual students in conjunction with the Travis County Bar Association. As a part of this service, upon initial contact with the individual student, the Students' Attorney shall advise him as to the substance of his civil and criminal legal rights.

3. The Students' Attorney may represent an individual student in any case which involves the interests of students generally; provided that the Students' Attorney shall accept no fee in such cases. *(Amended by Act B-75-68-69, Oct. 29, 1970.)*

4. If he can avoid problems of professional ethics, and only in such case, the Students' Attorney may extend legal services to individual students forcibly detained in criminal matters. His efforts shall be limited to having the student defendant released from detention or requesting dismissal, but he may not proceed to litigate such cases except in accordance with Advisory Committee policies as approved by the Student Assembly. In such cases legal services shall be extended to in-

dividual students according to priorities of time and severity of potential sanction, as consideration of the students' financial ability to retain other counsel. Records in such cases shall be kept confidential and shall not be disclosed to the administration of the University of Texas at Austin, nor to any other individual or groups. *(Amended by Act B–75–68–69, Oct. 29, 1970.)*

5. Services rendered on behalf of individuals shall be extended only to those students having a current blanket tax.

6. The Students' Attorney shall confine his activities to legal matters in conducting his office, assisting a student in matters affecting him in his role as a student.

7. The Students' Attorney shall not be used so as to invite, encourage or foster the breaking of any law by allowing reliance on his efforts.

Section 5. Authority

The Students' Attorney shall have the power to set up his office as he deems best, recruit law students to assist him, hire a secretary, and conduct such activity that he feels necessary and prudent within the intent of this act in maintaining his office.

Section 6. Funding and Budget

Funding shall come from appropriations of Blanket Tax Funds. Efforts should be extended to secure gifts, grants and donations to reduce the financial burden on students, to ensure continued operation, and to allow for expanded activities. Blanket Tax appropriations shall be channeled through Student Government funds, for disbursement consistent with the following budget:

funds available for attorney's salary	$14,000
funds available for secretary	5,000
office equipment	2,000
office expense	1,500
travel expense	500
library and miscellaneous	2,000
Total	$25,000

The salary of the Students' Attorney shall range from $9,000 to $14,000 yearly as decided by the Selection Committee, according to experience, ability, and other pertinent factors.

Section 7. Removal

The attorney may be dismissed according to terms of his contract, by recommendation of two-thirds (2/3) of the total membership of the Student Assembly. The recommendation shall be brought before a five member law faculty committee appointed by the Dean of the School of Law, which will decide independently and dismiss for good cause.

Regents' Rules and Regulations Relating to the Office of the Students' Attorney

[*Part II, Chapter 10, Section 11, as amended January 29, 1971.*]

Sec. 11. Employment of Attorney by Students' Association or other agency of Student Government

11.1 Any attorney retained in any manner by a Students' Association or other agency of student government at any component institution of The University of Texas System shall not act as counsel of record nor represent any student, faculty member, or staff member, or any group or combination of students, faculty members, or staff members, of System Administration or any component institution of The University of Texas System:

11.11 In any matter that requires an administrative decision to be made by any officer, committee, board, or agency of a component institution of The University of Texas System, The University of Texas System, or the Board of Regents of The University of Texas System.

11.12 At any stage of any criminal proceeding in any federal, state, county, or local court.

11.13 At any stage of any civil proceeding in any federal, state, county, or local court where such proceeding is directly or indirectly against or antagonistic to the interest of The

University of Texas System or any component institution thereof, or against or antagonistic to the interests of any person who is sued in his official capacity as an officer of the System or any component institution thereof.

11.2 Any contract or agreement for legal services entered into by a Students' Association or other agency of student government with an attorney whose remuneration will be paid from funds under the control and management of the Board of Regents of The University of Texas System, including funds from student fees, whether mandatory or permissive, is expressly subject to the applicable provisions of the Regents' Rules and Regulations, including, but are not limited to, the foregoing provisions of this Section 11 and the following: . . .

* * *

Students' Attorney Advisory Committee Bill B13-70-71

Section 1. The Student Assembly shall nominate and elect three students who shall comprise the Students' Attorney Advisory Committee, which nominations and elections shall be held in the same regularly scheduled meeting of the Student Assembly at which this Bill is enacted.

Section 2. The student members of the Committee shall serve a term of one [1] year.

Section 3. The purposes of the Committee shall be to consult with the Students' Attorney concerning the status of Constitutional liberties on the campus of the University of Texas at Austin and to receive from the Students' Attorney such advice as he may offer concerning the legal status, obligations, rights and privileges of the Students' Association.

Section 4. The duties of the Committee shall be to request from the Students' Attorney all opinions on legal matters that may be referred to the Committee by the Student Assembly and to report the opinions delivered by the Students' Attorney concerning such matters.

Section 5. The Committee shall elect one of its student members as Chairman, and within two [2] weeks from the date of his election, which election shall be held on the same date as the committee was established and its members chosen, the Chairman so elected shall report to the Assembly concerning the Committee's progress pursuant to this Bill.

Section 6. The Committee shall invite two [2] professors of the School of Law of the University of Texas at Austin to join the Committee in its endeavors, and the Committee shall maintain the number of such professors on the Committee at two [2].

Consultation Proposal R7-70-71

(1) Whenever any administrator or administrative body of the University of Texas System shall propose a rule or regulation that is jurisdictionally applicable to the students of the University of Texas at Austin, whether applicable to students individually or in association with other persons, and such rule or regulations shall vitally affect students and student interests in non-academic areas, said administrator or administrative body shall, prior to enactment and enforcement of the proposed rule, consult the Students' Association, its members, representatives and officers, concerning their opinions, thoughts, and beliefs in regard to the proposed rule.

(2) Whenever any proposed rule is such that consultation with the Students' Association is required, and after such consultation there is no agreement between the interested parties in regard to the Constitutional effect or questions involved, said parties shall invite the Students' Attorney to join them in consultation on such issues and in drafting of such proposed rules and regulations.

Infringement of Rights Resolution R6-70-71

Any and all such attempted influence, control, management, and infringement shall be deemed inoperative as against the Association and the Students' Attorney, regardless of the form that such attempted influence, control, management, or infringement may take, and regardless of the person, persons, office, or organization by whom such attempts are made.

Negotiation of Lease Bill B17-70-71

The President of the Students' Association is hereby authorized to negotiate with the aforementioned governing board of the Texas Union in order to secure physical facilities in the Texas Union for the use of such Association and its programs, under fair and equitable terms, and

The President of the Students' Association shall reduce the results of such negotiations to a writing in the form of a lease of the necessary and desirable space in the Texas Union; and

The President shall report as to the results of such negotiations whenever they they are complete; and

The Assembly may thereafter appropriate necessary funds as compensation under such lease, to be paid to the Texas Union Board.

Legal Aid Clinic for Students —
The University of Michigan*

When the Washtenaw County Legal Aid program was first started, indigent students were accepted as clients as well as other indigent members of the community. For approximately the last two years, the Legal Aid Clinic has refused to accept any students as clients. This decision was made because of the increased work load at the Clinic, and a determination by the Board that the first obligation of the Clinic was to the community poor. In order to aid students in their personal problems there is a need for the University to provide minimum legal advice and service as an extension of the University counseling service.

This memorandum represents the understanding of the University of Michigan and the Washtenaw County Legal Aid Society concerning the establishment of a branch Legal Aid Clinic on the University of Michigan campus.

(1) The University agrees to provide up to $20,000 on a twelve-month basis, and office space, including access to a core library (a first-year cost up to $20,000 plus space).

(2) The Washtenaw County Legal Aid Society will be responsible for providing legal services of approximately 1845 hours, attorney time during the twelve-month period, and for coordinating the volunteer work of law students to work in the Clinic. Records will be maintained, and a quarterly report and statement for services will be made to the University. Payments will be made quarterly. General policies of operation of the

---

* Approved by Board of Regents, The University of Michigan, January 21, 1971.

branch office will be determined by the Washtenaw County Legal Aid Society within the following guidelines:

(a) Legal services will be available for students and dependents meeting the tests of indigency. Legal service for fee generating cases are not permitted under standards of the Washtenaw County Legal Aid Society. Thus suits where significant amounts of money are involved and attorney fees normally would result, for example, suits challenging the University's residency policies, or use of University funds, which if successful would normally generate an attorney fee, would not be handled.

(b) Legal services on a non-continuing basis may be provided for student organizations when the University is not a defendant if the over-all work load of the office permits. The standards of the Legal Aid Society for determining eligibility will apply.

(3) The initial commitment to this program will be for one year from the time of commencement, and will be reviewed from time to time.

Civil Sanctions:
A Model University Bylaw*

1. Purposes: Relation to Criminal and Civil Law
University discipline is intended

(a) to deter conduct of members of the university which is harmful to others;

(b) to teach its members that individuals are accountable for harms they cause to others;

(c) to repair internal relationships which may be damaged by student misconduct; and

(d) to enable the university to continue its assistance in the development and rehabilitation of alienated or miscreant young people.

It is not a primary purpose of university discipline to vent the general public's indignation at the antisocial behavior of its students. For that purpose, the general public's own legal system should be employed. Members of the university community are subject to both civil and criminal laws in full measure, and university punishment will not be used as a substitute for the enforcement of such laws.

2. Academic Offenses
Students offending rules against cheating, or similar rules of

---

* This proposed bylaw is not offered as a complete provision. Additional, more specific, substantive provisions should be included, as well as provisions establishing a tribunal and a procedure. The proposal is made in such detail only with great diffidence. It cannot be presumed that all the problems arising from a shift to a civil model have been resolved. Premature publication is justified only for the purpose of stimulating more mature consideration. Paul D. Carrington.

a strictly academic nature, may be penalized by having a full
and fair statement describing their offense, in terms approved
by the judiciary, included as a part of their academic record.
In addition, the judiciary may approve an award of a failing
grade in the course in which the offense occurred, a forfeiture
of all academic credit for the semester, or exclusion from a
particular course of study, department, or school.

3. Restitution

Members of the university community who wrongfully cause
harm to the university or to other members or guests are
obligated to make restitution for harm resulting from their
misconduct:

(a) Restitution for tangible harms may include medical or
repair bills and replacement costs. Movable property which is
damaged or misappropriated as a result of misconduct may be
replaced at the option of the owner and then becomes the
property of the offending party.

(b) Restitution for intangible harms will be calculated according to standard formulae announced by the judiciary.
Thus, a student who is harmed by physical or extreme verbal
abuse which obstructs his study is entitled to restitution based
on a formula measuring the intangible harm by the economic
cost to the average student of the period of study obstructed.
Similarly, a student or employer who is harmed by the obstruction of an employment interview is entitled to restitution
measured by the average cost of such interviews.

4. Deterrence of Harmful Misconduct

The judiciary will impose additional obligations, not to exceed double the amount imposed for restitution, if restitution
is deemed an inadequate deterrent to similar acts of misconduct by the offender or other students. In fixing the
amount of such a deterrent obligation, the judiciary may take
account of the financial means of the offender, his motives,
penalties imposed by outside authority, and any other factors
bearing on the need for additional deterrence. A deterrent
obligation will not be imposed on a student who has been
prosecuted under the criminal law or who has been subjected

to civil liability for punitive damages for the same act of misconduct, or against whom criminal prosecution is pending. Any party seeking the imposition of a deterrent obligation thereby undertakes not to seek criminal punishment or punitive civil damages against the same student for the same act.

5. *Class Claims*

The students of the university are entitled to be compensated for any harm wrongfully inflicted on the learning environment by members of the university community.*Claims for such compensation may be brought by any student or teacher affected by the alleged act of misconduct. In such cases, the complainant, if successful, will be compensated for his trouble in the amount of fifteen per cent of the assessed recovery; the balance will be paid for the benefit of the scholarship fund.

6. *Payment*

Obligations are due when the decision of the reviewing authority is announced, or when the time for seeking review has elapsed, unless the judiciary otherwise provides, by the terms of its decision. Offenders lacking the means to make immediate satisfaction will be authorized by the judiciary to extend payment by installments over a period not to exceed one year. No degree will be conferred nor transcript issued for a student whose installment payments have not been completed. Employees may be required to authorize payroll deductions as a condition to the right to extend the time for payment.

7. *Limitation on Remedies*

In no case will an obligation of more than 1,000 dollars be imposed by the judiciary on a student for a single act of misconduct. For the purpose of this rule, each day of continuous misconduct will constitute a separate act. To the extent

---

* Formulae for computing the value of harms to the learning environment might be provided. Thus, the cost of an hour of classroom instruction might be computed by dividing the teaching budget by the number of hours of instruction. The product of that division might be regarded as an appropriate measure of restitution for a class disruption.

that obligations enforced under this bylaw are inadequate to compensate the university or individual members of the university community for harms caused by misconduct, resort must be had to the civil courts. Amounts paid in meeting obligations imposed under paragraphs 3 or 4 will be credited against any corresponding civil recovery.

8. Multiple Offenders: Joint and Several Liability

A member of the university community who has joined in an act of misconduct with others will be subject to full restitutionary and deterrent obligations. However, only one payment shall be required for each item of tangible or intangible harm; a member who fully meets an obligation for which others are also liable is entitled to equal contribution from all whose liability is established. A respondent may bring others into the proceeding for the purpose of having their joint liability established, in order that secondary obligations can be imposed.

9. Exclusions and Discharge

A student who has not met an obligation imposed by the judiciary within ten days after it becomes due will be excluded from the university until he meets the obligation. Exclusionary penalties will not otherwise be imposed. Students who are absent from the university for a full semester because of a sentence imposed pursuant to a criminal conviction must apply for readmission and will be considered for admission on the same terms as those applied to other applicants for readmission who have been away for the same period of time. A failure or a refusal of an employee to meet an obligation determined by the judiciary may be cause for discharge.

A LEGAL REMEDY

Temporary Restraining Order
with Self-executing Clause

IN THE DISTRICT COURT IN AND FOR THE
COUNTY OF BOULDER
STATE OF COLORADO
Civil Action No. 26035

THE REGENTS OF THE UNIVERSITY OF
COLORADO, a body corporate;
FREDERICK P. THIEME, President
of the University of Colorado,

Plaintiffs,

vs.

LYLE FULKS, et al.,

Defendants.

} MODIFIED TEMPORARY
RESTRAINING ORDER

This matter came on initially on the 14th day of April, 1970, at 10:45 o'clock a.m., and the Court, *ex parte*, issued its Temporary Restraining Order which would expire under the rules at 10:45 a.m. April 24, 1970, and which Order set the application of Plaintiffs for Preliminary Injunction for hearing on April 24, 1970, at 10:00 a.m. The matter subsequently came on to be heard on the Motion of the Defendants to Dissolve the Temporary Restraining Order at 1:30 p.m. Friday April 17, 1970, at which time counsel for the Defendants suggested that the Temporary Restraining Order could be modified so as to meet the objections of the Defendants, and counsel for the Plaintiffs offered to tender certain proposed modifications. The Court denied the Motion to Dissolve and set the matter for consideration of any Motion to Modify that might be filed, at 9:00 a.m. on Monday, April 20, 1970. Such a motion was filed by Plaintiffs on April 19, 1970, with the Judge, and with copies to attorneys for Defendants, and the Court, having read the file, the authorities cited by both parties, and having heard the statements and arguments of counsel,

DOTH FIND that from the allegations stated in the verified Complaint of Plaintiffs, immediate and irreparable injury, loss or damage would have resulted to Plaintiffs before notice could be served and a hearing had thereon; that this was and is a proper case for granting a Temporary Restraining Order, and for continuing the Temporary Restraining Order until the time fixed for factual hearing on Plaintiffs' application for a Preliminary Injunction; that unless a Temporary Restraining Order was granted and is now continued, the Defendants will engage in activities calculated to interfere with the lawful missions, processes, procedures or functions of the University; that the administrative and educational processes of the University will be substantially disrupted and a serious danger to the health and safety of its students, school officials, employees and invited guests will result; and that Plaintiffs, at the time the said Temporary Restraining Order was entered, had no plain, speedy or adequate remedy at law, and it is, therefore,

ORDERED that the Defendants, and their agents, servants, employees and attorneys, and any and every person acting or threatening to act in active concert and participation with them, are prevented, forbidden and restrained from:

(a) entering any academic or administrative building of the University of Colorado for the purpose of conducting any demonstration, protest, or remonstrance;

(b) willfully denying to students, school officials, employees, and invited guests of the University, lawful freedom of movement on the campus, lawful use of the property or facilities of the University of Colorado, or the right of lawful ingress and egress to any of the University's physical facilities;

(c) willfully impeding the staff or faculty of the University in the lawful performance of their duties, or willfully impeding any student of the University in the lawful pursuit of his or her educational activities, through the use of restraint, abduction, coercion, or intimidation, or when force and violence are present or threatened;

(d) engaging in any intentional overt activity designed or calculated to obstruct, disrupt, or interfere with any of the lawful missions, processes, procedures, or functions of the University. This paragraph does not prohibit orderly, peaceful, non-disruptive demonstrations or other activities within areas normally available for public use outside academic or administrative buildings of the University of Colorado; and it is

FURTHER ORDERED that if any of the Defendants, or any person acting in concert or participation with them, shall willfully disobey this Order, any peace officer be and is hereby authorized and directed to forthwith apprehend and arrest such person or persons and take said person or persons into custody and forthwith bring such person or persons before this Court to show cause why he or they should not be punished therefor and a fine or imprisonment imposed to vindicate the dignity of this Court, and it is further

ORDERED that the application of Plaintiffs for a Preliminary Injunction herein shall be and it is hereby set for hearing before this Court on April 23rd, 1970, at 2:30 p.m., and it is further

ORDERED that this Temporary Restraining Order, unless extended by the Court as provided by the Colorado Rules of Civil Procedure, shall expire at 10:45 a.m., Friday, April 24, 1970.

Done in Open Court this 20th day of April, 1970, at 11:15 o'clock a.m.

THE POLITICAL RESPONSE
TO CAMPUS DISRUPTION

Federal Law Denying
Financial Assistance
to Disrupters

The federal legislation reproduced below provides that various forms of financial assistance shall be denied to individuals who are guilty of serious disruption of educational institutions.

Department of Labor, and Department of Health, Education, and Welfare Appropriation Act, 1969
(Public Law 90 — 557)

Section 411

No part of the funds appropriated under this Act shall be used to provide a loan, guarantee of a loan or a grant to any applicant who has been convicted by any court of general jurisdiction of any crime which involves the use of or the assistance to others in the use of force, trespass or the seizure of property under control of an institution of higher education to prevent officials or students at such an institution from engaging in their duties or pursuing their studies.

Higher Education Amendments of 1968
(Public Law 90 — 575)

20 U.S.C.A. § 1060. Eligibility for Student Assistance

(a) If an institution of higher education determines, after affording notice and opportunity for hearing to an individual attending, or employed by, such institution, that such individual has been convicted by any court of record of any crime which was committed after October 16, 1968, and which involved the use of (or assistance to others in the use of) force, disruption, or the seizure of property under control of any institution of higher education to prevent officials or students in such institution fron engaging in their duties or pursuing their studies, and that such crime was of a serious nature and contributed to a substantial disruption of the administration of the institution with respect to which such crime was committed, then the institution which such individual attends, or is employed by, shall deny for a period of two years any further payment to, or for the direct benefit of, such individual under any of the programs specified in subsection (c) of this section. If an institution denies an individual assistance under the authority of the preceding sentence of this subsection, then any institution which such individual subsequently attends shall deny for the remainder of the two-year period any further payment to, or for the direct benefit of, such individual under any of the programs specified in subsection (c) of this section.

(b) If an institution of higher education determines, after affording notice and opportunity for hearing to an individual attending, or employed by, such institution, that such individual has willfully refused to obey a lawful regulation or order of such institution after October 16, 1968, and that such refusal was of a serious nature and contributed to a substantial disruption of the administration of such institution, then such institution shall deny, for a period of two years, any further payment to, or for the direct benefit of, such individual under any of the programs specified in subsection (c) of this section.

(c) The programs referred to in subsections (a) and (b) of this section are as follows:

(1) The student loan program under title II of the National Defense Education Act of 1958.

(2) The educational opportunity grant program under part A of title IV of the Higher Education Act of 1965.

(3) The student loan insurance program under part B of title IV of the Higher Education Act of 1965.

(4) The college work-study program under part C of title IV of the Higher Education Act of 1965.

(5) Any fellowship program carried on under title II, III, or V of the Higher Education Act of 1965 or title IV or VI of the National Defense Education Act of 1958.

(d) (1) Nothing in this Act, or any Act amended by this Act, shall be construed to prohibit any institution of higher education from refusing to award, continue, or extend any financial assistance under any such Act to any individual because of any misconduct which in its judgment bears adversely on his fitness for such assistance.

(2) Nothing in this section shall be construed as limiting or prejudicing the rights and prerogatives of any institution of higher education to institute and carry out an independent, disciplinary proceeding pursuant to existing authority, practice, and law.

(3) Nothing in this section shall be construed to limit the freedom of any student to verbal expression of individual views or opinions.

Guidelines on Questions
Relating to Tax Exemption
and Political Activities*

Recent activities on college campuses have given rise to expressions of concern within colleges and universities and on the part of members of Congress and others that institutions of higher education may inadvertently or otherwise involve themselves in political campaigns in such a way as to raise questions as to their entitlement to exemption under Section 501 (c) (3) of the Internal Revenue Code and as to liability under other provisions of Federal law. Activities which would bring into serious question the entitlement of a college or university to tax exemption could undermine the private support of higher education as a whole, so essential to the very existence of many such institutions. For this reason, educational institutions benefiting from the tax exemption should be aware of the problem and exercise care to make certain that their activities remain within the limits permitted by the statute.

Exemption of colleges and universities from Federal income taxes is dependent upon their qualifying as institutions organized and operated *exclusively* for religious, charitable, or educational purposes described in Section 501 (c) (3) of the Internal Revenue Code. For some years that section has provided that "no substantial part of the activities of" an exempt institution may be "carrying on propaganda, or otherwise at-

---

* Statement of the American Council on Education, June 19, 1970.

tempting, to influence legislation" and further, that an exempt institution may "not participate in, or intervene in (including the publishing or distributing of statements), any political campaign on behalf of any candidate for public office."

By the Tax Reform Act of 1969, the last-quoted prohibition was incorporated in companion provisions of the Internal Revenue Code dealing with the deduction of contributions for income, gift and estate tax purposes. As interpreted, this provision would deny exempt status to institutions engaging in legislative activities which are *substantial* in the light of all the facts and circumstances. Additionally, it *absolutely* proscribes participation in or intervention by an exempt institution in any "political campaign on behalf of any candidate for public office."

The mere rearrangement of an academic calendar for the purpose of permitting students, faculty and other members of the academic community to participate in the election process, without more, would not be deemed intervention or participation by the institution itself in a campaign on behalf of a candidate. Nor does it constitute proscribed legislative activity. This assumes that the recess period is in fact a substitute for another period which would have been free of curricular activity, and that the university itself does not otherwise intervene in a political campaign. During the period of the recess, members of the academic community should be entirely free to participate in the election process or not as they choose and should be so advised. The case may be different if the academic calendar, in fact, is shortened rather than rearranged for the purpose of permitting students, faculty and other members of the academic community to participate in the election process. In that case the question might be raised whether releasing faculty and staff members from normal duties, with pay, to participate in the process represents an indirect participation by the institution itself in a political campaign on behalf of a candidate for public office. Presumably those whose employment obligation is not limited to or governed by the academic year could be permitted to adjust their vacation period to permit time off during a political campaign in lieu of a vacation at another time. (Shortening of the calendar could also generate complaints that the institution is not providing a full term of instruction.)

Educational institutions traditionally have recognized and provided facilities on an impartial basis to various activities on the college campuses, even those activities which have a partisan political bent, such as for example, the Republican, Democratic and other political clubs. This presents no problem. However, to the extent that such organizations extend their activities beyond the campus, and intervene or participate in campaigns on behalf of candidates for public office or permit nonmembers of the university community to avail themselves of university facilities or services, an institution should in good faith make certain that proper and appropriate charges are made and collected for all facilities and services provided. Extraordinary or prolonged use of facilities, particularly by nonmembers of the university community, even with reimbursement, might raise questions. Such organizations should be prohibited from soliciting in the name of the university funds to be used in such off-campus intervention or participation.

Every member of the academic community has a right to participate or not, as he sees fit, in the election process. On the other hand, no member of that community should speak or act in the name of the institution in a political campaign.

In order to assure compliance with the requirements of Section 501 (c) (3), universities in their corporate capacities should not intervene or participate in any campaign by endorsing or opposing a candidate or taking a position on an issue involved in the campaign for the purpose of assisting or opposing a candidate. Those who in their official capacity frequently speak for the university should undertake to make it clear when expressing individual views that they are not stating a university position. Whether or not a university has participated in or intervened in a campaign within the meaning of the Internal Revenue Code can be determined only by looking at all past and present facts and circumstances relevant to the question.

We would make three further observations:

1. Colleges and universities may be subject to restraints of the Corrupt Practices Act which forbid corporations or labor unions from making direct or indirect contributions in connection with political campaigns (including primaries). Adherence to the Internal Revenue Code restrictions discussed above should eliminate any questions in connection with this Act.

2. State law governing all of the above may be more stringent and should be examined.

3. There may be special restrictions on the use of facilities provided in whole or in part with Federal funds.

A Compendium of State Legislation in Response to Campus Disorders

The extent of the public concern over tension, disorder, and violence on college campuses is reflected in the numerous laws enacted in recent years in response to the high visibility of the problems. While violence on campus has largely subsided since the May 1970 student strike, the school administrator must continue to plan his operations to conform to the requirements of whatever legislation was enacted in his state, and federal law as well. Some of these laws represent thoughtful and constructive attempts to aid administrators in performing their difficult tasks by carefully defining unlawful behavior and the administrative authority to control it. Others are clearly excessive, visiting upon schools and individuals alike extraordinarily harsh, unrealistic, and often unworkable penalties. Still others appear to be vague and ambiguous, perhaps to the point of questionable constitutional validity.

This Appendix X consists of summaries of the content of laws enacted in 1969 and 1970, and reproduction in full of a few selected laws, to illustrate the extraordinary range and the language of the legislative response to troubled campuses. An exhaustive survey of such legislation is beyond the scope of this volume. We have, however, gathered laws from some twenty-seven states, a substantial cross section of the legislative activity.

Assault or Battery on School Personnel

Arizona

Section 13–245 of the Criminal Code [as amended Laws 1970, Ch. 58, § 1] provides that an assault or battery is aggra-

331

vated when committed against a person whom the attacker knows is a teacher or school employee and is on school grounds or "grounds adjacent thereto." If the offender is unarmed, the penalty is a fine of $100 to $2,000, jail up to one year, or both, or state prison for one to five years. If armed with a gun or other deadly weapon, the first offense is not less than five years in prison; the second, not less than ten years; a third or subsequent offense is twenty years to life. If convicted of a second or subsequent offense, the offender is ineligible for commutation of sentence.

Declaring a State of Emergency

California

Section 22508 [added to the Education Code by A.B. 1286, effective September 4, 1969] defines "civil disturbance" and authorizes the chief administrative officer of any public college or university to declare a state of emergency under a number of circumstances, including civil disturbance.

Section 22509 provides for discretionary partial payment by the state of the cost of police assistance in campus emergencies.

Louisiana

Revised Statutes 17:3109 [Acts 1969, No. 59, § 1] authorizes the president of an institution of higher learning to request the governor to proclaim a state of emergency, under stated circumstances, upon a finding that safety of personnel is imperiled or likely to be imperiled, and that local law officers have failed, refused, or are unable to enforce the laws.

Revised Statutes 14:329.6 sets out the power of the governor to declare a state of emergency.

Ohio

One of a comprehensive set of statutes enacted in Ohio in 1970 [1970 H 1219, effective September 16, 1970], applicable to state universities, authorizes the board of trustees or president of a state-assisted school to declare a state of emergency when there is a "clear and present danger" of disruption. To effect control during the emergency, power is given to limit access, impose a curfew, restrict right of assembly by groups of five or more, and impose reasonable measures to enforce these restrictions. Notice of the action is to be posted or published. The power of the officials to impose restrictions necessary to proper operation, regardless of whether an emergency exists, is specifically preserved in the statute. [Ohio Rev. Code, Tit. 33, § 3345.26]

Direction to Adopt Administrative Rules

California
Section 22635 was added to the Education Code by Assembly Bill 1286, September 4, 1969. This provision directs the governing boards of public colleges and universities to adopt rules governing student behavior along with applicable penalties for violation. Students are to be provided with a copy.

Florida
Section 240.045 of Florida Statutes [S.B. 820, effective July 3, 1969] directs the board of regents of the state university system to adopt rules to discipline students, faculty, or administrative personnel who interfere with or obstruct campus operations. The rules may apply to conduct on or off campus, when relevant to campus functions.

New York
The statute reproduced below is Article 129-A, § 6450 of the Education Law [added by L. 1969, C. 191, effective April 29, 1969]:
§ *6450. Regulation by colleges of conduct on campuses and other college property used for educational purposes*
    1. The trustees or other governing board of every college chartered by the regents or incorporated by special act of the legislature shall adopt rules and regulations for

the maintenance of public order on college campuses and other college property used for educational purposes and provide a program for the enforcement thereof. Such rules and regulations shall govern the conduct of students, faculty and other staff as well as visitors and other licensees and invitees on such campuses and property. The penalties for violations of such rules and regulations shall be clearly set forth therein and shall include provisions for the ejection of a violator from such campus and property, and in the case of a student or faculty violator his suspension, expulsion or other appropriate disciplinary action. Such rules and regulations shall be filed with the regents and the commissioner of education not later than ninety days after the effective date of this act. All amendments to such rules and regulations shall be filed with the regents and the commissioner of education not later than ten days after their adoption.

2. If the trustees or other governing board of a college fails to file the rules and regulations within the time required by this section such college shall not be eligible to receive any state aid or assistance until such rules and regulations are duly filed.

3. Nothing contained in this section is intended nor shall it be construed to limit or restrict the freedom of speech nor peaceful assembly.

North Dakota

Century Code, Title 15, § 15-10-17.1 [S.L. 1969, Ch. 156, § 1] directs the board of higher education to adopt regulations for the conduct of students, faculty, visitors, and staff. The statute directs that the regulations shall provide for ejection, suspension, or expulsion of a student who willfully damages property or willfully obstructs operations. The expulsion is to be regarded solely for property protection and order, not as criminal punishment.

In cases of willful damage or obstruction, the board of higher education is directed to sue persons responsible, asking appropriate damages in civil court. The board may delegate the power to enforce regulations to the chief executive, the faculty, or any administrative committee of an institution.

Special police may be authorized by the board. It is the duty of the head of each institution to sign criminal complaints against violators.

Violation of any regulation by staff or faculty is a breach of contract, making the violator subject to dismissal or cancellation of contract after the hearing which must be provided by regulation.

Virginia

Additional powers were given to governing boards of educational institutions by § 23–9.2:3 of Title 23 of the Code [1970, c. 197]. They may establish rules for acceptance of students, the conduct of students, and their dismissal for violation of rules; rules for hiring and firing teachers and staff; and rules for parking and traffic regulation. Further, the governing board may obtain, by resolution, law enforcement officers to enforce statutes and local ordinances on the campuses.

Disruption on Campus

Arkansas

Sections 41–1447 and 41–1448 [added by Acts 1969, No. 345, § 2] prohibit obstruction or seizure of campus facilities by two or more persons acting jointly. The law is applicable to public and private schools and colleges. Violation is a misdemeanor subject to a fine not less than $200, or jail not less than six months, or both.

California

Section 602.10 [added to the Penal Code by S.B. 496, approved August 30, 1969] imposes a penalty for the willful obstruction of or attempt to obstruct, by physical force, attendance at classes on public college campuses. The penalty is a fine up to $500, or jail up to one year, or both.

Section 71 [added to the Penal Code by S.B. 1382, approved August 30, 1969] provides that threats of injury communicated to officers or employees of public or private educational institutions, with intent to obstruct their performance of duties, is a public offense. A first conviction carries a fine up to $5,000, or a term up to five years in state prison, or jail up to one year, or both. A previous conviction under the statute is required to be charged in the accusatory pleading, and if the previous conviction is found to be true, or is admitted, the penalty is state prison for a term up to five years.

Sections 415.5, 626, 626.2, 626.4, 626.6, and 626.8 were added to the Penal Code by Assembly Bill 534, September 4, 1969.

Section 415.5 makes it a misdemeanor to maliciously and willfully disturb the peace or quiet of any state school of higher education in a number of ways, including loud or unusual noise, quarreling, challenging to fight, and unacceptable language in the presence of women and children. Punishment is by fine up to $200, jail to ninety days, or both. The penalties are increased if the defendant has one or more previous convictions under the new §§ 626–626.8. The court may consider an official report of prior convictions, and it is not necessary that the prior conviction be alleged.

Florida

Section 239.581 [Laws 1969, c. 69–279, effective July 2, 1969; amended by Laws 1969, c. 69–106, §§ 15, 35] authorizes penalties which may be imposed against a student or employee after it has been determined that the individual "participated in disruptive activities" at a state institution of higher learning: (1) against the student, immediate expulsion for a minimum of two years; (2) against the employee, immediate termination of contract, and no future employment at any other such institution.

Maryland

Article 27, § 123A of the Annotated Code [Laws 1970, Ch. 726, effective July 1, 1970] prohibits disturbance of the orderly conduct of any school, college, or university, and the molesting or threatening of any one lawfully on or in the vicinity of a school. Violation is a misdemeanor subject to fine up to $1000 or imprisonment for six months, or both.

Ohio

Section 2923.61 of the Revised Code [1970 H 1219, effective September 16, 1970], reproduced below, establishes the dimensions of and the penalty for the criminal offense of campus disruption. Presumably it applies to offenses on public and private campuses.

§ *2923.61 Disrupting orderly conduct of a college or university.*

(A) No person, in circumstances which create a substantial risk of disrupting the orderly conduct of lawful activities at a college or university, shall willfully or knowingly do any of the following:

(1) Enter or remain upon the land or premises of a college or university, or any separate room, building, facility, enclosure, or area thereof, without privilege to do so, or, being on or in any such land, premises, room, building, facility, enclosure, or area, fail or refuse to leave upon request of proper authority, and without reasonable justification or excuse for such failure or refusal,

(2) Violate a restriction on access, curfew, or restriction on assembly imposed pursuant to section 3345.26 of the revised code;

(3) Engage in conduct which urges, incites, or encourages another to violate this section, when such conduct takes place in circumstances which create a clear and present danger of such violation.

(B) No person shall willfully or knowingly:

(1) With force or violence, disrupt the orderly conduct of lawful activities at a college or university;

(2) Engage in conduct which threatens or involves serious injury to persons or property at a college or university.

(C) Whoever violates this section is guilty of disruption, and shall be fined not more than one hundred dollars or imprisoned not more than thirty days, or both, for a first offense. For each subsequent offense, such person shall be fined not more than five hundred dollars or imprisoned not more than six months, or both.

Texas

Article 295a of the Penal Code [Acts 1969, 61st Leg., p. 56, Ch. 21, effective September 1, 1969] applies to all schools, colleges, and universities, public or private. The law defines disruptive activity as obstruction, restraint, seizure, threat of violence, or violence. Violation of the act is a misdemeanor punishable by a fine up to $200 or by confinement in jail for not less than ten days or more than six months, or both; and a third conviction requires a two-year ineligibility to attend any state-assisted school.

Utah

Chapter 142 [Laws 1969, effective May 13, 1969], titled "Enforcement of Law and Order at Institutions of Higher Education," declares the power of governing boards of private and state institutions to deal with interferences, trespass, and property damage on campus. Violation of the act is a misdemeanor. Property damage violations are subject to fine up to $1000 or jail to one year or both. Presumably other misdemeanors will be punished in accord with the general law.

Washington

Force or violence which interferes with college or university operations and threats of force or violence against students, faculty, or administration are punishable as gross misdemeanors, subject to fine up to $500, or jail up to six months, or both. [Ch. 98, Ext. Sess. 1970, H.B. 162]

Wisconsin

"Unlawful assembly" to obstruct use of any building, house or street, and refusal to disperse, is a misdemeanor subject to fine not to exceed $500 or a year in jail, or both.

Anyone causing or taking part in unlawful assembly on college or university property or an abutting highway is guilty of a misdemeanor. [Wis. Stat. Ann. § 947.06(2)]

Drugs

Florida

A 1969 Florida statute [Laws 1969, c. 69–366, effective July 8, 1969] requires that a student arrested for unlawful possession of drugs shall, after an administrative hearing, be suspended until the court disposes of the case. If found guilty by the court, the student is automatically expelled and cannot be readmitted to any other state school for two years. The law also provides for a discretionary waiver of suspension or expulsion if he gives information leading to arrest and conviction of his supplier, or if he voluntarily discloses his possession of the drug before his arrest.

Firearms on Campus

California

Section 626.9 was added to the Penal Code by Assembly Bill 1038, approved June 29, 1970. Except for certain authorized persons, one who brings or possesses a firearm on the grounds or in the buildings of any public school, including colleges and the state university, shall be punished by confinement in jail up to one year, fine up to $100, or both, or by a term in state prison up to five years.

Illinois

Public Act 76–1581, approved September 26, 1969, imposed penalties for possessing or storing weapons, without prior written permission from the chief security officer, on land supported in whole or in part by state funds or federal funds administered by state agencies. The penalty for violation is a fine up to $1000 or imprisonment up to one year. The statute declares that the chief security officer "must grant any reasonable request" for permission.

South Carolina

Section 16–141.1 of the Code of Laws [1969 (56) 319] prohibits carrying or displaying firearms in private school, public school, college, or university buildings, or in any publicly owned building. Violation is a misdemeanor, subject to fine up to $5000 or up to five years in prison, or both.

Texas

Article 295b of the Education Code prohibits interfering with school operation by the "exhibiting or using or threatening to exhibit or use a firearm." Violation is a felony, subject to fine up to $1000 or jail up to six months, or both, or by a term of not more than five years in the state penitentiary.

Forfeiture of State Financial Aid

California

Chapter 4.7 [§§ 31291–31294] was added to Division 22 of the Education Code by Assembly Bill 1286, effective September 4, 1969. A recipient of state financial aid who is convicted of a public offense arising from a disruption, or is found guilty of disruption in an administrative hearing, may be declared ineligible to receive funds for as long as two years. There is provision for notice and a hearing. Findings of the hearing board must be in writing.

Illinois

Section 30–17 was added to the School Code by Public Act 76–1581 (1969), effective September 26, 1969. This law directs that scholarships provided by state funds or granted by state institutions, whether used at a public or private school, shall be revoked if it is determined that the recipient, using means not constitutionally protected, took part in any disorderly disturbance or followed a course of conduct directed against the institution. Revocation cannot be accomplished until there is an opportunity for the recipient to present evidence in his behalf.

Michigan

Public Act 1970, No. 83, appropriating funds for Michigan institutions of higher education for the fiscal year ending June 30, 1971, contained the provisions reproduced below:

Sec. 4.(c) All institutions of higher learning shall be

required to submit a full report of any incidents that result from any physical violence or the destruction of property including the total damages in dollars incurred. Further, such report will include the number of students arrested, and classes missed due to strikes, boycotts or demonstrations. This report would be due within 30 days.

Sec. 8. Any student who receives scholarship funds under the provisions of Act No. 208 of the Public Acts of 1964, as amended, being sections 390.971 to 390.980 of the Compiled Laws of 1948, or receiving tuition grants under the provisions of Act No. 313 of the Public Acts of 1966, as amended, being sections 390.991 to 390.997 of the Compiled Laws of 1948, for or while in attendance at an institution of higher education, which receives appropriations under this act, and is either convicted in a court of law of the violation of any penal statute or ordinance prohibiting disorderly conduct, violence to a person or damage to property, which violation is committed while participating in any disorder, disruption of the administration of or the rendering of services, or giving of instruction at any such institution, or by the proper authorities of such institutions of violating its rules and regulations while so participating shall forfeit any right or qualification which he may otherwise have for the receipt of further benefits under either or both said acts. Upon final conviction of any such student of any penal violation or determination of violations of such rules or regulations, the president of such institution of learning shall cause report of the same to be forwarded forthwith to the awarding authority under said acts, which authority shall forthwith terminate any such assistance provided under either or both of said acts to such students. Any rule of any such institution relied upon to determine continued eligibility for said scholarship shall be in accord with due process of law including the right of appeal.

Sec. 9. No part of any appropriation made by this act may be used for the payment of any salary or wages to any faculty member or other employee or for the education of students convicted of the offense of interference with normal operations of any public institution of higher education as described in Act No. 26 of the Public Acts of 1970.

Sec. 10. No part of any appropriation made by this act may be used for the payment of any salaries, wages, or fees to any trustees, administrators, faculty member or other employee or for the education of a student, either full or part time, who shall possess or permit to be possessed, without being a peace officer employed by an institution of higher education, any firearm, not registered with the institution, or other dangerous weapon in any university, college or institution of higher education, including all the buildings and grounds under their jurisdiction.

Sec. 11. It is a condition of this appropriation that a student of a college or university who causes willful damage to public property on a campus or other facility of a college or a university and subject to all other legal penalties shall be expelled from the college or university.

North Carolina

Section 116–174.2 [1969, c. 1019] of the General Statutes provides that school administrators are directed to revoke and withdraw all state financial support from any student who is convicted or enters a plea of guilty or nolo contendere upon a charge of any of the unlawful activities listed, from rioting to sitting in.

Pennsylvania

Act No. 116 § 3 of the Session Laws of 1969 authorizes the Higher Education Assistance Agency to deny financial assistance to a student (1) convicted by a court of record of a criminal offense committed after the effective date of the act and which is a misdemeanor involving moral turpitude or a felony; (2) expelled, dismissed or denied enrollment in any college or university for refusal to obey regulations, if such refusal contributed to disruption on campus; or (3) who obstructs campus activities.

The institution is required to immediately furnish names of offenders to the agency, and if any institution refuses to execute an agreement to comply with this statutory mandate, the institution will be denied the status of an approved institution under the act (and thus ineligible for funds).

Wisconsin

Section 36.43 of Statutes Annotated [L. 1969, c. 89, effective June 27, 1969] provides for denial, after notice and hearing, of direct state support for educational purposes to students or employees of state and private colleges and universities. Conditions for denial: (1) convicted in court of record of a crime or violation of ordinance based on a crime; (2) crime must have been committed after November 23, 1969 (date of law); (3) crime must involve use of force, disruption, seizing control of property; (4) crime must be of serious nature, contributing to substantial disruption. The ineligibility term is one semester to two years from date of conviction or affirmation of conviction on appeal, if appealed. Additionally, refusal to obey regulations of a school, if the refusal is of a serious nature and contributes to substantial disruption, requires similar denial of funds, after notice and opportunity for hearing.

Interference, Trespass, Damage to Property

Colorado

The statute reproduced below, effective March 1, 1969, has been used as a model by a number of states, noted *infra*. It is found in Revised Statutes, Article 8.

40-8-21. Declaration of purpose

The general assembly, in recognition of unlawful campus disorders across the nation which are disruptive of the educational process and dangerous to the health and safety of persons and damaging to public and private property, establishes by this section and section 40-8-22 criminal penalties for conduct declared in this section and section 40-8-22 to be unlawful. However, this section and section 40-8-22 shall not be construed as preventing institutions of higher education from establishing standards of conduct, scholastic and behavioral, reasonably relevant to their lawful missions, processes, and functions, and to invoke appropriate discipline for violations of such standards. [Added by L. 69, p. 310, § 1]

40–8–22. Interference with members of staff, faculty, or students of institutions of higher education–trespass–damage to property–misdemeanors–penalties

(1) (a) No person shall, on the campus of any community college, junior college, college, or university in this state, hereinafter referred to as "institutions of higher education," or at or in any building or other facility owned, operated, or controlled by the governing board of any such institution of higher education, willfully deny to students, school officials, employees, and invitees:

(b) Lawful freedom of movement on the campus;

(c) Lawful use of the property, facilities, or parts of any institution of higher education; or

(d) The right of lawful ingress and egress to the institution's physical facilities.

(2) No person shall, on the campus of any institution of higher education, or at or in any building or other facility owned, operated, or controlled by the governing board of any such institution, willfully impede the staff or faculty of such institution in the lawful performance of their duties, or willfully impede a student of such institution in the lawful pursuit of his educational activities, through the use of restraint, abduction, coercion, or intimidation, or when force and violence are present or threatened.

(3) No person shall willfully refuse or fail to leave the property of, or any building or other facility owned, operated, or controlled by the governing board of any such institution of higher education upon being requested to do so by the chief administrative officer, his designee charged with maintaining order on the campus and in its facilities, or a dean of such college or university, if such person is committing, threatens to commit, or incites

others to commit, any act which would disrupt, impair, interfere with, or obstruct the lawful missions, processes, procedures, or functions of the institution.

(4) Nothing in this section shall be construed to prevent lawful assembly and peaceful and orderly petition for the redress of grievances, including any labor dispute between an institution of higher education and its employees, or any contractor or subcontractor or any employee thereof.

(5) Any person who violates any of the provisions of this section shall be deemed guilty of a misdemeanor and, upon conviction thereof, shall be punished by a fine not to exceed five hundred dollars, or imprisoned in the county jail for a period not to exceed one year, or by both such fine and imprisonment. [Added by L. 69, p. 310 § 2]

Florida

Section 877.12 of Florida Statutes declares intentional disruption or interference with the administration or functions of state educational institutions to be a misdemeanor, punishable by fine up to $500 or imprisonment up to six months, or both.

Idaho

Idaho law is identical to the Colorado statute, except for the omission of the last phrase found in Colorado Revised Statutes § 40-8-22(4). [Idaho Sess. Laws 1969, Ch. 223, approved March 21, 1969]

Illinois

Illinois, by Public Act 76-1582, approved September 26, 1969, added Article 21.2 to the Criminal Code, to define and set penalties for interference with a public institution of higher education. The article is substantially modeled after the Colorado statute reproduced *supra*. However, the penalty for the first conviction under the Illinois law is a fine up to $300, imprisonment up to thirty days, or both; a second or subsequent offense carries a penalty of a fine up to $500, or imprisonment up to one hundred twenty days, or both.

By Public Act 76-1581, approved September 26, 1969,

§§ 21–4, 21–5, and 21–6 were added to the Criminal Code. Noting the gravity of widespread campus disorders and the resulting damage, the general assembly imposed severe penalties for criminal damage to state-supported property and criminal trespass to state-supported land. For property damage, the penalty is a fine up to $1000, imprisonment to one year, or both; if damage exceeds $500, the fine may be as high as $5000, or prison up to five years, or both. Criminal trespass, which consists of going onto the land after receiving notice immediately prior to entry that such entry is forbidden, is punishable by fine up to $1000, or imprisonment up to one year.

Indiana

Chapter 45 of Statutes Annotated [1969 Cum. Supp.] deals with damage arising out of campus disorders: (1) property, § 10–4531; (2) entering property or remaining in to interfere with lawful use, § 10–4532; (3) refusal to leave on proper demand, § 10–4533; (4) interference in building, § 10–4534. Violations are misdemeanors punishable by fine up to $500 or imprisonment to six months or both, § 10–4535.

Louisiana

Section 328 of Revised Statutes [Added by Acts 1969, No. 58, § 1] substantially enacts the Colorado law on this subject. [Colo. Rev. Stat., Art. 8, § 40–8–21, reproduced *supra*]. However, the Louisiana law is applicable to high schools and junior high schools as well as institutions of higher education, and the jail term for violation is limited to six months.

Revised Statutes § 329.5 [Acts 1969, No. 176, § 6] is also modeled after the Colorado statute, except that it is applicable to elementary and secondary schools, and no penalty for violation of the statute is included in the section. Section 329.7 [Acts 1969, No. 179, § 9], however, establishes the punishment for violations of Revised Statutes 14:329.1–14:329.8, new provisions regarding riots, wrongful use of public property, declaration of emergency, and interference with the educational process. Rioting, inciting to riot, refusing to disperse, or wrongful use of public property is subject to fine up to $500 or imprisonment for six months or both. If serious bodily injury or property damage over $5000 results from violation of any of the provisions, the punishment is prison at hard labor for not more than five years. If a death occurs as a result of a statutory violation, the punishment is prison at hard labor up to twenty-one years.

Maryland

Article 27, § 577B of the Annotated Code [Acts 1969, § 3, Ch. 627, effective July 1, 1969] sets out the authority of school administrators to deny access to public schools and colleges and sets the penalty for trespassing and property damage. Violations are subject to fine of not more than $1000, or prison up to six months, or both.

Michigan

Michigan Compiled Laws §§ 752.581-3 [P.A. 1970, No. 26, approved June 2, 1970], declaring certain conduct at public institutions of higher education to be a misdemeanor, are reproduced below:

Section 1

A person is guilty of a misdemeanor, punishable by a fine of not more than $500.00, or by incarceration in the county jail for not more than 30 days or both:

(a) When the chief administrative officer of a publicly owned and operated institution of higher education, or his designee, notifies the person that he is such officer or designee and that the person is in violation of the properly promulgated rules of the institution; and

(b) When the person is in fact in violation of such rules; and

(c) When, thereafter, such officer or designee directs the person to vacate the premises, building or other structure of the institution; and

(d) When the person thereafter wilfully remains in or on such premises, building or other structure; and

(e) When, in so remaining therein or thereon, the person constitutes (1) a clear and substantial risk of physical harm or injury to other persons or of damage to or destruction of the property of the institution, or (2) an unreasonable prevention or disruption of the customary and lawful functions of the institution, by occupying space necessary therefor or by use of force or by threat of force.

Section 2

A person is guilty of a misdemeanor, punishable by a fine of not less than $200.00 and not more than $1,000.00, or by incarceration in the county jail for not more than 90 days, or both, who enters on the premises, building or other structure of a publicly owned and operated institution of higher education, with the intention to, and therein or thereon does in fact, constitute (a) a clear and substantial risk of physical harm or injury to other persons or of damage to or destruction of the property of the institution, or (b) an unreasonable prevention or disruption of the customary and lawful function of the institution, by occupying space necessary therefor or by use of force or by threat of force.

Section 3

This act shall take effect August 1, 1970.

This act is ordered to take immediate effect.

Minnesota

Interference with the use of public property of any kind or violation of any published, posted, or announced rule is subject to a fine of not more than $1000 or imprisonment for one year, or both. [Minn. Stat. § 624.72, Laws 1969, c. 767, §§ 1–6, effective May 28, 1969]

Nevada

An act of interference in a public building, refusal to leave after committing such an act, or aiding another to commit such an act is a misdemeanor. Any building in the University of Nevada System is a public building. [N.R.S. § 203.119, added by Laws 1969, 582]

New Mexico

Section 40A-20-10 of Statutes Annotated [Laws 1970, ch. 86, § 2] is a copy of the Colorado statute, except that the penalty for violation of the New Mexico statute is less—a fine up to $100 or up to six months in the county jail, or both.

Tennessee

Section 39-1214 [Acts 1968 (Adj. S.) ch. 554, §§ 1, 2] provides that trespassing in a school building and engaging in disorderly conduct there is a misdemeanor. Disorderly conduct is defined as property damage, drinking or being drunk, committing a breach of the peace, or refusing to obey requests of the school, including a request to leave.

Interference with campus operations and refusal to leave on request is trespass and a misdemeanor. [§ 39-1215, Acts 1969, ch. 257, § 1]

Obstruction of ingress or egress to campus facilities is a misdemeanor. [§ 39-1216, Acts 1969, ch. 257, § 2]

Entering campus facilities to incite to, take part in, or assist a public disturbance involving violence by persons in a group, which violence is a breach of the peace, an immediate danger, or injures persons or property, is a felony. [§ 39-1217, Acts 1969, ch. 257, § 3]

Entry on school property by nonstudents or nonemployees to incite or take part in a riot is a felony, punishable by two to five years in the state penitentiary. Riot is defined as violence by one or more of a group of three or more persons. [§ 39-5116, Acts 1969, ch. 223, §§ 1, 2]

Loitering

Colorado

Section 40-8-24 [added to Art. 8 of ch. 40, Rev. Stat. 1963, April 10, 1970] defines loitering and makes it a misdemeanor subject to fine of not more than $300, or ninety days in jail, or both. Included in the listing of acts which constitute the misdemeanor is the following:

(1) (f) Loiters or remains in or about a school building or grounds, not having any reason or relationship involving custody of or responsibility for a pupil or any other specific, legitimate reason for being there, or not having written permission from a school administrator; . . .

Delaware

A loitering statute, Code Annotated, Title 11, § 852, passed in 1969, apparently served as a model for the language of the Colorado law reproduced above. The Delaware provision is applicable only to loitering about schools supported wholly or partially with state funds. Punishment for the misdemeanor is by fine of not less than $25 nor more than $200.

Refusal to Leave Campus upon Request

California

Section 626 of the Penal Code defines terms used in the ensuing sections and asserts the authority of the court to consider official reports of previous convictions in determining penalties.

Section 626.2 declares that unauthorized reentry on campus by a student or employee who has been suspended or dismissed and denied access to the facility, with proper notice, is a misdemeanor, punishable by fine up to $500 or jail up to six months, or both. Previous convictions increase the penalty.

Section 626.4 details the authority of authorized officials to withdraw consent to remain on campus if it is reasonably believed that the person willfully disrupted the campus or facility. Unauthorized reentry or remaining after consent to be on campus has been withdrawn, with proper notice, is a misdemeanor. The penalties are set out in the statute.

Section 626.6 gives authority to proper administrative officials to ask nonstudents and nonemployees to leave if it appears that the person is there to interfere or obstruct. If he fails to leave, or reenters within seventy-two hours after being told to leave, he is guilty of a misdemeanor and the penalties are set out.

Section 626.8 applies similar sanctions to any person entering any school building or grounds, or adjacent public way, without lawful business and if his presence or acts interfere with the conduct of the school.

Oklahoma

Chapter 308 of Oklahoma Session Laws 1969 provides that any person not a student or employee or other authorized person who enters a campus or facility and commits or is about to commit an act of interference may be requested to leave by the chief administrative officer or his designee. Failure to leave when requested is a misdemeanor.

Virginia

The statute reproduced below is found in the Code of Virginia, in a chapter entitled "Offenses Against Property."

§ *18.1-173.2. Failure to leave premises of institution of higher learning when directed to do so.*

Any person, whether or not a student, directed to leave the premises of any institution of higher learning by a person duly authorized to give such direction and who fails to do so shall be guilty of a misdemeanor. Each day such person remains on the premises after such direction shall constitute a separate offense. [1970, c. 152]

Wisconsin

Section 36.45 of Statutes Annotated [L. 1969, c. 89, effective June 27, 1969] confers authority on designated college and university officials to declare campus off-limits to unauthorized persons in danger periods. Violation of such an order is a criminal trespass.

Section 36.47 [L. 1969, c. 26, effective May 16, 1969] prohibits unauthorized reentry on campus by one suspended or expelled, if reentry is within two years. Each such offense is subject to fine up to $500 or imprisonment for six months, or both.

Remedy of Injunction

North Carolina

Any chief administrator of any school, public or private, or his representative, may apply to any superior court judge for injunctive relief if a state of emergency exists or is imminent within his school. [Gen. Stat. No. Car. § 14–288.18 (1969, c. 869, s. 1)]

Sound-amplifying Equipment

North Carolina

General Statutes §§ 116–212 and 116–213 authorize the heads of state-supported institutions of higher learning to impose curfews. The unauthorized use of sound-amplifiers on the grounds during a curfew is a misdemeanor subject to fine up to $500 or six months imprisonment, or both.

Wisconsin

Section 36.49 of Statutes Annotated prohibits the unauthorized use of sound-amplifying equipment at a school, and defines its meaning. Violation is punishable by fine up to $100 or jail for thirty days, or both.

Suspension and Dismissal

Louisiana

Revised Statutes 17:3103 [Acts 1969, No. 59, § 1] authorizes expulsion or dismissal of students, faculty, administrators, or employees of institutions of higher learning who engage in any of the disruptive acts enumerated in the statute, upon written notice by the president or his designee. The person so notified has a right to appeal to a panel composed of members of the governing board, or a special panel appointed by the head of the board, if institutional rules allow it, and the decision of the panel is the decision of the governing board.

Revised Statutes 17:3104 specifies the content of the notification of dismissal, which must include statement of the right to request a hearing, within thirty days.

Revised Statutes 17:3105 authorizes the adoption of rules to govern the conduct of such hearings, and states that in all other cases of dismissal of a teacher, except for the commission of acts prohibited in these statutes, the state tenure laws apply.

Revised Statutes 17:3106 requires that details of the dismissal be recorded on a student's transcript. Ineligibility continues for a year. [R.S. 17:3107]

Ohio

Two 1970 Ohio statutes [Ohio Rev. Code §§ 3345.22–3] establish a special suspension and dismissal procedure to which faculty, students, staff members, and employees of state-assisted colleges and universities are subject if they are arrested for or convicted of certain criminal offenses.

The criminal offenses incorporated by reference into the new statutes and subject to this special procedure are:

§2901.19	Maiming or disfiguring a person
§2901.23	Intentional shooting, cutting, or stabbing
§2901.25	Assault and battery and making menacing threats
§2901.252	Assault and battery on law enforcement officers and firemen
§2907.02	Arson
§2907.021	Manufacture, distribution, and possession of fire bombs
§2907.05	Burning property of another person
§2907.06	Attempt to burn property
§2907.08	Malicious injury to property
§2907.082	Intentional injury or damage to public or private property
§2901.01	Malicious destruction of property
§2909.09	Injury to or committing nuisance in buildings
§2909.24	Destruction of public utility fixtures
§2923.01	Carrying of firearm or similar weapon
§2923.012	Carrying other concealed weapons
§2923.43	Interference with authorized persons at emergency scenes
§2923.52	Second degree riot

§2923.53   First degree riot
§2923.54   Inciting to riot
§2923.61   Campus disruption

Section 3345.22 provides that a student, faculty or staff member, or employee of a state-assisted school who is arrested for any of the offenses above shall have a hearing as provided in the statute to determine whether he shall be immediately suspended. The hearing must be within five days after arrest, with continuance for cause up to ten days.

The arresting authority must notify the school president of such an arrest. The president must notify the governing board. The board appoints a referee to hold a hearing in the county where the school is located. The referee is required to be an attorney admitted to practice in Ohio, but cannot be an attorney for, or a faculty or staff member or employee of any college or university.

Immediate notice of the time and place of hearing must be given to the arrested person.

The referee has the powers of a court, and may enforce order by contempt proceedings in the court of common pleas.

The adversary hearing must be fair, but the formalities of the criminal process are not required. The right to have counsel, to cross-examine, to testify, and to present witnesses and evidence is set out in the statute, but counsel need not be furnished to him. Unless he waives his right against self-incrimination, his testimony may not be used in later criminal proceedings.

The referee may bar all persons except news people from the hearing. He may, upon finding that the offense was committed, order suspension or permit return to the school on disciplinary probation. A violation of probation automatically effects a suspension.

A suspension continues until the case is determined in the court. If there is no conviction the suspension automatically terminates, the person is reinstated, and the record expunged. If convicted, he is dismissed pursuant to § 3345.23.

Failure to appear at the hearing requires suspension by the referee.

Appeal to the common pleas court must be filed within twenty days after the order. The court on appeal may change the suspension to disciplinary probation.

Section 3345.23 provides that conviction of any of the offenses referred to in § 3345.23(d) means automatic dismissal. If acquitted, or if conviction is reversed on appeal, reinstatement is required and the record is expunged.

Discretionary readmission or reemployment by the governing board after one calendar year is permitted by the statute, to any school in the system, but only on probation.

The person dismissed must be notified immediately by certified mail. If he is already suspended, the period of dismissal runs from the date of suspension.

No degrees, honors, credit or grades, and no funds of any kind may be credited or paid to one under suspension or dismissal for that period.

Although §§ 3345.22–3 must be carried out by the schools, they do not limit the administrative disciplinary authority of the institutions, including the use of suspension and dismissal, provided the person has a fair notice and hearing. The statute must be followed notwithstanding any inconsistent rule or regulation, however. [§ 3345.24]

Section 3345.25 prohibits entry or remaining on the campus of one suspended or dismissed without express permission of the board or the president.

Wisconsin

Section 36.46 of Statutes Annotated defines "campus misconduct" and "direct state support" and essentially repeats the provisions of § 36.43 as to forfeiture of state financial aid. Additionally, § 36.46 requires dismissal of the student or employee for the period of ineligibility, and permits petition for readmission, reemployment or reinstatement of support after one full semester.

A student or employee of a college or university who is

convicted of a misdemeanor for unlawful assembly may, additionally or alternatively, be suspended for as long as six months. If suspension is imposed, the institution cannot impose any other discipline for the unlawful assembly.

The court shall deduct the period of suspension already served in imposing sentence. A period of imprisonment counts as suspension. [Wis. Stat. Ann. § 947.06(5), Laws 1969, c. 262, amended by Laws 1969, c. 392, § 79, effective February 22, 1970.]

Bibliography

Books

Becker, Howard Saul, ed. *Campus Power Struggle*. Chicago: Aldine Publishing Co., 1970.

Bell, Daniel, and Kristol, Irving, eds. *Confrontation; The Student Rebellion and the Universities*. New York: Basic Books, Inc., 1969.

Brown, Michael. *The Politics and Anti-Politics of the Young*. Beverly Hills: Glencoe Press, 1969.

Califano, Joseph A., Jr. *The Student Revolution: A Global Confrontation*. New York: W. W. Norton & Co., Inc., 1970.

Cockburn, Alexander, and Blackburn, Robin, eds. *Student Power: Problems, Diagnosis, Actions*. London: Harmondsworth, Penguin Books, Inc., 1969.

Ehrenreich, Barbara and John. *Long March, Short Spring; The Student Uprising at Home and Abroad*. New York: Monthly Review Press, 1969.

Foster, Julian, and Long, Durward, eds. *Protest! Student Activism in America*. New York: William Morrow & Co., Inc., 1970.

Holmes, Grace W., ed. *Student Protest and the Law*. Ann Arbor: Institute of Continuing Legal Education, 1969.

Lipset, Seymour Martin, and Altbach, Philip G., eds. *Students in Revolt*. Boston: Houghton Mifflin Co., 1969.

Schwab, Joseph Jackson. *College Curriculum and Student Protest*. Chicago: University of Chicago Press, 1969.

Taylor, Harold. *Students Without Teachers; The Crisis in the University*. New York: McGraw-Hill Book Co., 1969.

Vaccaro, Louis C., and Covert, James T., eds. *Student Freedom in American Higher Education*. New York: Teachers College Press, 1969.

357

Periodicals
Colleges and Universities

Abram, M. B. *Liberalism: A Response to the Campus.* Sw. L.J. 23:662 (1969).

Anon. *Student Unrest In Michigan: One State's Protest Profile.* Coll. & Univ. Bus. 48: 72–5 (March, 1970).

Armstrong, T. J. *College Searches and Seizures: Privacy and Due Process Problems on Campus.* Crim. L. Bull. 5: 537 (1969).

Baldwin, F. N. *Methods of Social Control of Academic Activists within the University Setting.* St. Louis U.L.J. 14: 429 (1970).

Berland, John C., and Oglesby, Dwayne L. *Student Protest—Will the Art Department Be a New Target?* Am. Bus. L.J. 8: 26 (1970.

Bible, Paul A. *The College Dormitory Student and the Fourth Amendment—A Sham or a Safeguard?* U. San Fran. L. Rev. 4: 49 (1969).

Bowen, Howard R. *University Governance: Workable Participation, Administrative Authority and the Public Interest.* Lab. L.J. 20: 517 (1969).

Brechner, Judith A. *On Dissent, Civil Disobedience and Campus Demonstrations.* Women L.J. 56: 127 (1970).

Brewster, Kingman, Jr. *The Politics of Academia.* Sch. & Soc. 98: 211–14 (April, 1970).

Brock, William E. *Congress Looks at the Campus: The Brock Report on Student Unrest.* A.A.U.P. Bull. 55: 327–36 (1969).

Brown, Brendon F. *Natural Law Institutes 1969.* Loyola L. Rev. 15: 219 (1968–1969).

Brown, L. Neville. *Student Protest in England.* Am. J. Comp. L. 17: 395 (1969).

Callahan, P. F. *School and Vietnam.* Brooklyn Bar 21: 93 (1970).

Carreau, Dominique G. *Toward "Student Power" in France?* Am. J. Comp. L. 17: 359 (1969).

Carrington, Paul D. *Professionalism and Student Protest.* A.B.A.J. 55: 943 (1969).

Clarke, James W., and Egan, Joseph. *Political and Social Dimensions of Campus Protest Activity.* Gov. Research Bull. (Fla.) 7: 1-4 (March, 1970).

Coffman, L. D. *Campus Unrest—Why?* N.Y.S.B.J. 42: 106 (1970).

Comment. *Constitutional Law: College Regulations Employed in Suspension of Student Demonstrators Upheld.* Minn. L. Rev. 55: 116 (1970).

Comment. *Do College Students Have a Constitutionally Protected Right to Hear Outside Speakers?* Miss. L. J. 41: 135 (1969).

Comment. *The Fourteenth Amendment and University Disciplinary Procedures.* Mo. L. Rev. 34: 236 (1969).

Comment. *Higher Education and the Student Unrest Provisions.* Ohio S.L.J. 31: 111 (1970).

Comment. *Rules of Evidence in Disciplinary Hearings in State-Supported Universities.* Tex. Tech. L. Rev. 1: 357 (1970).

Comment. *Student Due Process in the Private University: The State Action Doctrine.* Syracuse L. Rev. 20: 911 (1969).

Comment. *Student Unrest in a Legal Perspective: Focus on San Francisco State College.* U. San Fran. L. Rev. 4: 255 (1970).

Costanzo, Joseph F. *Student Revolt: Law and Reason.* Loyola L. Rev. 15: 223 (1968-1969).

Crary, John C., Jr. *Control of Campus Disorders: A New York Solution.* Albany L. Rev. 34: 85 (1969).

Deener, David R. *On the Causes of the Present Discontents Between Campus and Society.* Loyola L. Rev. 15: 243 (1968-1969).

Finch, Robert H. *The Campus Crisis. Foreword.* Wm. & Mary L. Rev. 11: 575 (1970).

Fisk, W. M. *System of Law for the Campus: Some Reflections.* Geo. Wash. L. Rev. 38: 1006 (1970).

Friday, William C. *The Trustee and the Administration.* Popular Gov't 36: 15-16 (March, 1970).

Geck, Wilhelm Karl. *Student Power in West Germany.* Am. J. Comp. L. 17: 337 (1969).

Gerzon, M. *Whole World is Watching; A Young Man Looks At Youth's Dissent.* Harv. Ed. R. 40: 491-4 (August, 1970).

Goldstein, Alvin H., Jr. *Campus Violence—The Constitution, and Judicial Review.* Calif. S.B.J. 44: 568 (1969).

Goldstein, Stephen R. *Reflections on Developing Trends in the Law of Student Rights.* U. Pa. L. Rev. 118: 612 (1970).

Green, Edith. *The University and Society.* Wm. & Mary L. Rev. 11: 611 (1970).

Gutierrez, Carlos Jose. *Student Participation in the Government of the University of Costa Rica.* Am. J. Comp. L. 17: 390 (1969).

Herman, Joseph. *Injunctive Control of Disruptive Student Demonstrations.* Va. L. Rev. 56: 215 (1970).

Hoult, Thomas Ford; Hudson, John W.; and Mayek, Albert J. *On Keeping Our Cool in the Halls of Ivy.* A.A.U.P. Bull. 55: 186-91 (June, 1969).

Huddleston, Albert J. *Politics, The Natural Law and Student Unrest.* Loyola L. Rev. 15: 255 (1968-1969).

Humphrey, Hubert H. *Student Confrontations: Are They Inevitable?* Wm. & Mary L. Rev. 11: 580 (1970).

Jones, H.R. *Turbulence on the Campuses: Some Legal Aspects.* N.Y.S.B.J. 42: 502 (1970).

Jovanovic, Vladimir. *Participation of Students in the Administration of Colleges and Universities in Yugoslavia.* Am. J. Comp. L. 18: 172 (1970).

Lawson, Herbert G. *Courts and Campuses: Some Students Find They Can Win Demands by Suing Their School.* Wall St. J. 174: 1+ (November 25, 1969).

Mancini, Federico. *Student Power in Italy.* Am. J. Comp. L. 17: 371 (1969).

Mardian, R. C. *Student Unrest—The Role of the Federal Government.* A.B.A. Sect. Ins. N. & C.L. 1969: 211 (1969).

McCaughey, Robert A. *The Usable Past: A Study of the Harvard College Rebellion of 1834.* Wm. & Mary L. Rev. 11: 587 (1970).

Mitchell, Maurice. *The College Campus And Student Unrest.* Ins. Counsel J. 36: 529 (1969).

Morris, Arval A. *Student Participation in Law School Decision Making.* J. Legal Ed. 22: 127 (1970).

Mustor, Ray. *Concept of Student Participation in Governance Becomes Formalized and More Public As It Gains Momentum.* Coll. & Univ. Bus. 48: 12+ (March, 1970).

Note. *Civil Rights—Academic Freedom—Refusal to Rehire a Nontenure Teacher for a Constitutionally Impermissible Reason.* Wis. L. Rev. 1970: 162 (1970).

Note. *Civil Rights—School Officials Not Persons for Purposes of Section 1983 Regardless of Relief Sought.* Sw. L.J. 24: 360 (1970).

Note. *College Searches and Seizures: Privacy and Due Process Problems on Campus.* Ga. L. Rev. 3: 426 (1969).

Note. *Constitutional Law—Student Academic Freedom—'State Action' and Private Universities.* Tul. L. Rev. 44: 184 (1969).

Note. *The Emerging Law of Students' Rights.* Ark. L. Rev. 23: 619 (1970).

Note. *Legal Ethics—Constitutional Law—Despite Restrictions by the Board of Regents and Possible Ethical Objections, the Students' Attorney Act of the University of Texas at Austin Represents an Initial Effort Toward the Provision of Group Legal Services for Students.* Tex. L. Rev. 48: 1215 (1970).

Note. *Legal Relationship between the Student and the Private College or University.* San Diego L. Rev. 7: 244 (1970).

Note. *Student-Employees and Collective Bargaining Under the National Labor Relations Act: An Alternative to Violence on American College Campuses.* Geo. Wash. L. Rev. 38: 1026 (1970).

Ohles, John F. *A Revised Contract for College Students.* Sch. & Soc. 98: 23-4 (January, 1970).

Ozsunay, Ergun. *Participation of Students in University and Faculty Administration in Turkey.* Am. J. Comp. L. 17: 378 (1969).

Rosenthal, Robert R. *Injunctive Relief Against Campus Disorders.* U. Pa. L. Rev. 118: 746 (1970).

Salem, R. G., and Bowers, W. J. *Severity of Formal Sanctions as a Deterrent to Deviant Behavior.* Law & Soc. Rev. 5: 21 (1970).

Saxbe, W. B. *Student Unrest, and the Law.* Clev. St. L. Rev. 18: 429 (1969).

Schellhardt, Timothy D. *Defusing the Campus: College Officials Seek Better Ways to Deal with Student Violence.* Wall St. J. 176: 1+ (September 4, 1970).

Selvig, Erling, and Hambro, Christian. *Student Representation in Norwegian University Government.* Am. J. Comp. L. 18: 169 (1970).

Sepulveda, Cesar. *Student Participation in University Affairs: The Mexican Experience.* Am. J. Comp. L. 17: 384 (1969).

Smith, Benjamin E. *Student Revolt and the Natural Law.* Loyola L. Rev. 15: 259 (1968–1969).

Smith, Francis B. *Campus Unrest: Illusion and Reality.* Wm. & Mary L. Rev. 11: 619 (1970).

Tragesser, Gene. *Aspects of Student Activism on College Campuses.* Coll. & Univ. 44: 410–13 (Summer, 1969).

Van Alstyne, William W. *The Tentative Emergence of Student Power in the United States.* Am. J. Comp. L. 17: 403 (1969).

Wilkinson, Ernest L., and Rolapp, R. Richards. *The Private College and Student Discipline.* A.B.A.J. 56: 121 (1970).

Wofford, Harris, Jr. *The Campus as Battleground.* Trial 6:4:34 (1970).

Wright, C. A. *Constitution on the Campus.* Vand. L. Rev. 22: 1027 (1969).

Younger, E. J. *Violence and Education.* Lab. Bull. 44: 513 (1969).

Secondary Schools

Aldrich, Ann; Sommers, Jo Anne; and Ware, Russell M. *Fr dom of Expression in Secondary Schools.* Cleve. St. L. Rev. 1): 165 (1970).

Anon. *Constitutional Law: The Black Armbands Case—Freedom of Speech in the Public Schools.* Marq. L. Rev. 52: 608 (1969).

Anon. *Boardmen Reason: Share the Power with Students.* Am. Sch. Bd. J. 157: 27–8 (May, 1970).

Anon. *Hair Becomes the Plaintiff.* Saturday Review 53: 73 (November 21, 1970).

Anon. *Politics of Despair; Surveys of High School and College Students.* Saturday Review 53: 80 (September 19, 1970).

Anon. *Student Involvement; Channeling Activism Into Accomplishment.* Nation's Schools 84: 39–50 (1969).

Anrig, Gregory R. *Those High School Protestors: Can Boards Put Up with Much More?* Am. Sch. Bd. J. 157: 20–4 (October, 1969).

Barber, Donald. *K–12—Some Keys to Campus Unrest.* J. Sec. Ed. 44: 369–74 (1969).

Comment. *Public Schools, Long Hair, and the Constitution.* Ia. L. Rev. 55: 707 (1970).

Miller, Harriet. *Santa Barbara Has a Student School Board.* Am. Sch. Bd. J. 157: 29 (May, 1970).

Nahmod, Sheldon. *Black Arm Bands and Underground Newspapers: Freedom of Speech in the Public Schools.* Chi. Bar Rec. 51: 144 (1969).

Note. *High School Hair Regulations.* Val. U. L. Rev. 4: 400 (1970).

Note. *Symbolic Speech, High School Protest and the First Amendment.* J. Family L. 9: 119 (1969).

Spillman, Russell J. *Students' Concerns and Protests Merit Educators' Perceptive Response; High School Students, Chicago.* Contemp. Ed. 40: 334–42 (1969).

Taylor, Arnold. *With Temperate Rod: Maintaining Academic Order in Secondary Schools.* Ky. L.J. 58: 617 (1969–1970).

Index